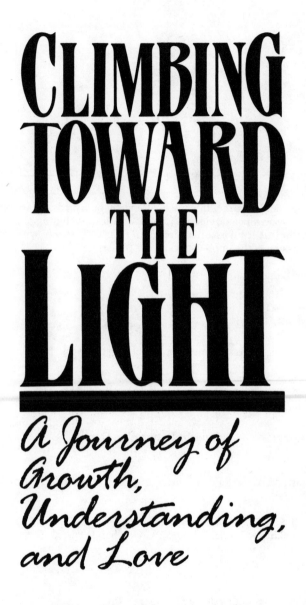

CLIMBING TOWARD THE LIGHT

A Journey of Growth, Understanding, and Love

By Ardath H. Rodale

THE GOOD SPIRIT PRESS Emmaus, Pennsylvania

Printed in the United States of America

Book design by Lisa Farkas
Illustrations by Maria Rodale

If you have any questions or comments concerning this book, please write:
Rodale Press
Book Reader Service
33 East Minor Street
Emmaus, PA 18098

Library of Congress Cataloging-in-Publication Data

Rodale, Ardath.
    Climbing toward the light : a journey of growth, understanding, and love / by Ardath Rodale.
        p.   cm.
    ISBN   0-87857-834-X   hardcover
    1. Spiritual life.   2. Life.   3. Rodale, Ardath.   I. Title.
BL624.R627   1989
646.7–dc20   89-32896
    [B]   CIP

Distributed in the book trade by St. Martin's Press

2 4 6 8 10 9 7 5 3 1   hardcover

To all the Davids and those who love them

Contents

Acknowledgments

I thank all those special people who were the encouragement on this journey of Climbing Toward the Light.

I send bouquets of appreciation to:

My Mother, Ardath Harter, who began my journey.

Bob, my husband, who has stood by me for 38 years.

Heather, Heidi, David, Maria, and Anthony, who made life so real and vital.

Tom Stoneback and Charles Norelli, my sons-in-law, for their loyalty.

Sarah Fitz-Hugh and Ellie and Guy Wagner for their faithfulness and care.

Frank and Jean Emerling and Mark Kintzel, who brought so much happiness to David's life.

Unity, Daily Word, and *Wee Wisdom* magazines for their inspiration.

Charles Gerras, my editor, and a friend since grade school, who made me dig deep into my consciousness.

Bonnie Gerhart, who from the beginning did the initial computer input and gave me valuable feedback.

All those people who worked as a wonderful team to make this book possible: Bill Gottlieb, Editor in Chief; Carol Keough, Senior Managing Editor; Sally Roth, Copy Editor; Dolores Plikaitis, Copy Manager; Dorothy Smickley, Senior Secretary; Ellen Greene, Marketing Director, Trade Sales; and Lori Goldman, Special Markets Manager.

There are many more who helped make a difference in my life. I circle all with love. . . .

Before you begin reading my life story, I would like to introduce you to the most important people in my life and describe for you several very special places.

I speak about my mother, Ardath, and my father, Stanley, my older sister, Joy, and my two younger brothers, Jim and Dave. I came to be called Ardie to distinguish me from my mother. We were a close family, living in a middle-class neighborhood in Allentown, Pennsylvania.

My husband Bob's parents, Anna and J. I. (Jerry), are also referred to as Nana and Papa in this book. They came to Emmaus, Pennsylvania, in 1930 to carry on the business of Rodale Manufacturing, an electrical wiring devices company. The company was a partnership with J. I.'s brother Joe and his wife, Esther. At that time Emmaus was an old mill town with a lagging economy. J. I. located his business in an old silk mill and also started Rodale Press that very same year. The first big magazine was *Organic Gardening and Farming*, followed by *Prevention*.

In 1941, Anna and J. I. purchased a 68-acre, run-down tenant farm, which became the first Organic Gardening Experimental Farm. We've always called it the Old Farm. Bob and I built our home there in 1956. Our property was four miles from Emmaus and at that time was real country. The farm was a constant source of entertainment for our growing children. They could cuddle newly born karakul lambs, pet our steer, collect eggs, and be wakened in the morning by the rooster's crow. It was ecstasy to eat vegetables picked fresh from the garden. Today the Old Farm is still as beautiful as ever, except the once-sleepy road in front has become one of the most heavily traveled in the area. The quiet is gone and the city has crowded in.

We purchased another farm in 1971–the New Farm, in Maxatawny, Pennsylvania. One of the most beautiful places on earth, this 305-acre property nestles in a gentle valley. From the top of the neighboring hill, you can see for miles and miles, and there is no main road in sight. Sunrises and sunsets can be enjoyed from anywhere on the farm. Our neighbors are Mennonites who still farm in the old ways. On Sundays and special days, horses pulling buggies clip-clop along the country road that winds through our fields.

The New Farm is actually a very *old* farm, owned by the Seigfried family for nine generations. The grant for the land was given to this family by William Penn. In fact, the houses and barns are on the

National Register of Historic Places. This New Farm is the location of the Rodale Research Center, where research scientists conduct and develop the most effective and regenerative growing methods. Last year over 6,000 people came to visit from all over the world.

It is interesting to note that all the important places I love are located within a 20-mile radius of where I grew up. Even though they are so close, when we take visitors to see them, there is so much to see that they are overwhelmed before we are half-way through.

There is one more special place I would like to describe to you. It is my son David's home, located five minutes up the mountain that serves as the southern border of Emmaus. Almost at the top of a very winding mountain road, you'll find a dirt lane that ambles off into the woods. At the end of that lane, in a clearing, David's tiny 200-year-old house sits, silent and peaceful and majestic. His land has become a sanctuary, a part of the South Mountain Preserve, where bird-watchers will always be able to come to observe all the wonderful varieties and to watch the hawks swoop over the meadow in the back of the house. Deer are plentiful, too. Oh, that he were still here to enjoy!

When Bob and I were married in 1951, the family company had grown in size to about 60 employees. It seemed right that I join the Rodale family, because they always had been known as pioneers in search of new ideas. Like me, they were always looking ahead. In the beginning, their new ideas met a lot of resistance. As a rebel, I joined the rebel force.

At the age of 28, Bob was named president of the company by his father. As the years went on, J. I. Rodale was thrilled beyond measure that his ideas about gardening and health were being accepted by the American public. He had become a celebrity. At the height of his achievements, at the age of 72, he died of a coronary attack. Bob then became chairman of the board of Rodale Press.

Through the years, Bob and I have followed parallel paths. His led to the expansion of Rodale Press, while mine led to the growth of our family. Today the company has 1,100 employees, and our one office building has multiplied to 14. The town of Emmaus has become our campus. Instead of building one big office complex, we have recycled an old school, a cigar factory, two silk mills, and various houses, turning them into office space. We have taken these old, vacant buildings and made them new again, while at the same time respecting their individual styles.

In addition to *Organic Gardening* and *Prevention*, the company now also publishes *Bicycling*, *Runner's World*, *Backpacker*, *Cross Country Skier*, *American Woodworker*, *New Farm*, *Mountain Bike*,

Adventure Travel, and *Men's Health.* Along with these magazines, we also publish nearly a dozen newsletters and about 40 books a year.

Rodale Press has succeeded and grown because it has both a message and a dream. The message urges one to live in harmony with his or her environment so that future generations may also find the world a beautiful and healthy place to live. Seeing that our efforts can help the world be cleaner, our food tastier, and our bodies healthier makes our dream become a reality. This dream has always been realized by the family as well as many of our dedicated employees. We live and believe the dream. When people work toward a dream, their steps will not falter as they reach for that high mountaintop goal, whatever it might be.

My path, just as important as Bob's, also took me someplace special—to my family. Our children, from oldest to youngest, are Heather, Heidi, David, Maria, and Anthony. You will meet each one in a separate chapter, but not in order of their ages. You will meet them as they presented challenges. Through the years, I have responded to the needs of others, and especially to the needs of my children. As a result, I sometimes had to revise my message to realize my dream. I have tried to walk in my children's shoes to try to understand. This meant that I had to walk part of their dream, too, and that's how I learned to understand. Today, our children have added a new dimension to our lives, as we all work together for the company, to carry on the dream of a better world.

This book is the story of my path taken.

I am excited about sharing this true story with you. My aim is to help others who face situations similar to mine and who look for answers and understanding as I did. My story is filled with hope, challenges, rewards, rebellion, happiness, sadness, and the triumph of overcoming obstacles. But at the core it is about love and growth through the changing circumstances of real life.

I want to tell you who I am as a person and how it's possible for anyone to gain self-esteem, courage, and dignity. I also want to demonstrate the importance of a commitment to dreams and goals.

I'll tell you about each of my five children, and how their strong individuality shaped their lives and mine.

You'll learn about the circles of influence in my life, how I responded to them, and how my family and my community of friends were affected by my responses. I want to tell you about the lifelines that turn from string to wire as they bind us together in love.

I'll tell you about facing tragedy, which we all do in life, and how we can become part of a network reaching out to care for one another in our suffering.

You'll see how love can soften the heart so that our lives can expand and we can reach out to make our own lives better while we enrich other lives we touch.

I point out how we can profit from old experiences by looking at them in new ways.

I stress making the most of each day, the importance of time, and how precious and fragile life is. I emphasize respect for other people and their lifestyles, a sense of sexual responsibility, and the value of having meaningful work to do.

You will find unexpected surprises within these pages—like an amaryllis growing in December or violets in October—and sometimes a childlike wonder about life that adds refreshment to the way we interpret it.

Why did I write this story? For many years, I have been writing letters to friends telling them what has been happening in my life. As a part of these messages, I have always included a bit of my philosophy of living. Often a return letter would tell me: "My friend needed to hear that message, so I sent it on to share." I am continually asked by my friends to "please let others know some of the valuable things you tell us." And I am getting a spiritual nudge from my son David, who died in 1985. I hear his voice in my heart saying over and over, "Mom, you have a story that needs to be told. You can help others. Hurry!"

I open my life to you. I put my arm around your shoulder as I share with you in friendship what I have learned. I hope my experiences and my philosophy will help you to gain in strength as we continue to Climb Toward the Light together.

RENEWAL

This is the day
you wake up whole
and find that the day
and your mind are clear,
your body blessed with perfection,
your senses keyed to kindness and delight.
You know that you have been renewed by night
and that the dawn has brought
that dreamed of day when everything is right.

John D. Engle, Jr.

It's coming back—the high energy and the excitement I always used to have about life! I particularly noticed these feelings of renewal before the first signs of spring last year. It felt as if something inside were ready to burst. Once again I felt invigorated and happy to be a part of this great, fantastic world. I could hardly wait to get outside and feel the warming earth in my hands, to pull off the old dried branches that were left from deep winter. Some voice inside told me that this joyous feeling was a symbol of rebirth after the past 2½ years. Climbing Toward the Light is very fast these days. I'm climbing with inspiration toward the light of understanding and I don't want to miss anything—nature, the family, the friends, and all other people I might contact. I don't want to miss growth, and, above all, I don't want to miss sharing with and helping others. I'm getting stronger every day.

In these past 2½ years, I have done a lot of thinking about what makes a person strong. What happens to a person after a tragedy that makes him or her able to bounce back, to rise above life's trials? It takes a strong will to break out of old paths when they become worn-out and no longer take us where we want to go. It takes courage to risk new choices. It takes a lot of contemplation, a lot of looking out the window of your mind to observe new things that are going on, so that you can set a new direction. It takes retreating behind the inner door of quiet time to decide which direction to take.

I was always a pretty good sharer, happy to help other people. But I was never a good receiver. This, I discovered, was the missing link in what I needed to be strong. Being a good receiver lets the strength of love come back to you as a gift from others.

I see each of us as an island, connected to one another by an ocean whose tides touch our beaches, then rush out to touch others, just as the tides from other beaches rush in to touch our shores. Our tides intermingle. This symphony of the tides brings the good to our shores and sends the good from us to others. It is this exchange that makes us strong.

I looked back over the past months in an attempt to give a broader perspective to this idea of giving and receiving. What led up to this return of high energy? A healing had taken place.

The two previous Christmases, after my son David's illness and untimely death, had been very hard. I was determined to make the Christmas of 1987 better, but I wasn't sure how to do it. Several ideas popped into my head, and I finally decided on one very special plan. It was almost time for David's birthday on December 12th. I would have a party. It was unfortunate that Bob, my husband, would be in Africa on that date. But I went ahead. I busied myself with the guest list and planned ways to make the day different and uplifting. The shopping began.

With checklist in hand, I started to make the rounds. The day was clear and sunny and I thought I could see forever across time and space. I was filled with anticipation as I waited in line at the checkout counter with my order. A woman about my size and age was directly in front of me. She smiled and we chatted briefly. She looked familiar, but I just couldn't put a name to her face. The woman paid for her order and left.

When my purchases were settled, I came out the door and saw the woman waiting for me. With a smile on her face, she said, "How long is it since David died?"

I was taken aback. I had only ever spoken of him as having left. How could she be so bold! I wondered if my face revealed the horror, and yet I automatically replied, "It's almost two years."

Then she pursued. "My name is Amy. I can't begin to tell you how often you have been on my mind during this time. How are you doing?"

"Oh, really well. David's birthday is just about due and I'm getting ready to have a party for his special friends." As I spoke to her, my eyes filled up with tears and I wondered, *am* I doing well? Turning these surprise corners of the mind sometimes leaves me with no defense. I must learn to be braver.

Still smiling, she said, "It's been eight years since my son died. He died at Christmastime, too. That's why I think of you so often."

Here were two of us standing in the sunlight, each trying to be strong, supporting one another in our common tragedy of sons leaving us too early in their lives—and ours.

My concern switched to Amy, as I asked her what had happened.

With a look of peace, she told me about her wonderful son. "For the first five years after he died, I didn't think I'd make it," she said. "I had to take stock. Then I realized that I had much to do and that I *wanted* to heal. I turned myself around."

We said good-bye, and as an afterthought I called to her, "Thank you so much for speaking with me."

Yes, Amy, many thanks for the gift of reaching out. How often I send her thought waves of love and appreciation.

As I approached the coming days, I tried to decide what this encounter meant to me. Something in my life was different.

December 12th, the day of the party, came near. I happily decorated the tree in the corner of the living room, choosing all the old Victorian silk balls that the children had helped to make and used to decorate the tree with about 12 years before. Things were falling into place.

One difference between David's parties and mine was that the preparations for his parties always had the spirit of community, while mine were one-person projects. He was never completely ready, so everyone willingly helped. Much of the fun and good humor came in doing the job. Everyone wanted to contribute. On the other hand, I was always ready. And once the party had begun, I was often separate from the guests, making sure things ran smoothly backstage, acting as the server, not really a participant at all.

This time would be different—more in David's style. When I asked 11 of David's special friends to come to a party on December 12th, their faces lit up with excitement. I didn't have to tell them what the party was for.

Mark, David's friend, dreamed the night before that David said he was hungry for fried potatoes. In the dream, Mark said, "But David, I don't know how to make them. I don't even know how to cut up the potatoes!"

"Here, I'll show you," said David very clearly in the dream, and he proceeded to dice the potatoes.

When Mark told me about this, we laughed and I said, "Of course, we'll add the fried potatoes to the menu of David's favorites— prime rib, salad, green beans with mushrooms, and moist chocolate cake for dessert."

What a wonderful night it was! I had decided to bring the large dining table into the living room so that the tree and the roaring fire in the fireplace would all be part of the scene. There was tremendous enthusiasm, lots of humor, great camaraderie, and delicious food. None of us will ever forget that strengthening time together. We shared in the joy of our special friend who, we all agreed, was still around in spirit and talking to us in wonderful, surprising ways.

Several days later, I packed a lunch and went to David's house on the mountain. The moment was enthralling. It was such a beautiful day, I couldn't help but share the experience with my large network of friends at work and everywhere else. When I came back, I wrote this to each of them:

I took my lunch to the mountain today. The sun was delightfully warm as I sat on the porch overlooking the woods. It was so quiet, not even the pampas grass was rustling in the breeze. The grass is still green and little white flowers are still in bloom by the side of the house. I wanted to linger, but I knew I had to leave. As I drove down the mountain, the radio played a song that added to my pondering mood, and I knew I wanted to share the words with you:

Cherish the love we have,
Cherish the life we live . . . .

I thought about the fragility of life and how much we take for granted and how important it is to touch our world and its people with tenderness.

Carefully, I place thoughts of each one of you Special Friends in my cupped hands, and these thoughts of love and appreciation overflow. I hope that with the holiday season and the approaching new year, your life will be filled with happiness and many of your dreams will be fulfilled.

Our youngest son, Anthony, was in Costa Rica. He had decided that this was one year he wanted to be away for the holidays. It was another reason why I thought Christmas would be hard. But Christmas would come and we still had to face it. Two years had passed since David left us on the evening of December 23rd. We all plodded onward, one day at a time.

On the evening of the 22nd, the telephone rang and a familiar voice said, "Hey, Mom, I've decided to come home tomorrow night!"

You could just feel the excitement in the family as they got the news. "Anthony's coming home!"

Since he wasn't expected for Christmas, nobody had shopped for presents for Anthony. So on the 23rd, we were all scurrying around, happily singing while we finished the shopping we thought had been completed weeks ago.

That evening, Mark and the whole family went to David's favorite restaurant for dinner. This could have been a sad time but we were all jubilant, for afterward we would go to the airport to welcome Anthony home. We all grew another step in strength that Christmas, as love and caring for one another was given and received.

I look back on how we as a family have stuck together and have grown in love. How did it all happen in this way? How is it that all of the children wandered away from home for a while (as I did) but eventually found that home was where we all wanted to be? It takes strength to leave, and love's ties to bring you back.

I recall my early goals—to be a good wife and to be the best mother I could be. It took plenty of soul-searching to realize that these goals were set originally to please other people. But I needed some goals to please myself, too.

Writing this book has given me the opportunity to step back even further and look at my life with some objectivity for the first time. It has led me to place in perspective those events and interactions with others that brought me to the point of reaching out to share in love. Who was Ardie? How did I become the person I am now?

STAGE I

Beginning the Climb

I was a middle child searching for my space. I had unlimited energy and walked as if my feet had springs. I was curious, spunky, skinny, rebellious, and my fingernails were always bitten way down. The look in my eyes gave people the impression that I was seeing far beyond the path I walked.

I waded through the trials of growing up. I found someone to love and became the mother of five children. I expected my life to follow an orderly pattern, and I worked to make that happen. In the process I lost sight of my personal potential. My spirit was worn down. At age 37, I contracted two major illnesses in one year. Then a doctor's leading question changed my life.

CHAPTER 1

Me, Ardie

---

*So I went, as he directed me, into the field which is called Ardath,
and there I sat among the flowers and ate the plants of the field,
and the nourishment they afforded satisfied me.*

2 Esd. 9:26

I was born in a hurry on October 17th, right before the Depression years. I was the second of four children. Mother's name was Ardath, and it was decided that I would be named for her. Soon I became known as Ardie.

We lived in a small six-room row house in Allentown, Pennsylvania, that Grandpa gave my mother and father for a wedding present. It was one of 17 red brick houses, all exactly the same, that lined each side of our block. The neighborhood was a stable one with a good mixture of old and young people. But in retrospect, I wonder how we did it—Mother and Daddy, Joy, my older sister, my two younger brothers, Jim and David, and myself, all living in a small house with one bathroom!

It was a time of large families, so many of the houses were as crowded as ours. Within our block there were 52 children, so you can imagine that there was always plenty of excitement and the sound of everyday living—especially in summer when windows were open and people rocked on their porches. There were wonderful street sounds that are no longer part of our experience—"Bananas! Rags! Ashes! Umbrellas! Horseradish!"

A little Italian fruit peddler with a huge curved mustache pushed his well-stocked cart through our back alley, crying "Bananas! Bananas!" A whistle and the call "Ashes! Rags!" announced the rag man, who drove a slow-moving truck up the alley as he collected ashes from our coal-burning furnaces and took away our cast-off clothes and goods, which he managed to sell somehow.

In front of the house there were other sounds. "Horseradish!" We imitated this man with his "spinning wheel" grinder by setting our tricycles upside down and turning the front wheel as if we were grinding the sharp-smelling horseradish as he did for each order. And the call of the umbrella man was familiar to everyone: "Umbrellas! Umbrellas! Anybody need umbrellas fixed?" If only this service were available today! I hate to think of all the almost-good umbrellas I have thrown away in my lifetime.

In those days before air-conditioning, open windows were a must and such sounds were a part of living. In many ways it was necessary to live outside of ourselves in frequent contact with others. Today, people hibernate in houses kept closed to be cool in summer and warm in winter; they huddle alone with TV for entertainment. No wonder we're more prone to live an interior existence, in every sense of the word.

The happy voices of children was another regular sound as children of all ages played street games together in the evening—red light, Mother may I?, hide-and-seek.

There were subtler, not-so-pleasant sounds that also characterized those Depression years of the thirties—the knock on the door around meal time: a shabbily dressed man stands on the back porch, always polite, "I'm hungry, could you spare some food?" The food from our house always came on a china plate with a napkin. No one was ever turned away. We kids were always curious about these people who we called tramps. We didn't talk to them; we just kind of hung back and watched. What interesting stories they might have told us!

In the evening, we often heard a familiar knock on the back door that filled us with happy anticipation. We knew it would be Mrs. Redfield with a basket of fresh, still warm, raised doughnuts for sale, protectively covered by a crisp white cloth.

As children, we were never afraid to answer our door, day or night. We might have been afraid of the dark or of our parents, but there was no fear of our environment.

Times were tough in those days, and every household had to stretch resources. I had an insatiable desire for meat, and this caused me a lot of trouble. Mother said I was greedy because I always looked for an extra piece. (I was a middle child, and being small for my age, I had to make sure that I had a place!) I was given the bone of whatever meat was served as my portion to chew on. When I complained, my parents said, "Remember, the meat is always sweeter next to the bone!" I wasn't greedy, I was *hungry*.

I was looked upon as a child hard to cope with; I was rebellious and I knew it! Now I realize that I was just trying to establish a place for myself.

When I remember Mother, I think of her seated, reading or knitting. One year she made 24 sweaters—everyone in the family had enough sweaters! Aside from the sisters who taught at the nearby parochial school and lived in the corner house, Mother was the only one in our block with a college degree. She felt that her education set her apart and above her other neighbors. So I believe that mother's knitting and poetry and scrapbooks were the vehicles she used to escape them to contemplate and to expand her mind.

Sometimes I would come to talk to her while she was off with some of her cloud thoughts and I could sense that she was not giving me her undivided attention. That made me feel like screaming, "Listen to me!" But I didn't.

For over 40 years, my mother was the sole teacher of the Mothers' Class at church. She also donated her time to the Girl Scouts and later became the local commissioner of that organization. She was a great speaker and much in demand for inspirational and uplifting messages. All her life she shared her thoughts and philosophy with us. Mother always had high ideals for her children. Most of all, she inspired us to dream beyond the day, to look toward the future.

In the meantime, we did chores while she dreamed and inspired and did her needlework. Somehow, when I think of her I compare her to Mary, the sister of Martha, in the Bible. The rest of the women in the neighborhood were the Marthas who busily scrubbed, cooked, and cleaned. I had the best of two worlds. I had Mother, the Mary, and Aunt Anne, the Martha.

When I felt unappreciated at home, I visited Aunt Anne, who lived next door. She always assured me that I was loved and had value. At her kitchen table I learned how to make and roll dough, always using the coffee cup for measurement. At Aunt Anne's I learned how to bake pies and cakes and the most wonderful Cornish pasties. For this last item alone, she deserves a monument from our family, because the pasties have become such a great part of our lives. Just to think about them starts the saliva juices flowing. Just to smell the pasties as they bake tantalizes the appetite to great anticipation! Just to see the not-large-enough pastie in front of your eyes makes you think, *More, more, more!* After all these years, I am still the only one in the family who can make them right. Every once in a while someone will say, "Gee, Ardie, I'm so hungry for a pastie. How about it?"

Aunt Anne taught me to sew on her treadle sewing machine. She also taught me how to iron, showing me how to squiggle the iron around so as not to scorch the fabric. From her I learned how to produce wrinkle-free masterpieces.

And after all the chores were finished, we enjoyed our leisure on the front porch glider, laughing and eating ice cream.

Many years later, at a seminar I attended, the leader took us through a directed dream. We closed our eyes and visualized the experience in our minds. A shortened version of the direction we were given goes something like this:

It is a beautiful day. You are a child again.

You are enjoying a leisurely walk in the country. All nature is green and beautiful. There's a fence along the side of the road. You step to the side of the road and peer over the fence. There is a wonderful meadow. You are enchanted and decide to get over the fence to explore what prizes you might find. What do you see? You notice the blades of grass, the refinements of the Queen Anne's lace, the lavenders and pinks and purples of the wild phlox, the singing of the birds. It's paradise. Look over there. Under the arms of a spreading tree are your mother and father. What is each of them doing? You are playing. What is their reaction to you? (My father was reading the newspaper and my mother was sitting, doing her knitting. Neither of them looked up as I played. They appeared not even to notice I was there. I felt sad.)

All of a sudden a storm comes into the scene. There is real danger and you are scared. You fear for your life. What do you do? Who saves you? (My parents didn't move or look up. Aunt Anne came to wrap me in her arms. I cried in reality.)

This was an amazing revelation to me. I guess Aunt Anne—not Mother, not Daddy—was really my symbol of security!

All through life, I felt that I didn't know Daddy well. Outside of telling us stories when we were small, he didn't talk to us children much. He stopped going to school after the eleventh grade, and his philosophy was "You have to work hard and prove yourself." How to "prove yourself" was left to our own interpretation. I don't think any of us ever asked Daddy what he meant by that statement.

Daddy was the Master of Punishment in our family, and I got punished often. Mother would say, "You just wait till your daddy comes home!" And I knew what was coming. We always had dinner together in the dining room because the kitchen was too small for a family meal. I would retreat under the dining room table. (Perhaps for protection, or to be harder to reach.) Mother would relate the tale of my naughtiness while I listened from down under. Eventually, I would be hauled out. If Daddy thought what I had done was really bad, and if he was in an ornery mood, I was spanked and taken to my room—and the door was shut tight till morning. I cried and cried, and sobbed and sobbed, until no more sound would come out of my mouth. No one ever came to console me. I was left to my own misery. Because of experiences such as these, I believe I harbored a lot of anger toward my father.

As general traffic manager, Daddy carried the troubles of Mack Trucks on his shoulders. So all the time I knew him he was a very stressed person. His favorite way to relieve stress at the end of the day was to have his hair combed. I was usually the one called upon to do the job. Daddy would sit in his chair with his eyes closed, and if he would have allowed himself to, I'm sure he would have purred. To me it seemed like a never-ending chore, so every once in a while I deliberately combed too hard. Of course this got a rise out of him! Was this my way of getting back at the "punisher"? Knowing myself as I do, I'm sure it was!

The loves of Daddy's life were (in this order): Mother, playing the violin, dancing, and taking care of his roses. In season, seven days a week, a fresh rose always adorned his lapel.

My best fun was outside the house, as it was with most children. Joan was my very first best girlfriend. She lived three doors away and next to the Sisters of Saint Francis convent. To us, the sisters were very special, and we loved to be involved with them, whether it be chores or play.

Joan and I were used as models when the sisters chose the floral crowns to be used in the church processions. (At that time, they used real waxed flowers to make these wreaths.) In return for this privilege, we did odd jobs like fixing flowers at church and running errands. We were delighted because it gave us an opportunity to leave the neighborhood for a little while. Of course, we loved our neighborhood (with so many kids around we never wanted for companionship), but we were curious to know what the rest of the world was like.

Saint Anthony was a very special saint for Joan and me. She once told me that if you prayed to Saint Anthony when you couldn't find what you were looking for, he would help. We were always misplacing our favorite toys, so we prayed, "Dear Saint Anthony, it is lost and cannot be found." To this day Saint Anthony helps me find the items that I lose.

We had the usual pastimes, like digging to China or spending hours making a cardboard boat that we knew would float. It was also fun to jump off the high porch railing at the front of the house using an umbrella as a parachute. (The bigger the umbrella, the better the ride. Daddy's big black *bumbershoot* had uses beyond the rain!)

After a summer rainstorm everyone would come out on the front porch to view the damage and to watch the sun reappear, forcing its way through the diminishing rain clouds. We kids would throw off our shoes and socks, then run through the puddles and sail our cardboard boats down the flooded gutters. We'd have to follow the fast-moving boats closely so that we could pluck them from the water the second before they would be lost to storm sewers at the street corner.

Many of those summer days were unbearable because of the heat. The radiant fever from the sun penetrated the uninsulated brick of the row houses, the concrete walks, and the macadam streets. We were reluctant to use the energy it took to breathe. There was no relief. No one had air-conditioning. I don't even remember any fans, except the hand-held reed ones and the printed paper ones (with advertisements) that funeral parlors gave out free.

At night, my sister and I would try not to move in the stifling hot bedroom. We would lie there, half-dreaming of the breeze that never seemed to come. And we listened through the open windows to the boisterous laughter and jokes from the neighbors as they sat around the kitchen table playing cards and drinking beer.

Our only break from the summer heat came on some longed-for weekends when Daddy was off from work. Then the whole family loaded into the car to go to a cabin set on the mountain above the town of Rockport, a small abandoned coal mining town in the Pocono Mountains area of Pennsylvania. The cabin was owned by old aunts, who shared it with our family. And there, under the pine trees, we found relief from the heat. We were lucky. Many of our friends didn't have an oasis to go to.

The simple hunting cabin had a wonderful charm—a huge open fireplace, a kerosene cooking stove, and *only* ice-cold refreshing springwater flowing from the tap. At night we needed comforters and blankets to keep warm!

We children thought the outhouse was much too far away, and we shuddered at the idea of venturing out there alone with a flashlight. My brothers relieved themselves over the porch rail. I thought to myself, I'm afraid of the dark. I'll try it over the porch rail, too. To me, it was worth hanging over the edge of the porch instead of facing the unknown night. Daddy *shlumped* me because I messed up the porch. He said I had to learn that women *waited* till someone else had to go, too. And I learned that, sometimes, we women fidgeted around till that time came.

The cabin was all alone in the woods. In contrast to the swarms of children in the neighborhood at home, here we had only the family to turn to for fun. With just a few toys at hand, we had to use our ingenuity and be innovative with our entertainment. My brothers, Jim and David, and I would spend hours making villages of all kinds out of sticks and stones and moss. We all hunted for orange salamanders after the rain. At night we read or did jigsaw puzzles by the kerosene light and the light of the fire in the fireplace.

Mother taught our family simple crafts early in life. I have always found real delight in making things with my hands. She inspired us to make our Christmas presents for all the relatives—and there were many relatives. We made blanket-stitched coasters, oilcloth covers for cleanser containers, string holders, hot pan holders, painted tiles for hot mats, and many other items.

Mother had a secondary reason for challenging us with handiwork all summer long. It kept our hands and minds busy, and kept us out of trouble. By the end of the summer, my brothers and sister and I had produced a lot of items and we felt a real sense of accomplishment. More than that, we were ready for Christmas! This training began a lifelong habit of keeping my hands creatively busy.

In contrast to the ruggedness of our weeks at Rockport, I had several summer vacations with my Aunt Mary, my father's sister, and Uncle Charlie. Every now and then they invited me to join them for part of their vacation at the elegant Chalfonte-Haddon Hall Hotel in Atlantic City. Peter, their only child, was my age, and we were always great companions during my stay.

Oh, what an event that was! I could hardly wait for Homer, their chauffeur, to come for me. With suitcase packed and white gloves in hand, I yearned to start the splendid ride alone. I felt like a little princess, sitting in the backseat of their big car.

I can still see the beautiful dining room of the hotel, with its huge, magnificent murals. At the end of the dinner meal, if we had behaved well and cleaned our plates, we knew we were sure to have a special treat. Later, we might be allowed to accompany the adults to the Saturday dance in the ballroom. It was fun for me to get all dressed up in party clothes and watch the dancers twirl across the floor. I tried so hard to be perfect during those weeks, in the hope that I would be invited again the following year.

One great fear of mine was the dark. I was absolutely petrified by it. Not until someone gave me a loud ticking clock to keep by my side did I feel a sense of companionship that comforted me, and then the fear of the dark became almost tolerable. Years later, Mother said, "Why didn't you tell us you were afraid of the dark?"

"I did," I said, "but everyone was too busy to listen."

Naturally, in a neighborhood of 52 children, there were squabbles—sometimes with words; often with fists. Occasionally, confrontations occurred between children and adults, usually because parents sided with their children in a disagreement. If the adults hollered at me, I hollered back just as loud, with no respect for age. A lot of parents went to bat for their kids, but mine took no sides. I had to fend for myself. And I did!

By the time I got to third grade, I had vowed to make my mark in life. I was very visible and active and I got into lots of trouble as a young girl. If anything was misplaced or broken, it was always Ardie who did it! Because I was always so busy doing things, Mother called me fidgety. But the truth was, I just had a lot of energy that needed to be put to use.

Saturday was chore day at our house. The list of to-dos was posted on the blackboard in the kitchen before we awoke. We took great relish in crossing off the accomplished jobs; we were that much closer to fun!

We were blessed with a large assortment of old aunts and uncles and family friends. On May Day it was our custom to make baskets, fill them with wildflowers, and hang the baskets on the doorknobs of their houses. Then we would run away to hide and watch their pleasure in discovering our gift.

It was always a treat to visit these dear people more formally. Each home looked as if time had stood still inside. There were so many interesting things to see—old grandfather clocks, beautiful china, books and pictures, the kind of old furniture we didn't have at home. I am amazed to realize now that my visits must have meant something special to them, too. We would always sit in the best room and aunts and uncles would come to talk with me and give me their undivided attention. It gave me a feeling of worth because I, little Ardie, was being treated as a real guest! I felt important. There were never any hugs or kisses, just warm smiles and conversation, and a sharing of experiences. Were they bored? No, it was an exchange of dignity in life for both generations.

On a summer's day, it was an absolute delight for us when Mother decided that we would take the 20-minute steam train ride from Allentown to Topton for a visit with Grandma and Grandpa Lessig, Mother's parents. Even today, the smell of sulphur in the air from the smoke of a steam engine stirs the nostalgia in my brain. Specks of soot adorned the windowsills; the horsehair-filled velvet seats with their brass trim were stiff and regal.

Grandma and Grandpa's house was across the street from the railroad station, so naturally life in this house revolved around the trains. We didn't need clocks: the 8:00 A.M. train from Reading to Allentown announced breakfast; we were to be at the table for lunch when the noon train rumbled by; the evening mealtime coincided with the train at 5:00 P.M.

The large house provided room for us to stretch—a welcome change from our tight home quarters. I could roam around in *unused* rooms, and live history in the attic. Or sit on the 17-windowed sun porch to watch the whole town come by to pick up mail at the post office across the street. (There was no mail delivery in Topton.)

Grandpa was a butcher and Horace, the hired hand, traveled around town in a horse-drawn butcher wagon to sell the meat. When I slept over, it was routine for me to awake early and go with Horace on his route. I sat on the passenger side of the wagon as we wove through the town streets, and it was my job to ring the butcher bell, like a school bell, at each stop. The women who responded to the bell would hurry out to the sidewalk in their sunbonnets, carrying a plate for their purchase and always a black coin purse.

"*Wie geht's*?" Horace would greet the customer. "Oh, all *recht,*" was the usual response. The conversation and the sale were conducted in Pennsylvania Dutch. There was always some conversation about little Ardie. (Yes, she was growing up a bit!) I felt important and special.

Thursday was butchering day, and Grandpa was very protective of us children on these days. We were not permitted to watch the slaughter; in fact, we were confined in the office until that part was over. But the door had a large keyhole so we could see what was happening. Once was enough.

Another hand was always welcome on sausage-making days. The meat had been cooked in huge cast-iron cauldrons. A hand grinder was attached to the counter and the casings were slipped over the nozzle like a long white balloon. With two hands, I would turn the crank as the meat filled and stretched the casing until it resembled a huge snake. And, lo, sausage was made!

We packed into the car every other Sunday during the winter to go to Topton for the rest of the day. All four kids huddled under a blanket in the backseat for the cold half-hour journey in the unheated car. When we got there, the first place I darted for was the heat register in the hall floor, where coal-fed hot air sent up a warm breeze. My Sunday dress puffed out like a balloon and I would stand there, in euphoria, until I was warm, kind of sleepy, and calm.

Meanwhile, the smells from the kitchen invaded my consciousness. There were turkey, chicken, roast beef, gravy, homemade mashed potatoes or filling, and corn and tomatoes. A favorite fresh lemon sponge pie or a hickory nut cake awaited on the cold windowsill for dessert.

The gastronomic delight, the joy of the company, the fun of sharing in the cleanup and the wonderful stories—while the men went to take a nap—will never be forgotten by the women who were there. Our family always stayed for the evening meal of leftovers.

Microwave cooking? I am forever faithful to the nostalgia that comes with old-fashioned cooking—and the exhilarating smells and anticipation while the meal is being prepared.

With great fondness I think back to Topton and my many, many visits with Grandpa and Grandma Lessig. I think back to all the interesting experiences and I remember the wonderful smell of the guest room, the beautiful painted china mirror, the crystal pin box, and the big soft bed. (How luxurious it was to wake up in a room by myself!) I loved those times. I was the Grandest Tiger in the Jungle. This was the only place I had a room to myself where I could stretch and feel special—and feel free!

I'll never forget one Sunday in December 1941. After we had finished the evening meal and the dishes were all cleared away, it was a ritual to listen to the Charlie McCarthy and Edgar Bergen radio show. This was the time to go to the special place in the parlor near the radio in the corner. We all sat very properly in this room to listen. The children had better not talk, because it was Grandpa's philosophy that children should be seen and not heard. The radio was tuned in, but instead of hearing jokes and laughter, we heard the shocking report that Pearl Harbor had been bombed by the Japanese. There was silence. We packed up the car and left.

Even we children felt the impact of the event, and all the way home hardly a word was spoken. Daddy drove into downtown Allentown where a newspaper boy on the corner was shouting, "Extra! Extra! Read all about it!" This was my first experience with tragedy.

I was in junior high school when the Second World War broke out. My sister, Joy, was four years older than I, and many of her high school classmates went off to war. Her friends were my friends, too;

when they were at our home, I always hung around with them. How I cried when Bill Whispel was killed in the South Pacific. I can still see his wonderful face and his beautiful smile. I guess I had a real childhood crush and it hurt so much to know that he would never come home again.

Mother was a USO hostess. As a Girl Scout, I worked a few hours a week at the ration board office. Meat, butter, sugar, shoes, and gasoline were on the ration list, but the scarcity of these items never really affected our family. We always seemed to have what we needed.

During this time, I learned to play the violin, and it taught me a valuable lesson. When I joined the orchestra, there was a wonderful awakening to beautiful music that thrilled and enriched me. But I never got to play the melody. As the time wore on playing second and third violin, I found it less and less gratifying. I wanted to be first! If I wanted to lead, whether it be in friends or music, it was clear that I must find ways to do so that were personally rewarding.

On the night the war ended, I was home by myself. Mother was on duty at the USO. When the thrilling, long-awaited announcement came over the radio, I was anxious to get in on the excitement, so I took the bus downtown. The streets were filled with people cheering, throwing confetti, laughing, drinking beer. Soldiers and sailors were kissing girls. Sirens were sounding, church bells ringing. Everyone seemed to be in the middle of the greatest party of their lives. I wandered around in the midst of the merriment, jostled willingly by the cheering crowd, taking in all the wonder of this once-in-a-lifetime event—alone.

As we grew, our six-room house became increasingly tight. I wanted to move to a bigger house in a better neighborhood. I was determined to make it happen!

Mother and Daddy weren't particularly interested in granting my desire for more space. So I began to read the ads for houses for sale and started to call real estate agents on my own. The agents would call back, and my mother would put them off. At my urging, they became such pests that Mother gave in and decided to look at some of these properties. Mother and Daddy found their four-bedroom dream house as a result.

I left our row house on my bicycle for the last school day of my ninth-grade year, and at the end of the day, I rode to our big new house at the other end of town. A new era had begun. Mission accomplished!

When I got to high school, I set my eye on the social crowd that I wanted to belong to. I couldn't gain the acceptance I yearned for, so instead of being a leader, I tried to become a follower of the pack. I pushed down my free spirit and lost a lot of self-esteem.

I took on various jobs, from baby-sitting to working for a florist. I even started my own summer day-care program—unique in those days. When school started that fall, I got a job as a salesperson in the gift department of Leh's department store. The job was ideal for the oncoming holidays.

The following year I worked after school in the credit department at Hess's department store. I learned something there that affected my life. I saw red markers after certain people's names to designate that they had not paid their bills on time. I was shocked and embarrassed for them. I vowed that this would never happen to me. If I didn't have the money to pay for an item, I wouldn't buy it! I still feel that way.

After high school, I went on to Kutztown State Teachers College, now Kutztown University. There I learned the personal discipline necessary to meet the constant deadlines an art student faces. As a freshman, I set high goals to make sure I would survive in the art field. At the same time, my ability to lead began to surface, and once more things were on an upward swing.

Life must have a master plan. Shirley, who was my "big sister" at college, got me involved in the Student Christian Movement, which stressed caring for the total person. We learned that there were four important areas of life: heritage, personal responsibility, the need to care for the community, and a commitment to world responsibility. The friendships I made and the programs I became a part of were uplifting and wonderful.

One of the programs included a summer spent in Europe on a work-study seminar. I participated and my eyes were opened to broader horizons as a result. I loved reporting on the happenings and new ideas I learned through the Student Christian Movement to the family at home. But this turned into a source of aggravation for Daddy, who would shake his head to say, "That organization is all pink. . . . Pink!" In his eyes, Russia and Russian ideas were all red. America and American ideas were all pure white! And yet he never once said, "Stop what you are doing."

The dean of women at Kutztown was a matriarch even though she had never married; she viewed all of us women as her children. We were being educated as teachers; therefore, we had to dress at all times as if we were already professionals—neat, no bare legs, and no shorts on the main street of the campus. We had *daily* room inspection. The rooms had to be in order and clean. Though young people today would probably rebel at such treatment, I know it taught us a discipline and an appreciation for neatness and order in our lives that has been a tremendous plus to me.

I made up my mind that as soon as I finished college, I would get away from Allentown. For me, Allentown was a dead end. I needed to get out, to see more of the world–even though it turned out to be only the next state, New Jersey, where I accepted a supervisory and teaching position in art.

The three schools that made up my jurisdiction were at least five miles apart. I should have had a car, but I had no money to buy one. An old relative offered to sell a car with 15,000 miles on it. I pleaded with Daddy to help me buy it. The answer was flat no, without explanation. And it was final. So I had to rely on the bus and on other people to transport me. And I hated it. I wanted to be independent! It was hard, but I stuck with it because I loved the teaching–especially the spontaneity of the little children.

The name Rodale was a familiar one in our house as I grew up. Bob Rodale's parents and mine were friends, since both our mothers were active in the art museum auxiliary. Ruth, his sister, was in my class in high school, and Bob was in the class behind.

The summer before I went to New Jersey to teach, Bob's parents gave a square dance at the farm where they lived. My gypsy dancing feet worked well, and I heard later that, at the end of the evening, Bob's father had said, "Now, that Ardie Harter is the girl you should marry. She has real spirit."

That year, at Christmastime, I invited my high school friends to my mother's house one evening to see the slides I had taken in Europe two summers before. Of course, I called Ruth, and as a last thought I said, "If your brother isn't doing anything, why don't you bring him along?" She replied, "Oh, I'm sure he is busy."

The night of my party arrived, and when Ruth came, Bob was with her. That night Ruth confided to *my* mother that *her* mother was upset because Bob was not dating any girls. I must have inspired a change of heart. The very next day, Bob called and asked me to go to a play. We had several more dates over the holidays, but all too soon the time came for me to go back to teaching.

On January 21st, less than a month after our first date, Bob asked me to marry him. Of course I said yes. He told me he would probably have to go into the service. Would I go with him? Yes, I said. It was all decided.

The next day at lunch, Bob said to his family, "Guess what! I'm getting married!" Everyone laughed. They thought it was a joke.

When he persisted, someone in the family finally asked who he was planning to marry. "I'm marrying Ardie Harter," he said.

"Over my dead body you will!" his mother said. She wasn't comfortable with the idea of having our families joined.

Bob wanted to do everything right. He went to visit my father, who was in the hospital after one of the several heart attacks he suffered in his later years. When Bob told Daddy that he wanted to marry me, my dear father said to him, "Are you sure you know what you are doing?" I believe he thought no one would ever want me.

Bob came from a Jewish/Christian marriage. The choice of religion had been left to him, and he had none. The wedding would be in my Lutheran church. We made an appointment with the minister because we were very concerned about his reaction to our interfaith marriage. We came to his door with much apprehension. When we left after the interview we couldn't believe the trivial questions he had asked us. He wanted to know what color the bridesmaids would wear and such things; we had come to talk about commitment, responsibility, and family. We left the parsonage disillusioned and confused.

It was February 12th and the night was rainy and very foggy. Mother would be waiting to hear all about what went on, and we were upset because we didn't know what to tell her.

We took a drive so we could figure out what to say. After we'd gone about 20 miles, Bob pulled into the driveway of a hotel to turn around. A pine tree blocked our view of the road as we emerged. We both looked and saw nothing coming, so we pulled out and found ourselves in the path of a tractor trailer's headlights. As it hit us, we were both thrown out of the car. I thought, I better put my head down, or the truck will break my neck. Another crash followed, as the truck completely demolished a car in front of the hotel. Bob and I escaped with only scrapes and the shivers from shock.

Mother asked very little about the disappointing meeting we had had with the minister. She was just glad we were safe.

It was a long four months until the wedding. My teacher's salary of $2,300 a year was barely enough for me to get by on. The salary checks were spread out over 12 months, so my take-home pay was about $45 a week. Anna Laura, another teacher, and I shared a studio apartment that cost us $100 a month. With our other bills, we barely made ends meet. Bob's visits on most Wednesdays, when he brought an armful of meat from his family's freezer, were our salvation. If we entertained during a week when Bob didn't visit, our guests had to settle for soup and salad.

The night before payday was always touchy. We often ended up with knockwurst for the evening meal—50 cents for two generous pieces. When I left teaching in New Jersey, I vowed never to eat knockwurst again. I have kept that vow.

Our wedding in June was perfect. At last I had found the perfect father for my future children—one who would laugh and play and be happy with them throughout their lives! He would be an inspiration.

Life was great. Bob and I did everything together. He went to night classes at Lehigh University, and I went with him. Part of this togetherness was due to my fear of being left alone in the dark, a powerful holdover from my childhood.

We bought a wonderful new six-room home in Emmaus and took great pride in furnishing the rooms. Bob liked modern furniture and I liked colonial, so we compromised by furnishing the living room in modern and the rest in colonial. I worked hard to make all the draperies by moving day, so that we would start our new life in a completely furnished house.

Our first daughter, Heather, was born in March, and to me, this was a dream come true. I had found utopia.

Those early days in the new home with a new baby were wonderful. Grandma Lessig gave us $200 for a hi-fi record player. This was a thrilling purchase. And when Bob came home unexpectedly with our first record, *Scheherazade,* it was just as exciting. We played it over and over again!

Another day, Bob came home, all excited, with a box. He had been to New York and purchased a beautiful replica of the bust of the child Christina by Houdin. My heart melted. This highly sentimental treasure has a place of honor in our home today.

At my family's home, family dinners consisted of everyone's telling about personal activities. Sometimes several people talked at once. The noisy get-togethers didn't happen often, but to me they were fun. To Bob, these times were often confusing.

Bob's family got together more frequently for a dinner—mostly every week. Here, instead of talking about what family members were doing, the excitement was in sharing new ideas. It was always very stimulating, exciting, and mind-stretching.

J. I. Rodale, or Papa as the children called him, was a nonstop idea man for new ventures. He was always trying out new health ideas, new sleep patterns, and new diets. In frustration, Nana would scream, "Jerry, I need 24 hours' notice of diet changes!" He was also presenting new ways of garden experimentation constantly. Papa was way ahead of his time.

I remember before we were married, my father would say to friends, in almost a whisper, "Jerry Rodale is a genius!" I felt lucky to be a part of this group. Papa often referred to the family as a big melting pot, and he was very proud that this mix of religions and backgrounds had happened.

As the years went by, the grandchildren were always included in the family gatherings. While they may not have understood all that was being said, I'm sure the children felt the electricity, the sense that something of great importance was going on in all of our lives. Some-day its meaning would all become clear to them.

Life was shaping up for me, but my parents faced serious trials. My father had had three heart attacks, each a year apart. Recuperation took longer with each attack. Daddy was lagging, so he decided to go to our cabin in the mountains. This had been his "no-stress retreat" for all his married years. He often went alone. This time he went with Mother.

The neighbors drove them there. Unwisely, Mother and Daddy had chosen to stay in the middle of the woods without a car and without a telephone. Soon after they arrived there, Daddy had another heart attack. Mother finally walked to the village to call the doctor. The old family doctor who tended Daddy called us and said, "Go up there at once. This is the last time you will see him alive."

Daddy's two sisters, a brother-in-law, my cousin, and I went to Rockport. We came in the door and stood there looking at Daddy lying on the daybed by the side of the fireplace. I saw his pitiful sadness as he cried softly, and I saw the child in him for the first time. Was he contemplating that his life was almost over?

Not one of us moved from the doorway to go over and take his hand, to console him, to tell him he mattered in our lives. Why were we so distant, when we thought of our family as being so close? We should have rocked Daddy in our arms. But the silent understanding was clear: We didn't share our emotions; we didn't touch.

Mother finally realized that Daddy should be in the hospital. But how could we get him there? We were so inexperienced. Even though we didn't own a station wagon, we could have rented one and made a bed in the back. Instead, the village undertaker, who was a friend of my parents, said to Daddy, "Stanley, as soon as I have to go down to Allentown to pick up a body, I'll take you there." It was agreed, and it was an unfortunate omen.

Daddy got to the hospital and succumbed to his final coronary shortly after. I was petrified of death. I didn't want to go near a dead body. Mother had her own ideas of what we would do at the funeral. She wanted us to pile our hands on top of hers, all resting on Daddy as though we were all part of a team in a huddle. I cried and sobbed in an effort to get out of doing that. But Mother insisted that the funeral wouldn't go on until I agreed to do it and become part of the group. I hated it! I was almost hysterical. I was 25 years old.

Soon after Daddy died, our daughter Heidi was born and then our first son, David. We had the perfect family and I, as leader, had almost everything under control. The children always had the best manners; they could be taken anywhere and they always behaved properly. I was on my way to being the best parent I could possibly be and teaching everyone to perform as expected. For now, life was predictable. They were the reasonable years. I took care of the children and Bob took care of me. It felt good.

Our neighborhood was largely composed of young couples, many of them new to the area. Again I experienced the need to fit into the group. Everyone was a do-it-yourselfer—painting, paperhanging, decorating, fixing. I thought that Bob should learn to do these jobs so we could blend in. I was convinced that husbands should do this kind of work. I didn't want to stand out from the crowd by paying to have someone else do it.

But Bob had his own priorities—working at Rodale Press and reading—and this type of activity was not on his agenda. Finally he said in exasperation, "If you want do-it-yourself projects, you do them, because I will not, and that's that."

A spark of old-time rebellion began to flame. I said to myself, O.K., if that's the way you want it, I'll show you. I soon learned to be first-rate at painting and paperhanging.

The families in our neighborhood became a community, enjoying one another as close friends. None of the women worked outside the home and we all coffee-klatched and chatted over the washlines, solving all life's problems.

Instead of traveling over summer holidays, we all stayed home and had our own clambakes and barbeques. We banded together for bridge and we celebrated every birthday. Covered dish parties were frequent. Then we moved on to progressive dinners and scavenger hunts.

Bob read a column in the *New York Times* about neighbors having parties with themes. Our group was not to be outdone. We divided into committees and each committee tried to have the best, most unusual party. The themes included a Backwards party, where everyone entered the house by a ladder through the window and at dinner the dessert was served first. A Poor Taste party gave the "worst" trophies to qualifying guests. A Hobo party featured cocktails served in tin cans. Of course, appropriate costumes were worn for each occasion.

Other winter evenings, we loaded at least 12 people into a station wagon to go to the burlesque. Those crazy fifties were loaded with laughs for us.

One summer day, life was going smoothly when a neighbor woman knocked on the door and asked us to sign a petition to have the yards sprayed by air to get rid of the bugs. We were horrified. "The bugs aren't bad," we said. "No way will we sign!" It was against our convictions.

"Well, we'll try to omit your yard," we were told. "Chances are some of the spray might float over. We can't help that."

The neighbors on each side of us refused to sign, in support of our stand. They didn't spray *that* year, but the possibility would always be there in some other year.

Bob and I were devastated. We owned our own home and our surroundings, or so we thought, but we still didn't have control over our space. We decided to move out! Bob's parents offered us land on their farm for a house and we took it.

We found our house plans in a book from the newsstand. This would be the perfect house. We started building right away.

The number of things we had accumulated during our six years of marriage was unbelievable. As the moving date came closer, the boxes to be moved piled higher and higher. The neighbors came to our rescue. Station wagons were loaded with boxes, and the car caravan drove to our new house, filling the driveway. After unloading, and amid all the boxes, we sat on the living room floor and enjoyed our beer party by candlelight.

The frenzy of putting life back together in a new location was exhausting. I said to Bob, "Don't ever ask me to move again! I'm here for the rest of my life." I meant it.

We enrolled the three children in private school and I began teaching part-time as art instructor at the same school to help pay the tuition.

David had just turned six when Maria was born. We were delighted. The doctor said, "She's perfect. Maria has the tiniest ears I have ever seen!" The three older children became assistant parents and life was still reasonably predictable. We all fit the mold.

As we grow up, certain things that happen make a strong impression. Later we sift through our conscious memories and say to ourselves, This was a good experience and I would like to carry this on throughout my life. Other times we say to ourselves, I want to drop this nightmare out of my existence.

As I remembered the postponed punishments I had anguished over, I vowed that my children would be disciplined on the spot. If they were sent to their rooms, I always went to them after allowing for some contemplation time and put my arms around them. We discussed what had happened and how the situation could have been different. The child was assured that, although his or her actions made us upset and angry, as a person the child was much loved. Then bedtime became a time of peace. I have always kept this promise to myself for my children.

Our home became a very busy place. We entertained a lot of visitors and our children were never excluded from the group. I got summer help to cope with the busy schedule of entertaining, freezing fresh garden vegetables, and taking care of the family, while I worked gratis for the family company. I was busy decorating a brand new building that was to house our company offices.

Three years after Maria was born, along came Anthony. This would be a breeze. I knew exactly how to cope. By this time I was a pro at child rearing. But Anthony challenged my comfortable sense of predictability. Suddenly, everything seemed to be out of kilter. We didn't know what was wrong. We tried to keep the family settled in the usual mold, but it wasn't working. For example, we always went on traveling vacations together, but Anthony in a car seat became a Houdini who could escape from anything. Though the assistant parents and I tried to hold him, he would dive from the front seat to the backseat, front to back, continuously. After ten minutes of this on a trip, we were all exhausted. We decided to stay home for a while. Life would be easier. We had to alter our pattern.

There was a lot going for me, yet I became increasingly sad. I was, in my neighbor's words, "only feeling medium." I was tired, and I had a pain in my chest that did not want to leave. I couldn't get beyond feeling blue, blue, blue.

One day, I happened to look at my two beautiful Haitian wood carvings; one showed a woman picking up a load of charcoal, and the other, a woman bent over her broom, sweeping. I thought to myself, These are me! My diary often contained this entry: "Today I've been the doormat again."

I was 37 years old and stuck in my own trap. How did I get where I was? And what about the four or five meetings a week for church, PTA, and other duties I thought I owed to society? I was filled with "oughts" and "shoulds" and a need to make sure that everything I did was done well.

Time passed and the pain in my chest got even tighter. I kept thinking of how sad life had become in spite of all I had. It was Lent and as I sat in church one Wednesday evening, the tears never stopped falling. I thought about losing sight of my dreams and goals. But what were they now? Were they still confined to being a good mother and having a good marriage, and working for society? I was so tired.

Was this all there was to life?

CHAPTER 2

Today my life is like the rain,
A constant drip of depressing thoughts
Sogging the soil of myself.

Ardie

It was Friday. I couldn't take the pain any longer. I called my internist and he let me come in for an examination that very day. "Ardie, I want to put you in the hospital right now," he said. "I think you might have myocarditis, an inflamed heart muscle. Please make arrangements with your family."

I called my mother to help out at home and I was admitted to the hospital that afternoon. Instructions were complete bed rest. I could sew if I wanted, but all I wanted to do was to lie in bed—no reading, no nothing. Cardiograms were taken every day, as the doctors tried to discover whether there was heart damage. I was told that my life pattern might have to be altered. I thought of a life with no more painting and wallpapering and no more dancing till the last dance. I thought about the possibility of not being able to wrestle with my kids. And I cried more and harder.

Eventually, I was allowed to go home. But still the slightest effort was too much for me. Even pushing in a thumbtack caused chest pain that lasted for several days. It was hard, being unable to pick up my baby boy, Anthony, when he came to me pleading, "Mamma, up." My sadness continued. Heather, at 14, became the assistant mother, and we couldn't have survived without her.

The doctor wanted me to have an angiogram. We decided to get a second opinion from a specialist at the University of Pennsylvania. The appointment was set for two months later.

Meanwhile, I slowly began to get better. Only a dull headache persisted. I kept testing myself to see how far I could go. I started walking, then bicycling, and, finally, running at my own pace. As they observed my activities, the doctors shook their heads in amazement at the speed of my recovery.

The day came for the examination–July 3rd. After the testing and questioning and prodding the doctor thought hard and said I seemed to be OK. It was cause for a celebration. We were exhilarated, and my life accelerated.

Bob was a member of the U.S. Skeet Shooting Team, and he left for 2½ weeks to compete in Chile two days after my examination. By the time he got back, I had the trailer all loaded up, ready to take off with the family the next day for the National Skeet Championship in Rochester, New York. Anthony, our baby, would stay home. The rest of us were eager to go on vacation. We planned to stay at a motel and use the trailer as our clubhouse at the gun club. It provided a good base for all the family to be together while we were at the club.

The circus was in Rochester, and we looked forward to giving the two younger children their first big top experience. The summer had been very dry and the dust filled my head. The vague headaches of my postmyocarditis days got worse.

The next day, a trip to a big shopping center for the wives and children of the skeet shooters was planned by the hosts. We were bussed there for a treat my children enthusiastically anticipated. (They all inherited their mother's love of shopping and scouting for new ideas and for trends in clothing.) On the return bus ride, I was shivering and shaking all over. What could be wrong with me?

We all went to see the movie *Born Free* that night, and the shaking started again. I knew I had a fever. All night I kept shivering and by morning I had such stiffness and pain that I could barely walk. I couldn't keep anything in my stomach. The house doctor was called.

The doctor arrived and I cried in agony when I had to get up to open the door. My illness was diagnosed as spinal meningitis. I had to be hospitalized immediately.

I was admitted through emergency and taken to my room. Bob had tried to get a private nurse for me, but none was available.

Then the tests started. The first was a spinal tap, for which I was told to curl up like a sleeping cat so a needle could be inserted in my spine to draw fluid. Something went wrong. The doctors probed five times; finally, when they switched to a larger needle, they succeeded. I remember how the perspiration rolled off my body, how the hand of Dr. Kneidle, the resident doctor, reached up to hold my hand in comfort as I felt the pain. When it was all over, the nurse said, "Roll over. Now don't move for 12 hours." She left the room and I was all alone.

I believe Dr. Kneidle was the very first person ever to show me compassion by touch when I was in pain. He was on emergency duty that night. It was a busy night. It seemed as though the ambulance sirens sounded every couple of minutes. I knew he was very busy, and yet he came every hour to check on me.

I couldn't sleep. My body was racked with unbelievable pain. I wanted to thrash around for relief—but I was not allowed to move. How would this all end? When would the pain decrease?

Bad as it was in those dark hours, I never thought about dying. My family needed me.

The wives of the other shooters worked out a plan for taking care of the children. Bob was scheduled to shoot his second day of the two-man-team event. He went to the gun club to report that he couldn't shoot because I was in the hospital. They asked him if he had brought his gun. Yes, he had. "Well, just shoot," they said. "It won't take long." As luck would have it, Bob and his partner tied for first place, and that meant he had to wait around for a shoot-off late in the afternoon.

I was alone all that day. Where was someone to help me? I couldn't even raise my head from the pillow. The only way for me to eat was to take the food in my hands, since managing a spoon or fork was out of the question. Didn't anyone care? I thought of my kids happily watching the White House wedding of Lucy Johnson on TV. If only one of them were here with me to help! I didn't know how to reach them, but even if I could, there was no way for them to get to the hospital.

I couldn't manage decisions in my condition. I felt as though I were at the farthermost outpost of the world. It was what I imagined hell to be like. There was only fire and brimstone in my agony. When Bob finally was able to come back to me at the end of the day, he found me desolate, devastated, and heartbroken.

Medications, including penicillin and painkillers, were started. All of a sudden, my mind played images for me. It was like watching a TV spectacular, with the channel being flipped every couple of seconds. I had never seen anything like this in my life. The part that I remember best was a wonderful happy clown standing on a tightrope with a big paintbrush in his swooping arms as he painted the most glorious rainbows across the sky! Wow! I thought, I can't believe this! It didn't last.

The birch doors in the room were beautifully grained, and I started seeing images evolving from the grain of the wood. The forms took on the appearance of people I was at odds with, and everywhere there were faces, faces, the same ugly faces. They wouldn't go away. The faces became more and more gruesome until they were only skulls looking at me. I closed my eyes, but the images were still vividly there.

The subject of the images changed. I saw a whole series of old, old photographs–family portraits, in grays and blacks–taken around 1900. I found myself as a child in the crowd. I was always in the front row. And I always looked so very sad!

I told the doctors about these experiences. Could it be the medicine? They said no. Finally, to the chagrin of the nurse, I refused to take the painkillers anymore, and gradually the grim images disappeared.

Telephone calls started coming in from relatives. To comfort and cheer me? No. They wanted to make sure that my children would be isolated from other people after they got home! My children were devastated. But the doctors told me there was no reason to fear that they might pass the infection on to others. The dissension this unfounded fear caused was too much for me to handle, and I started to relapse. All incoming phone calls were stopped by the hospital.

As I improved again, X rays had to be taken. I was wheeled down to that department in a wheelchair and required to sit and wait until the pictures were developed. The pain from holding my head up for so long became excruciating.

When I finally got back to my room, the nurse said happily, "I held lunch for you!"

"No, take it away! I can't ever leave this bed, ever again." And I sobbed and sobbed. Where was the hope?

But good things happened to me at the hospital, too. My bed had a small radio speaker under the pillow, and the sound was soft and beautifully mellow. I kept the classical music station tuned in almost 24 hours a day, and the fantasy music calmed my soul, eased the pain, and gave my spirit the wings it needed to survive.

Perhaps the most important of the good things occurred one day when my doctor, Richard Shaw, came to visit. His words would gradually change my life. He said, "I can't understand it. Here you are a young woman and you have had two major illnesses within the past five months. Some people believe that thoughts can make us sick or well. What are your thoughts?" I didn't know what to say.

Dr. Shaw's words haunted me. I just couldn't forget them. I asked myself over and over again, Why did I get sick? Subconsciously, I must have known that my depression would make me ill. Perhaps I had been denying the probable consequences for a long time. In retrospect, I think I stayed too long in that emotional state, and I never once asked myself what I was going to do about getting out of it. I don't know why. I was paralyzed with sadness.

My friends at home had contacted their friends in Rochester to tell them about me. I received notes and flowers and short visits from these people during my stay. I had never had that! It was soothing and heartwarming to know that even strangers really cared enough about me to reach out. I will never forget this enlightenment to a wider vision of community. I would reach out to others, too, when I was better.

I thought back to my father after his heart attack at Rockport and how we all remained at a distance from him on that visit, not attempting to touch. Times were changing in my life. Those around me were becoming sensitive to the comfort conveyed in reaching out. Now I think of it this way: Instead of people in my life living behind closed doors, they were willing for us all to stand in the sun together!

I finally became well enough to be transported home for the rest of my recuperation. The trailer was hitched and a bed was made for me on the backseat of the car.

Before I left the hospital, the doctors came to visit me for the last time. I asked, "How long will it be before I can start to do things?" They looked at each other and shrugged their shoulders. One doctor replied, "Maybe three weeks. Your cells must regenerate and each person regenerates at a different rate. We can't tell how long it will take you." I thanked them for helping me get better.

Little did I know how long the full recuperation of my inner self would take! It was a time to think and to begin a long process of a much-needed healing–of the body and the spirit. It didn't happen in a minute. The process took several years.

Again Mother and Heather became lifesavers for me by pitching in as I recuperated.

As I wrote this, I remembered just how I felt, but in all these years, I had never thought to ask Heather how she felt then. Now I wanted to know, so I called her on the telephone. "Heather, remember back when I was ill for almost a whole year and you came to my rescue by taking care of the family and me? You were only fourteen. Did you resent having all that responsibility fall on your shoulders? Were you angry?"

She was silent for a moment and then she replied, "Mom, I was afraid you were going to die. I thought that if I could help you, I would have you with me longer. I still feel that way about you. I feel that such challenges are given for special purposes."

I welled up with emotion. "Heather, you have truly touched my heart," I said. "It took me all these years to find out how you felt. I'm very proud that you're my daughter!"

Can it be that I am still healing in a wonderful way? That I am still discovering and appreciating those who really care that my life made a difference in theirs?

Precious Years

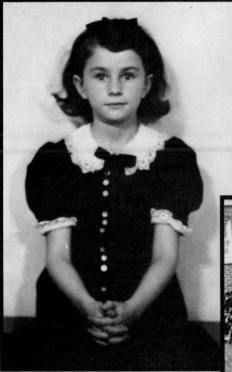

Even at six years old, my eyes were always looking far ahead.

Joan and I created new styles.

This was my engagement picture,
which was taken by Bob. 1951

June 23, 1951, was a very
happy day in our lives.

Heather, Heidi, David. Here's to the team! We always stuck up for each other. 1957

Heidi, Heather, David, Ardie, Bob, Anthony, and Maria, the year after my illness. 1967

There were fun times of togetherness. We loved making gifts for others to enjoy. 1965

Ardie, a model for Organic Gardening and Farming, *in the minidress era. 1973*

Bob, David, Anthony, Heather, Ardie, Heidi, Maria. Wishing you love now and for all seasons. Christmas 1975

David's place. This picture of the porch was Anthony's Christmas gift to David, given to him several hours before he died. When David saw it, he said, "Oh, it's so good to see home."

The Workplace. I have always believed that an innovative company needs creative work spaces.

T. L. Gettings

Jim Cook

Ardie and Bob. Thirty-eight years of growing together.

I hear David urging and calling me in spirit, "Mom, you have a story to tell. Please hurry! Please help people to understand."

STAGE II

Storms on the Mountain and the Umbrella of Protection

Tragedy had struck several of our relatives and friends who had children. I was so shaken by this that I made a pact with myself that I would be the best parent I could possibly be. The children would come first. Each child would be given the opportunity to grow to his or her highest potential. If and when any problems arose, this Mom would go to bat for each one! My children would all survive!

To make sure of this, the children were placed under my huge Umbrella of Protection. It was a shield against all the harmful elements out there in the world. For a long time, the children were content to live under this Umbrella. Because we lived in the country, it was easy to keep them there. The children developed strong bonds among themselves. Not only were they brothers and sisters, they became best friends and they watched out for one another.

School friends had to be imported, but the farm had wonderful places to explore, the house was loaded with books, and good food was always available for them. I did the usual chauffeuring for Scouts, for music lessons, and for David's drama classes. The children and I also had lots of craft time together. The family always gathered for the evening meal, where we exchanged happenings of the day. Bob and I took our turns at being PTA presidents. The children were included in all our formal entertaining, and they grew up learning to be comfortable with older people.

The family seemed secure—and then each of my children darted out from under my Umbrella of Protection at different times in their lives. They left not necessarily in order of age, so I speak about them in the order in which they left the Umbrella. I, too, was forced out from under the Umbrella so I could learn to understand them. These are their stories of self-discovery—and mine.

CHAPTER 3

Anthony -
Hurdling
Obstacles

---

*Today I am sharpening my perceptions. I can do a lot of things
well, but I want to strive for perfection in one field.*

Anthony

Our youngest son, Anthony, was the first one to dart out from
under the huge Umbrella of Protection. Strange that the youngest
would be the first.

Anthony came into our lives with boundless energy and a strong
will. He joined a family that had established a pattern of sticking
together. Maybe, small as he was, he sensed, I'm Anthony. I'm different.
I have to find my own place or be swallowed up in the crowd. *Look at
me.* I'll make you notice me!

He started by wandering from his bed at night. I often awoke in
the morning with a little warm bundle lying beside me. Preparing the
evening meal with Anthony the toddler around was particularly hard,
because this was the time he wanted my attention most. More than

once, in his frustration at trying to get more time from me, Anthony bit me on the backside. I was torn between keeping him happy and getting ready to feed my hungry family.

Along with his endless diving from the front seat to the backseat of the car as we traveled, this two-year-old delighted in jumping from the coffee table to the couch at home, not realizing where the next jump might land him! Anthony was a nonswimmer, not yet three, when he would put the life preserver near the rim of the pool and, with arms outstretched, jump into the ring and paddle to the ladder so he could come out and do it again. One time he forgot to extend his arms and he slipped right through the preserver. All the kids laughed. "Look, Anthony is swimming." All the terrified adults jumped in to save him from drowning. To him, this was the greatest fun! He went right back for more.

The summer he was three, Anthony's activities expanded to wandering around with the farmers and doing little tasks—learning how to plant and how to pull weeds, following along to feed the animals and discovering his love of the outdoors.

That fall, Bob was a member of the United States Olympic shooting team representing our country at the Games in Mexico. While families were discouraged from going to Mexico, it was acceptable for them to be present during the training period in Santa Fe, New Mexico. It was Bob's idea to take the two youngest children with us. I was too scared of flying to go by plane, and driving there would take too long. The only alternative was to take the train. I knew Maria, who was six, would do fine, but could we manage with Anthony? Would he cooperate? Till the time came for us to leave, I talked to him every day about being a good boy if he wanted to go with us. He would have to behave and be a part of the group.

The trip went surprisingly well. We took little games with us for the long train ride. The children enjoyed walking through the other cars to the domed car of the Super Chief, and even Anthony was fascinated as we viewed the vistas of huge open spaces and the tall mountains in the distance—and, finally, the majestic snow-capped El Capitan. The other passengers engaged the children in conversations and games, and those who had traveled the route before pointed out sights the children and I would long remember.

Santa Fe is a tremendous place to see things that would delight the eyes. We walked through the Plaza every day to look at the wares the Indians were selling—jewelry, rugs, baskets, trinkets. And every day we made a few purchases.

A side trip took us to San Ildefonso where Maria Martinez, the great potter, made her famous black pottery. As we entered the village, there was no one in sight. We felt as though we should whisper. The brown dusty earth was devoid of green, and as our feet touched the ground we had the hushed sense that comes when walking on sacred ground. It was a memorable moment.

Bob and I were grateful that all went well. Then he flew on to Mexico to compete in the Olympics and I brought the children home.

This had been Anthony's first experience in real cooperation. Maybe it was the way he would learn, by having his awareness challenged and by experiencing life in fresh and unusual situations. His energy continued to be limitless.

When it came time for kindergarten, I sent Anthony off with a sigh of relief. He was the only one of my children I didn't shed tears for as he boarded the school bus for the first time. Life at home finally took on some order again and I had time to take a few deep breaths.

In April of that year, I was called to Anthony's school for a special meeting. In a very kind way, I was told that Anthony had shown some learning disabilities in a standard test given to kindergartners. His score was just under the norm. Anthony was one of 17 such children who would be entering first grade in the school district.

Many of these children were designated as hyperactive. All had an above-average IQ, so it wasn't that they were incapable of learning. Rather, it was felt that they had a disorder in one of the learning processes. In order for learning to take place, a child's brain must input information and then send a message back which is output of that information. These children were experiencing problems on input and output, which was causing them difficulty in reading, writing, spelling, or math. No one knew then, or knows now, what causes this to happen. Among the members of Anthony's class, there were more boys with learning disabilities than girls. Was it possible that this tendency in Anthony was inherited from me? I looked back to my own unlimited energy and rebellion that I felt through life.

We were told that some children who had a hard time coping with school would gain the attention they craved by becoming the class clowns. Many became high school dropouts because they lacked a sense of belonging. What's the matter with me? they thought. I must be stupid. I can't learn. I don't fit in anywhere. I don't understand why I have to learn this. These children suffered from low self-esteem. Parents often label these children rebellious because they can't empathize with the terrible worry and frustration these children feel.

The school district proposed a pilot program for children such as Anthony. The students would get more individual training, and new teaching methods would be put in place to help children overcome their difficulties.

"There's no problem," we were assured. "After a couple of years, your children will fit right into a regular classroom."

School trips were part of the plan. Willingly, I signed up as a school trip parent to help with the children on their excursions. The content of the lunches some children brought on these trips amazed and appalled me. Most of them contained lots of sweets; one little boy never brought anything but a bag of candy. After seeing this repeatedly, I went to the principal and asked for permission to advise the parents about nutrition and healthy food. His answer was no.

The class continued through second grade. That year there were some new strategies. One morning a week, the 17 children were divided into three groups. The teachers rotated the groups, seeing each group throughout the morning. One teacher had a reading class, another math, and I taught an art awareness class. Since I was anxious to see these children become winners in life, I had volunteered my services.

I loved teaching, and it was fun to go back to doing lesson plans and coming up with arts and crafts lessons that would stimulate the children. Some of my most carefully prepared lessons bombed, while others, not nearly so well planned, were a terrific success. I tried to find out why. The other teachers had the same problem. We all came to the same conclusion that it was not the preparation of the lesson that made the difference, but the temperament of the children on that particular day that counted. What the children had for breakfast had a lot to do with that. One or two children with excessive hyperactivity on a particular day could destroy concentration and disrupt the learning effort of the whole class.

By the end of the second year, the program still had its problems, and the emphasis in the school district changed. The program was abandoned. All the children were absorbed into the regular classroom environment.

Bob sometimes became exasperated with Anthony's running, running, running. Bob would tell him, "Stop it! Sit down and read a book." I would see Anthony tighten up, and his emotions revved up to match his actions. His response was to run, run faster!

I discovered something very important through all of this. Sometimes, as a parent, I had to step out from under my own Umbrella of Protection to go where Anthony was. Then I could feel as he did—feel the rain in my face and my clothes getting soaked, feel the coolness of the moisture on my body, as well as the warmth of the summer drizzle. I had to experience what my son must be feeling in his good times and in his unhappy ones, when life seemed so hard as he faced the elements. There must be an escape from the traditional system; there must be a way—and we must find it!

The first in a series of very important learning experiences for Anthony happened at this time. We bought a second farm in Maxatawny, Pennsylvania, about 20 miles from our home, in 1971. We planned to use it as the Rodale Research Center. It was a large farm, an unspoiled one that had been held by a single family for eight generations. When Johannes and Gertraut Siegfried were granted the land from William Penn, it was inhabited by the Lenape Indians. Part of it had been a campground, and the land abounded in wonderful forests, many streams, and cool, refreshing springs. Today, many of the surrounding areas, now cleared of the forests, are owned and farmed by the Plain Mennonites. The soil is rich, and the land carries an aura of peace, the same sense we experienced in San Ildefonso. The landscape is different, but the reverence for the land is the same.

Ben is the neighbor at the next farm. He and his Mennonite family lease some of our land. Ben took a liking to Anthony at once, and said to him, "I would like to be a grandfather to you. I will show you many parts of living you do not know."

It was Ben's habit to walk the land silently in early morning and at evening time. His hands clasped behind his back, he would walk with his eyes concentrated on the earth. Ben was always hunting Indian arrowheads. His eyes were so keen and attuned to the soil that he sometimes stopped his tractor in the midst of daily plowing to pick up some unusual thing exposed when the soil turned over.

This was the learning Ben brought to Anthony, who was an awestruck, enthusiastic student. Ben told Anthony stories of how the Indians traded their stones between one tribe and another. He taught Anthony how to identify various rocks and recognize those artifacts that originated locally and those that came from other areas of Pennsylvania. Anthony learned a lesson from Ben that was to become one of his most valuable assets—the art of perception.

Often I looked out the window to see the two, the old man and the young boy, walking side by side as they observed the land. One of the most important elements of perception is to know what you are looking for! This is the generous gift Ben gave to Anthony in the many hours they spent together.

After a while Anthony began to venture through the fields by himself, walking slowly for the first time in his life, and never failing to find a treasure. Time and time again, Bob and I have wandered over the same paths—and we have never found a single arrowhead!

Ben took Anthony on other excursions too, riding with him on the horse-drawn buggy to family get-togethers on a Sunday afternoon. There the children played barefooted in the barnyard. There *he* was the child others were curious about, and *he* was the boy the girls looked at shyly out of the corners of their eyes. He was tasting the challenge of being on his own, making new friends.

It was customary for each of our children to attend camp for two weeks during the summer. Anthony hated it, but made the best of it for three years. It was his way to seek out the person who seemed most out of place, or one who was disabled, and give that person special attention to help make him feel in tune with the rest of the crowd. Anthony must have realized how it felt to be the odd one, or low man on the totem pole. There was a need inside him to help such people overcome their difficulties.

A milestone in Anthony's life was the arrival of a new family with two boys in the house next to us. Chris and Anthony were two days apart in age, and Mike was four years older. The parents, Pat and Mark, were younger than Bob and me. And the family was very different from ours. We tended to be introspective; they were very outgoing. Mark was a former football star from Syracuse, so the family emphasized sports—football, wrestling, skiing, camping. Anthony was adopted in spirit as Pat and Mark's third child. He was included in every vacation, all of which were sports-oriented. Often Anthony would finish his evening meal at home and quietly go next door for another meal an hour or so later.

Mark was a stickler for discipline, so if Anthony wanted to belong to the group, he had to comply. And he did, because he wanted so badly to be part of this family.

Outside interests always had priority over school for Anthony. He knew he was a winner in certain fields, but school was hard for him and he lagged. When it came to traditional learning, a feeling of low self-esteem persisted in Anthony. By the middle of his eighth-grade year, it was evident that as far as school was concerned, Anthony was in trouble.

Maria was attending Lawrence Academy, a private school in Groton, Massachusetts. Most prep schools have only one program and that program is geared to preparing the student for college courses. Lawrence is different. They have a course in which the creative student is allowed to write his or her own learning program, with the supervision of the staff.

Anthony decided that as much as he loved home, it was time for him to go there, too. This kind of learning was a godsend for Anthony. He worked hard and developed his confidence with the help of very caring teachers, who were also friends. His interest in photography zoomed. A special school program took him to the island of Belize, and later he joined a work study program on the island of Kalymnos in Greece. His knowledge of the world and its people was forever expanding. He loved the simple people and the sense of being close to the land. All the while, he was making mental lists for accomplishing new tasks. He organized his mind and set goals for himself.

To my great pride, the wife of the headmaster said to me one day, "You know, if any of us here wants a job done well, we ask Anthony to do it. He sees it through to the finish, and we don't have to go back continually to check on him. We are going to miss him when he leaves."

During the summer between Anthony's freshman and sophomore years at Lawrence, his assistant father, Mark, became critically ill. Life for Anthony and the two boys next door became very dismal and confusing. The boys were truly devastated. Pastor Tom, from the nearby church, came to counsel and comfort the family as they faced Mark's impending death, and Anthony was included in those meetings as a family member. He was very grateful. He said, "Mom, I hurt, too!"

Mark did die, but along with the fine legacy of love he left to his wife and two sons, he left an indelible memory of affection and respect in the heart of Anthony, the boy next door.

After graduating from Lawrence Academy, Anthony went on to Brooks Institute of Photography in Santa Barbara, California. Long distances and few vacations made communication between us hard sometimes. I often planned a little extra loop into my work travel for a visit with Anthony. It was important that he not feel pulled to entertain me at the expense of his schooling, so both of us had our days free and enjoyed wonderful meals and conversation in the evenings when we were together. On one of those visits, close to the time of his graduation, Anthony said to me, "Today I am sharpening my perceptions. I can do a lot of things well, but I want to strive for perfection in one field – photography."

As a part of his schooling, Anthony had the opportunity to go to Bombay, India, to make a documentary. The slide show, set to music, is called *Dabbawalla,* which means *box man.* It portrays the unique daily delivery of lunch from a worker's home in the suburbs to his workplace. The box passes through many hands and is carried on bicycle, on people's backs, on carts and trains to reach its destination. It is amazing to see that this business is conducted by men who cannot read, but who identify only by symbols. We swelled with pride at the quality of Anthony's work, especially the perception and sensitivity his slides revealed.

When Anthony graduated from Brooks, he was already leaning toward work in third world countries. Because he would need to speak Spanish in order to communicate, he went to Costa Rica to learn Spanish firsthand.

Today, working with his father, Anthony is a photographer for Rodale International. This nonprofit organization is developing an international network for sharing practical information and training techniques for regenerative agriculture and gardening, preventive health, and community development. The organization's goal is to help poor farm families around the world control their own lives. Anthony is specifically working to develop educational programs. He uses his photography to develop visual communication among the agricultural third world countries, and also within our own agricultural community.

Recently he said to me, "Mom, I love my life and my job. I'm living on the edge of tension, and that's the way I like it. There are so many wonderful challenges to be met. Last night I worked until 2:30 A.M. Today I am so invigorated because I see my life and my work coming together. It's great!"

I think back over these years, and what stands out in my mind is the importance of allowing children to make decisions and choices for themselves, as they grow. Parents, teachers, and other adults don't always know what is best. After all, they haven't walked in the young person's shoes.

To help a child develop self-esteem, it's vital to believe that your child will succeed. Find out what the young person's interests are, give him or her the opportunity to develop those interests, and then love your child through thick and thin. What's left for the parents is for them to be the best cheerleaders they can possibly be.

All through the years, I have tracked new developments for people with learning disabilities. About six years ago, a teacher who had been in charge of the remedial reading program for Anthony's first-grade class established the Hillside School, a school for learning disabled children, and I was asked to be on the board of directors. I am helping in whatever way I can to see that today's young people have all the opportunities Anthony didn't have when he started school.

Last Christmas, my heart was deeply touched when Anthony's present to me was a donation to the Hillside School.

If we believe we can make a difference . . . we will!

CHAPTER 4

Heidi
Taking a Stand

We called the neighbors. "Come on over for a party. We'll have a baby by tomorrow, so let's celebrate!" The neighbors came, but the party's atmosphere was very awkward. I realize now that the guests must have been sitting on the edge of their seats wondering, What is this woman doing? She's happy and laughing and we're scared to death because the baby might be born any minute! To the relief of one and all, Bob and I finally left for the hospital. By morning, we had a beautiful, tiny five-pounder whom we named Heidi. She was our second child.

From the time she learned to walk, Heidi showed a strong determination in everything she did. There was a fiercely independent air about her. "I want to do it myself!" was her most frequently used phrase. Heidi seemed fully aware of her every destination.

As soon as she was old enough to choose her own clothes, it was clear that Heidi would create her own style—tailored, never full and frilly. Look-alike dresses to match those of her older sister were out!

She was her own person, artistic and introspective. Heidi became a whiz at puzzles, loved books, and was gifted with a remarkable memory.

Though she started out as a talkative toddler, Heidi gradually became a very quiet child, talking only to the teacher throughout her nursery school years. When she did talk, her voice was almost a whisper.

Heidi and Heather would spend hours getting set up to play dolls, something Heather loved to do. Then, when everything was ready, and much to Heather's dismay, Heidi would sometimes suddenly announce, "I don't want to play anymore. I quit!" We were to learn this about Heidi as a child: She liked the planning much more than the play.

The summer weeks she spent at camp were important for Heidi because being there challenged her and taught her neatness, or so she said. I must say there were periods when this prized trait in her was hidden from me.

Through school, Heidi made friends easily. Perhaps her winning smile coupled with her shy way were the reasons. It was a challenge to get to know Heidi, but once committed, she was a faithful friend.

Whenever I wondered where Heidi was, I was likely to find her tucked in a corner with a good book. Sometimes it exasperated me that she seemed so content to be alone. She didn't seem to need me, and that thought bothered me. The rest of the family would be carousing around, talking and laughing, and often as not, Heidi would be missing from the scene.

Years later, I was amazed to discover the real reason that she went off alone so much. "I was angry with you because you gave so much time to Heather and David," she told me. So this was why I sometimes caught Heidi looking at me as though she didn't like me, or didn't approve of me! I also learned that Heidi hated the dancing classes and many, many of the other things we had her do as a child. These were things I wanted for her, not what she wanted for herself, she said. But how could I have known? Heidi never told me what she wanted for herself.

For a long time, Heidi stood under my Umbrella even though she really didn't want to be there. She rebelled inwardly, in contrast to the way I spoke up as a child for what I wanted. It's hard for me to imagine now how far apart we were as we went through those trying periods, and harder still to understand why we weren't aware of our distance at the time.

I found a letter I wrote to Heidi when she was 15 years old.

Dear Heidi,

We are all pieces in a puzzle of life. Each piece has a function in creating the whole picture. If one piece is missing, there's a hole. The picture is incomplete. So it is with the family. Each one has a function to perform in making a harmonious picture of life. We all have to work together toward that masterpiece.

You don't know how hard I as a mother try to teach everyone to be pleasant and to work together at home. It often seems that you act as if you don't like me. These are the times I'm most tired . . . and perhaps out of sorts from too much to do. I know I'm not presenting my best self sometimes, but I do try hard to please.

I want the best for you in life, but you must be willing to cooperate, to help and appreciate and give more of yourself . . . then things will start coming your way. We can't sit back and wait for people to come to us . . . because that isn't the way life works. I realize we are all far from perfect, but we can't stop and analyze our lives and try to plan where we are going and above all what kind of person we want to be. Every day we must practice to be a success in life. It's like the story of the Great Stone Face. We grow toward the image of what we admire.

I love you, Heidi, in spite of the fact that we have disagreements. My love for you never stops even then. . . . I'm just disappointed that we can't come to an understanding.

The best gift anyone can ever give anyone else is a smiling, happy, willing heart!

Love, Mommie

After her junior year in high school, Heidi decided to take summer art classes at Carnegie Mellon University in Pittsburgh under a program that allowed high school students to explore their interest in the arts to see if this were the direction they wanted to follow as a career. It was a wonderful summer for Heidi. Her eyes were opened to wider vistas.

Later that summer, Heidi and I went to look at other colleges she might want to attend after high school. On the way up to the New England states we stopped briefly to look at Cornell University and

Ithaca College. On the tour of Ithaca College, we entered the perform-
ing arts building while the symphony orchestra was rehearsing. The
beautiful music was enthralling. It seemed perfect to us. But the
conductor tapped his baton impatiently. "No, no, no! This is all
wrong! You are merely playing notes. *You must get excited!* Now let's
begin again." The music flowed again and as it touched our hearts, the
tears came to my eyes. What a wonderful lesson this was for life. We
bring so much more meaning and beauty to everything we touch if we
are excited about living! Neither of us ever forgot this experience. Life
was good just then as we looked forward to Heidi's finding a school
where she would be happy and feel inspired.

Soon Heidi's senior year of high school was completed and
graduation night arrived. She looked forward to the big party we
planned to have by the pool after the ceremony. All kinds of wonderful
food had been prepared and decorations were in place. As we dressed
to go to the ceremony, the telephone rang. It was a reporter from New
York who told Bob he had heard a report that Bob's father, J. I. Rodale,
had died. Was it true? he wanted to know. "There must be a mistake,"
Bob said. "Someone is playing a bad joke."

We had to get to the root of all this fuss, so we sent Heather on to
the graduation with the family. Bob and I would follow shortly, as soon
as we got this all cleared up.

We never got to the graduation. It was true. On that day in 1971,
Papa had had a fatal heart attack while taping Dick Cavett's television
show. Bob and I left for New York immediately.

When the children came home from the graduation ceremony,
they heard the sad news. Of course, the party had to be canceled. Cars
drove up loaded with young people all raring to go for a good time, only
to be turned away with the news about Papa. A sad punctuation to a
happy event.

But life continues, and with great anticipation, Heidi planned
her first year as an art major at Carnegie Mellon. I was delighted at
her choice of such a challenging school. And there were many challenges in store, for Heidi and for me.

Shortly after Christmas, Heidi called me. "Well, I gave almost all
my clothes away to the Salvation Army, Mom!"

I cried. "Heidi, what for? All those beautiful clothes! How could
you do a thing like that?" She had really made a dash away from
my Umbrella!

Heidi's astonishing actions made me feel as though I'd been hit
on the head, and I flailed around in my inability to understand what
was happening. I was miserable, and I felt unloved and lonely, even
though there were people all around. Why were my daughter and I at
such odds? Why would she want to rebel against the values and

lifestyle of her secure home? The advantages were here. She had it all, I thought.

Heidi told me later that giving away her clothes was a symbol of clearing out the junk of her life and taking a stab at her own independence. She was erasing the traces of everything we wanted her to be and do—the dancing classes, the charm school, and the rest. All the things we had thought would be good for her, to help her get a head start in life.

And this was only the beginning, the first of many startling ways Heidi showed that she was taking off in her own direction. Heidi the quiet one; Heidi the reader.

What Heidi did next was a tremendous breakthrough in her own self-searching, and among the most significant things she contributed to my life. Heidi began a serious study of Gestalt, a theory and technique for dealing with life and life's problems.

Basically, Gestalt teaches that all of life's experiences should have a beginning and an end, a completed circle. Each experience has a continuity that leads to a definite conclusion. That means any problem can be resolved, and that resolution releases you to go on to another experience. A life situation whose continuity somehow stops abruptly and hangs unsettled is called an open Gestalt. It results in a bad or uncomfortable feeling because the cycle of the experience isn't finished. We must find a way to finish the experience, for that's how we heal our wounds. It is essential to get rid of anger and frustration and disappointment before that healing can take place.

The first thing Heidi felt she had to do was get rid of her anger towards me and to break away from what she thought were my unreasonable expectations of her. She had to become the pilot of her own plane, and this would come through a progression of lessons and experiences in Gestalt.

The next summer Heidi announced her plan for an extended stay at The Farm, a commune in West Virginia. I huddled under my Umbrella of Protection and feared for her, because at that time the idea of a commune scared *me!* It was a concept I didn't fully understand, nor did I want to. Heidi came home about a month later and brought Jane with her. Jane was close to 30, and I was puzzled at Heidi having an older friend. As it turned out, Jane was not only a friend but acted as an older sister who understood Heidi's striving for independence. Jane provided time and a sympathetic ear for Heidi when it was needed desperately. Later I wrote to Jane to say thanks, and I meant it from the bottom of my heart.

In October, after Heidi had gone back to Carnegie Mellon, I wrote her the following letter. At age 43, I had made a thrilling discovery I simply had to share!

Dear Heidi,

I feel that I must write to you. I know now what I want to do in life!

Remember a couple of times this summer, we talked about this subject and my answer was always, "I don't know, but not really what I'm doing now." When I started to tell Dad about my new ideas, I had to laugh because some of it, I think, is what you are striving for, too.

I want to feel the pulse of life! I want to know everything I can learn about people and awareness in all aspects of daily association with people and experiences. I want to experience so many things, to know how it all feels, and how others feel, and how all of this fits together. I want to be so sensitive to life that I know how even the smallest thing feels in life. Some of this might be called empathy.

How is it that I used to have ESP and now it's gone? How come I no longer am able to express my thoughts in writing? How come I stopped having the real feel for life?

Now it's almost like stepping out into a dream, like Alice in Wonderland. All of a sudden, I'm really happy and filled with anticipation for all these new experiences. Perhaps my sleeplessness is a sign that I don't want to miss any of this. It's one life and I've got to know!

Evolving as a more aware person calls for being more aware of others, knowing how they feel and think, feeling their emotions with them. Perhaps along the way, we can help one another to be our real selves.

Much of this has been on my mind for a long time, and for one reason or another, I was afraid to express it, afraid, perhaps, of what others might think.

When you were home from Virginia with Jane, one night Jane and I sat out on the grass and talked about many things, what all, I don't remember. But what is important is that I think that experience opened the door. I couldn't sleep that night and got up and wrote 14 pages of how I felt about a lot of life. Perhaps a person must come to a low point in life before she can break out in desperation to live.

Lately, life has really been beautiful . . . work gets done, I'm enjoying my jogging in the beautiful world . . . and even picking persimmons in the rain . . . association with new people . . . and perhaps even the rug-hooking is helping to force my creativity and time to think.

Along the way, I hope that life becomes better for our family and friends. While each of us is distinctive, some of us are also similar. There are so many people in this world who are merely existing and I don't want to be one of them.

So, these are my thoughts. Perhaps some will change, but above all, I don't want to go back to what I was before. I wanted to tell you this.

Love, Mom

Life never continues long in a smooth stream. Heidi's next bombshell was her plan for a trip to California during the coming summer—hitchhiking and camping across the country with another girl! I blew up when she sprang that one on me.

Dear Heidi,

I'm sorry about the outburst tonight. I know how important it is to discover yourself as a person and to be independent. It's something each person must do to find out where they belong in life. Some people find it with no trouble. Some take a whole lifetime and some, in that time, never find what they are looking for.

Life is a progression of steps . . . mountains or obstacles . . . whatever you call them. Each one gives us incentive to climb beyond . . . or . . . if we are weak, give up! I shudder to think of giving life to anyone who gave up on life. I want to fight for it!

But, Heidi, believe me . . . there's a right way and a wrong way about doing it. Please listen and don't close your mind yet.

This week while at work, Peter, who works in the company's kitchen, cut off the tip of his finger and I had to rush him to the doctor's office. The doctor's office was crowded and I had lots of time to sit and think and observe. There was a very young couple, homely as you could find anywhere, obviously very much in love. They had brought their baby to be checked. With amazement, I looked at this mite and thought . . . they sure don't come any smaller or more perfect! The mother proudly announced, "She's two weeks old and weighs five pounds one ounce."

A quick flash passed through my mind. This was just like Heidi . . . beautiful and perfect. My love for you has never stopped all of these 19 years even though we have been at opposite ends many times. Dad and I brought you life and it's precious to us and we hope that life to you will be that way . . . an ever unfolding experience . . . with the beauty of an opening flower . . . one that can withstand the sun and the storms of

*life . . . one with stamina and dignity that will not mar the
miracle of that life.*

*I'm not against you wanting to find out about life . . . but
when one deliberately throws one's self in the path of danger to
that life . . . I want to fight too, for your life that I brought into
this world. If you feel that the answers are in California then by
all means go . . . but travel by bus, train, or plane. I can't
understand why you have placed such little value on life and
my heart cries for you. I'm wondering how long it will take for
you to grow up and realize that each of us is not an island and
it's caring . . . and sharing . . . and loving other people that makes
the world a better place in which to live . . . and in helping
others, we discover ourselves.*

With love, Mom

Gratefully I report that the California trip never came to pass that
summer. However, Heidi did drive to California with a friend the
following summer. While Heidi was away, I became the caretaker for
Heidi's dog, Kazak, a Siberian husky. It was another chore for me,
and a hard one. Kazak liked to run away, and he discovered the
neighbor's sheep where he wreaked havoc. He killed!

I wrote to Heidi in California.

Dear Heidi,

*You asked if Dad and I minded some of your decisions
about what you were doing.*

*I told you that we brought you up for 19 years trying to
instill in you a way of life that we thought was right. Perhaps it
was an extension of our lives. What is right for one person might
not be right for another. There comes a time when each one
must branch out on his own to find out what is right for him.
Your time is here.*

*It's taken me a long time to grow up because I never had the
chance to express my true self when I was younger. I had lots of
ideas . . . not as broad as yours . . . but I only thought them. My
life was governed by fear of bad reflections on my parents
. . . what other people might think of me, and fear of spoiling the
image I wanted people to see. In the words of my father, "Prove
yourself." This facade or fear has traveled with me for many
years . . . spreading into many other areas. I had to keep my
dreams private and guard them with care to keep them safe
from others. It was my own private world . . . and I spent a lot of
time there. Perhaps this was an escape . . . and when I was
sad . . . this world lifted me up and it was beautiful.*

Because of all of this I held grudges, especially against my father, because I felt that he was to blame for my being where I was. I said to a friend at Christmas that I never related well to my father, and after I said it, I realized that the grudge was gone. I climbed a mountain and saw him in his own light . . . someone who was trying to do the best he knew how. His vision was not mine. I am finally free of this barrier that he made . . . and I kept all these years. I am now seeing myself grow in ways that I never expected to be possible. It's almost a year since you came back from The Farm which was perhaps the beginning of it all. I am reading so much these days as I feel starved for finding ways to expand. I want to hold on to all these new ideas and thoughts and use them as a ladder to climb higher.

This is what I am trying to do now with my Couples and Singles class at church. I am so filled with the idea of change that I think everyone must be made aware of the potential of being more of an alive and growing person. I've been trying to give them a jolt! Some of them are challenged, but some still just sit there and listen, and you wonder whether anything will change them.

The choices you make now, Heidi, are basically your own. Perhaps you will be better able to cope with some of life's later problems as you exercise your ability now.

No parent knows all the answers. Lately life is tumultous and fantastic. I don't want to live in dreams anymore, but in reality of this great expanding world of now.

One poster I have says, "Love is giving someone room to grow in his own way." Do you understand what I am trying to say?

Love, Mom

I was still getting upsetting messages from Heidi:

Mom, I'm busy. . . . I have work to do. . . . I don't want to talk to you.
Mom, can't you see I don't need your advice?
Mom, hurry, I'm late. . . . Hurry, I can't wait.

Heidi completed her junior year as agreed (I'm ashamed to admit that I bribed her to do it), then informed me very decisively, "I'm not going back to college for my senior year." And she didn't.

That summer Heidi was ailing. She had been to the doctor a number of times, but it was she who initiated each return visit. Whenever he did see her, the doctor just gave her more medication with no follow-up appointment. One day, we were sitting on the back porch as Heidi returned from one of the doctor visits. She dragged herself up the steps and told us that she had three infections, according to her doctor. I asked if she was scheduled for another appointment. She said no.

Our son-in-law, Tom, who has a Ph.D. in microbiology, took me aside and said, "Ardie, Heidi must see a specialist. I'll see that she gets an appointment tomorrow."

I went with Heidi the next day and this doctor admitted her to the hospital immediately through Emergency. We could have lost her.

Something in the relationship between Heidi and me began to change at that time. Maybe it was because I gave her my undivided attention throughout her illness. Maybe this was time together that we should have had long before. Just the two of us. It was a beginning.

After her recuperation, the first thing Heidi did was to move out of our house.

Rodale was developing a velodrome in Trexlertown, and the touring cyclists who rode there needed a place to stay over the summer. Nana owned a house in Allentown that she was willing to let these young men use. They would need someone to run the house and to cook, and Heidi volunteered to do it. It was Heidi's job to provide a healthful, appetizing breakfast and dinner every day to satisfy those hungry appetites. Much of the produce was freshly picked from our farm. Heidi did comparative shopping to get the best prices for whatever else she had to buy. She introduced the riders to granola, brown rice, and yogurt, health-giving foods most of them had never tasted before. I believe the high-nutrition diet might have played a role in the miraculous way everyone got along so well.

Sometime after Heidi's velodrome summer, Nana invited Heidi to accompany her on a trip to Egypt, Lebanon, Turkey, Greece, and Iran. The Shah was still in power and Iran seemed serene and beautiful. The trip was a lesson in how people from two generations, miles apart in their thinking, can learn to get along. When I asked her how it all went, Heidi replied, "The amazing thing was that, even though it was the two of us traveling together, we were never alone. Nana talked to everyone, so we found ourselves eating most meals with people she picked up in those conversations."

On the last leg of the trip, Heidi made arrangements to spend some time in London with her brother David, who was studying there. It would be good for the two to be together. I got a phone call from them late in January, and it made me so happy to hear their voices, to know that all was fine. But they were only calling because they wanted something. Money, what else? My ire was aroused immediately, and I had to let it out, so I wrote a letter. "Another of your famous letters, Mom . . ."

Dear Heidi and David,

There's a lot on my mind these days and I wonder whether I have done the right thing by you in helping you grow up. Even though I have released you to your own decision making and living your own lives, I hope that my efforts to impart my thoughts and ideals all these years have not all been in vain.

One of the prime things that bothers me is the question of consideration. In nine out of ten cases in the past . . . you came first willingly. . . . I wonder about the other side of the coin and I think that as far as Mom was concerned, you considered me one in ten. The money I was saving for my vacation has now been sent by Western Union across the ocean. . . . When I asked a simple question out of curiosity and not out of reprimand, I got the message, "Why must I tell you? It's not your business." Yet, it's my business to send the money . . . take care of the cars . . . the animals . . . the bills . . . whatever needs doing from this end. I have done so willingly.

Everyone wants to be free and independent . . . and the more I see, the more and stronger I want it for myself . . . but I still have a caring and a consideration for other people's feelings and their needs.

You have reached for your independence, but you must learn to live within your means. I want you to know that I no longer feel obligated just because I am your mother. I am an equal, with equal rights. All life is a struggle to find our way, and to be appreciated and loved . . . each one in his own right . . . for his own uniqueness. I still love you and appreciate the good that is there. . . .

Mom

After Heidi returned, she started working for Rodale Press as library promotions manager in the Book Division, and life with her and me was reasonably quiet. There was still a distance between us, but the worst of rebellion was past and we were working toward an improved understanding.

When the time came for my annual working visit to a branch of our company in England, Heidi asked if she could go along. I had taken her younger sister, Maria, with me before, and now I was glad to have Heidi to myself because life for us seemed so much better when we were alone. We took side trips to Bath and wandered through the art museums; we went to plays and restaurants, and just enjoyed life.

Nana decided to come to England while we were still there and she arrived on the second-last day of our stay. All three of us went out to visit the company offices in a town outside of London, and we had a wonderful day giving Nana a rundown on all that was happening there.

At the end of a full and eventful stay, we boarded the return train to London. We planned to have a nice dinner together at Nana's hotel that evening. The train pulled into Euston Station at about four that afternoon and we walked easily through the uncrowded concourse. Nana walked between Heidi and me and I was thinking about how simple it would be to get a taxi before the rush hour. I turned to say something about it to Nana and Heidi, and, very calmly, I said to myself, Why is Nana lying on the ground, moving backwards?

Everything happened so fast that Heidi and I were stunned and confused. Nana had been mugged while we walked on either side of her! Now she was being dragged along the terminal floor because she wouldn't let go of her purse. Fortunately, a passerby chased the mugger away, but not before Nana's shoulder was broken.

When we finally made it back to the hotel, the doctor there sent Nana to Middlesex Hospital. Because it was Friday, most of the doctors at Middlesex were off for the weekend, so we spent endless hours in the waiting room. The emergency room staff was practicing triage, and they didn't consider Nana's shoulder as a priority. Finally it was her turn. On the following morning, all three of us left London for the long journey home. It was an unfortunate and upsetting end to an otherwise happy reunion time between a mother and her daughter.

At 26, Heidi returned to Carnegie Mellon to finish her fine arts degree. Now she painted with real determination. There was a marked difference in her work. That spring she was given a one-woman show at the school. I went to see the show and to visit Heidi for that weekend. Her work was outstanding and well received. I could have burst with pride over Heidi's accomplishment! One of her teachers took me aside at the exhibit and said, "Sometimes Heidi is a puzzle. She is a person of real depth, who is waiting to be discovered. And it will happen when she is ready. . . ."

Heidi's work is beautiful, if occasionally elusive, with some impressions left to the imagination. Looking at her work is like entering a garden and being continually surprised by the treasures that can be found there. She is a deep well, and what comes to the surface is cool, imaginative, and refreshing.

Heidi and Maria moved into a house in Emmaus together. While there were times of disagreements and growing pains for each one, a strong bond developed between the two. Heidi and Maria became strong pillars of support for each other as they strove to find their way.

Heidi resumed her interest in the velodrome races and became a regular there on Friday nights. She renewed her acquaintance with one of David's close high school friends, Charlie Norelli. Their friend-ship grew into love, then marriage.

Charlie is a doctor of rehabilitation medicine and the delight of their lives is their two sons. Motherhood has brought a love to Heidi's face and heart, and she shares the joy that is now so obviously hers. She is seriously committed to equality for all people and strives to help achieve it the world over. Heidi is presently working on a new magazine that deals with the human spirit.

As all the children grew and began to move off in different directions, we began to lose track of what each one was doing. Heidi started a family newsletter as a way to bridge the gap. The first issue was in the works when David died. She finished that issue, but with it the drive was gone. She said, "David did it all. . . . "

Heidi and I had been to Canyon Ranch Spa, a favorite retreat in Tucson, Arizona, separately. Now, the spring after David's death, the two of us decided to go together for a week-long session on Stress for Women in Family Business. The session was canceled, but we went anyway and met a number of women who had signed up for the seminar, too. Our informal discussions with them showed us that others in family businesses had some of our problems, and we came away with some possible solutions. That week was one of the most healing experiences we could have had together. Finally, we saw each other as equals, with genuine lines of love connecting us.

Using the gift of hindsight, I can see now that we should have asked each other earlier, "How are we doing together?" Perhaps I should have done more things with Heidi, just the two of us. Maybe we both needed to listen more sensitively. I've discovered that true understanding just doesn't happen. It must be pondered over and absorbed, and then experienced.

As Heidi grew up, I thought she *must* be a part of our free-for-all wrestling matches and the other happy, crazy things that we some-times did as a family. I thought that she *must* want me to dance with her until we fall, and laugh with her until we can't laugh anymore. She *had* to want that, I thought!

This is where I think my relationship with Heidi might have gone wrong. I wanted her to enjoy *my* idea of good times. I loved her too much to let her miss them. I couldn't admit to myself that she could be so different from me.

Now I watch Heidi play with her sons and have fun and giggle. I see that she's finally the kind of free child I always wanted her to be—but on her own terms. Always on her own terms.

CHAPTER 5

David

A Different Path

Families must not be sacred. Individuals must be. So, too, relationships and involvements, although held in high regard, must never include sacrificing your own individuality.

David

As I sit here ready to write David's story, I smile to myself. Without realizing it, I am wearing his favorite color, turquoise. Maybe he loved it because turquoise was his December birthstone.

I think this chapter should be subtitled "David the Creator . . . Ardie the Expediter."

With tears of joy we greeted our first son, David Evan, born two weeks before Christmas. How lucky we were to have three healthy children! Heather, 4½, was constantly at the cradle's edge, checking to see if he was all right.

Early in his life, it was evident that David was a dreamer. He was content to sit quietly on my lap for long stretches, thinking his own thoughts. He was a *good* little boy, with a deep, wonderful chuckle that bubbled to the surface whenever he was amused.

We lived on the Organic Farm, an experimental center for Rodale Press, about 500 feet from the house where Bob's parents lived, and David loved to go there to spend time with his grandparents. He enjoyed eating Nana's good soups, and most of all, he like to sit at the huge table with Papa while he worked. Papa had a strong influence on this little lad. Even before David knew how to write, Papa would hand him paper and say, "Here, write a play." And David would seriously scribble page after page of his "play."

We had a collie dog named Sparky, and the farmer who worked our land owned one of her puppies. Naturally, we saw both dogs running and playing together all the time. One particularly cold morning, I dressed David in his warmest snow outfit, and I wrapped a long scarf around his neck to protect him from the bitter wind. As I watched this lone little soul pass through the garden area on his way to see Papa, the two dogs suddenly appeared. Playfully, each dog took a different end of the scarf in its mouth, and the dogs tugged at the scarf ends in opposite directions, pulling David to the ground. I screamed at the sight, and Bob ran as fast as he could to rescue his petrified child, whose face was now white with fear. David never could forget this terrifying experience, and neither could I.

David was gentle and peace-loving. Even as a first-grader, David never joined in the fights small boys sometimes seem to relish. He would take any abuse that came his way, but he refused to fight back.

David was clever and innovative–always busy making things with his hands, playing music, or writing. He would sit by the piano for hours making up little tunes, sometimes driving me crazy as he repeated the same several bars over and over again. He seemed to be trying out concepts in his mind, and he wouldn't give up until they were perfected. All the children took piano lessons, but with David, Mr. Norman threw up his hands. He said David would never master the piano. Undoubtedly, David was bored with the lessons at the time. Later, as a young adult, David composed beautiful music in a classical vein.

David was always plagued by sore throats, and his repeated bouts with them seemed to wear him down. When he was in first grade, we decided to get rid of the tonsils. On the morning of the operation, I waited impatiently at home until the doctor called to say all was well. Then I rushed to the hospital to be with David. When I got to his room, he wasn't there! The nurse assured me he was probably in the recovery room.

I waited a long, long time, and as I walked absent-mindedly around the hallways, I noticed a nurse wheeling a small child on a litter. I looked at this child and thought, Oh, that poor child, he must be awfully sick. He has absolutely no color. . . . Oh, my God! It's my son! I became almost hysterical. David had hemorrhaged and had been rushed back to the operating room. That's why he was gone so long.

It took six weeks for David to get well enough to go back to school. I was so thankful my Umbrella was there keeping him safe and nursing him back to strength.

Like the rest of the family, David went to camp for two weeks each summer. Traditionally the boys' and girls' camps held a Brother-and-Sister Day, on which any camper who had a brother or sister at either of the camps was eligible to meet between the campsites for a picnic. David and Heather would meet there and cling to each other, crying because they missed each other so. In time, David would develop an interest in the boating and swimming activities at the camp, and he would willingly return there for six more years.

David liked to help those who seemed to be misfits at the camp. One year, Mike, who was mentally retarded, was a cabin mate. David spent a lot of time helping him to master various skills. On the last night of camp, Mike chased David around the cabin swinging a pipe, screaming that he was going to kill David. "Why?" was David's only question.

In grade school, David was not in the brightest class. He complained that the kids and some teachers didn't like him. One day, I met with the principal and told him I wanted David moved to an advanced class, where he would be challenged more. After this was done, David's school life improved, both in performance and relationships. Years later, David met a grade school classmate and they talked about David's difficulty in making friends at that time. "What was it that stood in my way?" David asked.

The friend replied, "*You* always wore clothes that matched!"

When David learned to play the alto saxophone, his interest in the school band soared. Later he played the baritone saxophone and became an avid member of the school's dance band. He also acted in the class plays and even wrote some (the humor of which I did not understand). He loved to dance.

Mom was the family chauffeur, because public transportation didn't extend out to our house. When the call came, "Mom, would you pick me up?" I'd be expected to drop everything. Sometimes it wasn't convenient; sometimes it was downright annoying!

One particular Saturday, right before Christmas, sticks in my mind after all these years. David had gone Christmas shopping in downtown Allentown. One-way streets were just beginning to appear to help ease the flow of traffic. The lines of cars waiting to pass through traffic lights were endless. David called to say he was ready to be picked up. I fought the traffic and finally made it to the designated corner—but there was no David! My temper flared and all kinds of angry thoughts raced through my brain as I bucked the traffic, going around the block to make another pass. Just wait till I get my hands on him! I thought, as I approached the intersection for the second time.

Then I saw him, my young boy, standing on the corner and straining his neck, looking for me—with a bouquet of roses clutched in his hand. The door swung open. "Hi Mom! These are for you!" My heart melted in a second; the anger I felt was replaced with only love.

The summer after I was ill with meningitis, the three older children were packed off to summer schools. David was to attend Tabor Academy in Marion, Massachusetts, and he left from New York with a whole busload of other young people. It was hard for him to go, and hard for me to see him go. For two weeks after he got there, he called every day. "Hello, Mommie, I miss you all at home so much!"

At first I listened and sympathized, then I got tougher. "David, enough!" I said. "Get hold of yourself." But the letters continued to be grim all summer. Bob even went to Tabor on a morale-boosting visit, halfway through the summer. In the meantime, I had all kinds of guilt feelings about doing this to David.

Later, I read David's diary of that summer. He wrote about the wonderful things that happened at Tabor (especially the opportunity to sail) and concluded that this was one of the best summers of his life!

The relationship between Bob and David grew closer when they took a trip to Mexico for a meeting with philosopher Ivan Illich. They did some skeet shooting together, too. But perhaps their deepest camaraderie resulted from a mutual interest in kayaks and the desire to maneuver the whitewater rapids in a kayak of their own. Those adventures required sharp skill and keen judgment as well as a willingness to roll with the spills and cope with several hair-raising near accidents. They both loved the challenges and the fun of the sport.

Bob always wanted to learn weaving, but he just didn't have the time. One day, he asked David if he would like to go to weaving school. David was ready and willing, so he studied with the Mannings in East Berlin, Pennsylvania, and eventually became a master weaver. At local crafts fairs his fine work always sold out early. David wove coverlets and wall hangings that we cherish today.

As he matured, David developed a fine singing voice that landed him the leading male role in most of the high school musicals. For fun, he started a kazoo band with his friends, and they frequently won prizes when they participated in local parades.

The summer between his junior and senior years in high school was momentous. The summer school where Heather and Heidi went, Burnham by the Sea in Newport, Rhode Island, became co-ed, so

David was able to attend. He really bloomed there, becoming more outgoing and making many new friends.

But when he came home from Burnham, David was antagonistic toward me for the first time. We didn't get along at all, and life for me was painful.

"David, what's wrong?" I asked. I didn't realize it, but he no longer wanted my Umbrella of Protection. He had adopted a path that would lead him through a lifestyle I knew nothing about. He was almost 18.

The antagonism between us continued for almost three months. Then, literally by accident, our mini-cold war enjoyed a truce. Often David rode his bicycle to school and came home when band rehearsals or play rehearsals were over. One such evening, Bob and I were eating dinner in the kitchen when we heard a screech of brakes from the busy road in front of our home. "There must have been an accident," I said. Then we saw that a line of cars was stopped, so we raced out of the house to the road, and found David lying there! He had decided to come home in time for dinner that evening. With his head up in the clouds, perhaps humming a tune, he had steered directly in front of a car and was hit. David suffered a loss of memory for about 24 hours, plus a very badly bruised leg and a few scrapes.

Over the next six weeks, I drove David to therapy sessions for his leg and we had time to talk. It was then that some of the friendship and understanding between us came back.

Senior year in high school was packed with activity for David— president of student council, band, drama, model United Nations, planning and photographing the senior class movie, and much, much more. He graduated from high school in triumph. College would be next.

I was always the person who took my kids to college, and I loved doing it. We took at least two extras days for the trip so that my child and I could share the start of this new adventure together, one on one. David went to Ithaca to study drama. He and I wandered through Treman Park there; we walked on the rocks and quietly contemplated by the waterfalls. On those trips, David led me deeper into the delights of gourmet dining. We'd purr over the scrumptious meals we ordered, and I discovered that he was a master at seeking delightful new places to go.

Part of Ithaca's school program offered a semester in London to study the theater, and of course David took advantage of it. I went to England for a week's work while he was there, and we spent some time together. We went to see *The Rocky Horror Picture Show* and *A Chorus Line*, and David took me on a tour of his school. We continued in our newfound hobby of sampling the good food at some fine restaurants.

During spring break, David and a group of friends vacationed in Greece, climbing seaside rock formations and sleeping in Minoan caves. They traveled to majestic ancient ruins and reveled in exploring these fragments of history, imagining what life was like there thousands of years before. The trip ended with a weekend in Amsterdam. All the while, David wrote detailed stories of his experiences, each illustrated with delightful cartoons. I found them after he was gone.

Shortly after his return to London, David developed a throat tic. He often called home about it, very upset. He stopped singing because it seemed to aggravate the problem. I thought perhaps he was just homesick. When David finally consulted a throat specialist, the doctor recommended surgery. David called and said, "I want to come home!" It was spring.

The doctors in America could find nothing wrong. Still, the tic persisted. Then, some months later, it simply disappeared. Perhaps the tic was a subconscious manifestation of the conflict within David's own mind—an inner struggle to discover *who* he really was.

David transferred to Lehigh University, and after one semester, he went to New York City to find his way. Our relationship broke down again, and I tried to ride it out, as I had before. People were beginning to notice a change in David—a brusqueness and a cynicism utterly unlike him—and question me about it. I wrote to David, telling him how sad I felt and how confused I was.

A response written on turquoise paper came back to me immediately. I'll never forget how it began.

Yes, Mom, you may have suspected, I'm gay.

It was a touching letter that went on to tell me he was sorry for any hurt he had caused me, and above all, he hoped his lifestyle would not make a difference in the love our family felt for him. He was 20. The letter continued:

Homosexuality is not easy to deal with when it is part of yourself and not part of the world around you. Contrary to old wives' tales, you can't blame the basic feelings on anyone or anything. It may be a surprise, but I feel I must tell you now that this is not one of the many paths which I could have taken. I've had homosexual feelings ever since I was very young. It's something that, if I would have suppressed it, would have built up inside to a point where, sometime, I would have to let it out to maintain my sanity. If I didn't I would go crazy.

Homosexuality is not a place where I want to end up. It's a transition. Don't think I'm copping out by saying that. I've given it a lot of thought and tried many ways to deal with it. If I

63

wanted to spend the rest of my life as a homosexual, I would have to tell you that, and would have been extremely adamant in holding to my beliefs.

No. There's nothing I want more than to have a wife, children, and a happy married life. That's what I'm aiming for. Please don't think that homosexuality means sex. It does, but that's not all. It means feelings and love just as you feel love. It's not sick as some people consider it. It's emotional and natural. Homosexuality has been present since the beginning of man. It doesn't come and go with the eras of man. It doesn't go in and out of fashion. It's not vice. Please don't see it that way.

I know where I'm at, I know where I've been, and I know where I'm going. I do not regret my past. I really think things work themselves out if you give them a chance. If you don't let yourself go to explore your feelings, how can you know what you feel? How can you know love? I think you can identify with that, only on a different level. Please trust me. Not all people are alike and there is not a magical age where everyone does the same things. The sooner we all realize nature's capabilities and all its ins and outs, the sooner we will all understand each other.

Several years later, in one of our discussions, he said, "You know, Mom, the one thing I regret about my life is that I will never have children." We hugged each other and we both cried.

Was David's uncharacteristically sullen, antagonistic attitude in those teen years an expression of his becoming aware of who he was? Did he fear the penalty of not conforming to society's ideas? How did he honestly feel in exposing the real David? I look back at my own life as I try to find an answer. I remember doing many rash things at times when I wasn't comfortable with myself and didn't know how to cope. I could understand David's feelings.

Having David, someone I loved, announce to me that he was gay was a shock. I knew nothing about homosexuality. So I went to a professional counselor for information and guidance. In essence, all he told me was, "There is very little known success in trying to change a person from gay to straight." I was no better off than before.

When I got home, I told Bob what was going on with David. I asked him to speak with David about it. But that was something he just wasn't able to do. One thing was perfectly clear in my mind: Under no circumstances could I ever be alienated from this son whom I deeply loved. Sometimes I allowed myself to think that maybe the problem would just blow over and life would be normal again. I was grasping at straws. I was hoping for an easy solution, but I knew deep down there was none.

David had made a strong move away from the Umbrella of Protection, and I had to deal with it. But I had no experience, no sense of how to proceed. It was clear to me that I, too, had to step out from under the Umbrella to look for a new direction. Our family was under stress. We had just discovered Anthony's learning disability, and it was the most intense period of Heidi's rebellion. I was 44 years old.

My father-in-law, J. I. Rodale—Papa—had died in 1971, the year before David announced that he was gay. My mother-in-law was diligently engaged in keeping the name of J. I. Rodale alive, and perpetuating his myriad projects and interests. As part of that effort, she had bought an old church in downtown Allentown and had had it renovated into a 248-seat theater. Because of his interest in the theater and his training, David applied for the job of artistic director. He was qualified, and at the age of 21, he filled the position at the J. I. Rodale Theater. He came in early enough to be involved in all the renovations. In fact, the whole project was done under his direction. What evolved was a fantastic theater, the finest in the whole area surrounding Allentown. David wrote to his grandmother:

> *The other day when I walked into the theater, a wave of satisfaction and anticipation swept over me. Finally the fruits of our planning can be seen and the realization that it will soon be a working facility becomes more concrete as each piece is put into place.*
>
> *I believe that the goal of the J. I. Rodale Theater should be to create and support new works as well to produce the classics and other established works. In order to cover a wide range of theatrical experiences and augment the culture of Allentown . . . it should be decided to do a set number of new plays, working with the playwright if possible, a certain number of classical, contemporary, and musical productions. The planning of a season of productions should be carefully thought out as to cover the widest range of interest and audience.*

The response was enthusiastic, the theater prospered, and the standards David set are still in force today.

David knew he didn't want to continue in this position for the rest of his life. While he was on the job, the toll in personal stress was high. Friction developed within the family because of the theater, and the wild lashing out resulted in emotional devastation for David. I knew what he was going through. I had experienced it, too. I commiserated with David. Often it would take us a whole week to recover our self-esteem after the latest crisis.

What we should have done was to write a play about *anger!* David and I didn't do that. Both of us still heeded my mother's message: "You suffer in silence."

Why don't more people understand how painful it is sometimes to be human? Why do so few reach out to aid and comfort those who need it? After two seasons, David left the J. I. Rodale Theater and went back to New York.

Through this period, David was trying to sort out his feelings and work through some of his many frustrations. He went through a time of deep depressions. In his journal he wrote:

> *I am trying to hide from my depression. It seems to haunt me more and more when I don't have to deal with it on a day to day basis. All that I have been trying to hold on to for balance is crumbling, not in reality, or so I tell myself, but in mind . . . crumbling as the last possible handhold at the top of a cliff. Many times I've stumbled and recovered. But now I am forever falling, falling farther from what is and where my purpose lies than ever before.*
>
> *This is how I choose to express myself for now. I may not have reached the depths which I am digging for, but unless you dig to China, all you do is walk around. By digging, I'm closer; I know what's inside the circle. If I circumnavigate, I know how wonderful the surface is. The surface is there to be seen, what's inside remains to be explored.*

Several months later he wrote:

> *Families must not be sacred. Individuals must be. So, too, relationships and involvements although held in high regard must never include sacrificing your own individuality.*

· · ·

> *As I go back and read that which I have been writing, I find that what I dwell on is expelling the difficulties, working out problems, quelling manifestations. Little do I expose of the wonders and the joys I have felt, the many exciting experiences and discoveries. So far, the bad has overshadowed the good so much that does it not appear in my writing and it disappears from my thoughts. I have been dwelling on negatives, but now I see it is not that I enjoy doing that. It is a way of dealing with discomfort, dealing with disturbances.*

Finally, a note of hope comes through:

Before my eyes one of the most important tests I have known. . . . I will be asked to look beyond my own sufferings and wants, to change my patterns. I will be asked not to judge, but to let each one judge for himself.

Each day I see more things that are wonderful and ugly about the world. I constantly experience surprises and disillusionments.

You must use them to the best of your advantage so you can grow beyond them. All these things, and more, are going through my mind. This thing I have learned to depend and rely on so much, this thing which I have been living for, which I have set my eyes on for the future, this thing which I have felt crumbling under me now becomes clear or at least clearer at times.

This thing of course is none other than love which has supported me and uplifted me. Love which has helped me grow. But we always want things to be wonderful, and I guess they can't be.

David was always a very loving person. He needed to love and be loved. Can any of us live without love? It makes no difference whom you love, but that you do love, and learn to love very deeply.

David met Jesse while standing in line to see a production of Shakespeare in New York's Central Park. They became fast friends, sharing their fantastic intellects, enjoying the plays and the music New York had to offer. It is because of Jesse that I am able to record all these events. In 1982, as a birthday gift, David presented Jesse with 22 volumes of a work he called *DVO My Body*. It was a compilation of David's writings accumulated throughout his life. (David never threw anything away.)

Well, David came home again and lived at the New Farm in Maxatawny where there was a beautiful peace. He continued his weaving. One day, David went to the local mall to purchase a new pair of shoes–taking just enough money for the purchase. He passed a music store along the way, and stopped in to try out a Yamaha baby grand piano. He played for a long time, losing himself in another world. Finally, the clerk said, "You know, you can't leave this. You should have this piano."

David's fingers caressed it lovingly. He replied, "I have less than $50 with me. Would you take that as a down payment?" The clerk said yes.

David raced home to tell me. "Mom, guess what I bought! Wait till you hear it. You'll love it!" He was *so* happy! In a frenzy of energy, he composed wonderful music in the style of the classics. He also bought a Great Pyrenees puppy to keep him company at the farm. I thought, "Thank God, he has come home!"

But David's contentment didn't last. I could see his wanderlust beginning to surface, and one day he announced, "Mom, I've decided to go to Provincetown for a while. I think I'll try my hand at being a waiter there. It will give me plenty of free time, and I want to write a book. I'll really miss my piano–but it will still be here when I come back."

Off he went, leaving Mom in charge of Obie the dog until David got settled. We gave Obie lots of love and affection, but it wasn't the same. Obie sorely missed David. Each time David came home to visit and then drove away alone, it was easy to see that Obie was sad because he missed being part of David's life. I'm sure Obie missed the car rides he used to have in David's convertible with the top down– sitting in the passenger seat, tall and regal. (All that dog needed was a pair of sunglasses!) We had many good laughs remembering the sight of the two of them together.

David got a job at a great place, the Terrace Restaurant, on the first day he was in Provincetown. Shortly after he started to work, David served a couple, the Emerlings, who were destined to play a very important role in all of our lives–but especially in David's. They came from Falmouth; Frank was a pediatrician, and Jean, a Doctor of Dentistry at Boston University, specializing in jaw reconstruction. "FrankenJean," as they became known, were a source of nonstop energy, intellectural stimulation, delightful and unbounded fun that was sorely missing from David's life. When the family members visited David in Provincetown, there was always a stop with FrankenJean for the kind of fun and laughter that were missing from Bob's and my life, too.

Twice a year, in September and May, when delivering or picking up Maria or Anthony at school, I'd loop around to visit with David. These were always very special times. The small pine-paneled studio house he rented sat on top of a deck that extended out over the bay. I would sit on the porch of the house and the relaxation would grad-ually take hold. It was as though someone were slowly pulling a blanket over me, until I felt cozy. As the salt air filled my lungs, the sea gulls called and gracefully swooped over the water. The evenings blessed us with beautiful sunsets, and I felt sure that this must be a special corner of paradise.

Later, I was amazed to find myself sitting in my son's living room surrounded by pillows, under a gazebo made of sheer cotton, as

David, the gourmet cook, put the finishing touches on a Chinese dinner.

The low oriental-style table was perfectly set with simple classic accessories and flowers. Soft flute music in the background added to the atmosphere. I had never experienced anything like this. And David had done this just for me! It was an evening that brought a new dimension to my life.

During the day, David took me to the special stores he knew in Provincetown. The friendliness of the people was reminiscent of a small town. They all held David in high regard, respecting his creativity as he respected theirs. We wandered in and out of antique shops, looking specifically for brass and copper urns that might fit in at home. That way, the family could surround itself with a bit of the Cape and feel that David was somehow closer.

We often climbed the high Provincetown dunes, and I can still feel the heat of the burning sand on my feet. I remember an amazing moment when we become aware of the sky, the sand, and the clouds mingled together as one. We were the only audience for this spectacular play of space. In this time we spent together in Provincetown, I felt a real caring as he held my coat or removed a speck of dirt from my face. There was tenderness.

At the end of his second summer in Provincetown, David took Obie back with him for companionship. David was delighted to have him as part of his life again, but Obie didn't have the same spirit. Often as they walked along the road, Obie would just stop and lie down. David said, "Boy, Mom, he sure got obstinate while he was with you. He just must have it his way." Finally, David took Obie to a veterinarian; the diagnosis was bone cancer. Oh, how David nursed and cared for that dog! Still Obie went down and down.

As much as Obie had missed David, I believe that Obie's being taken away from the surroundings he knew and loved to an unknown territory was a fatal jolt for him. Great Pyrenees don't handle change very well. Even though David was with him, Obie lost his will to fight. And one thing that is imperative in adversity is the will to fight! Because the end was imminent for Obie, I was ready to fly to Provincetown to be with them both. But when I called to ask, "David, should I come?" I had waited too long. . . .

David decided to spend a winter in Provincetown. "I have the opportunity to house-sit for some friends whose house is much cozier for the winter than my apartment. I'll stay here and work on my book. You know, Mom, Provincetown gets to be a real bleak place in winter. Most of the town closes down and there is real isolation—and many suicides I'm told—but I'll be here."

David had some terribly lonely and depressing periods that

winter. He was missing someone to love, and you need that when profound loneliness takes over. He was always close to the family, but as you get older, you need the companionship of a mate. The love is different.

In spring David called. "Mom, I'm coming home. I've decided I want to come back to stay and be a part of the family again and work for Dad." His apartment at the New Farm was still intact. The piano was waiting for his return.

Mom rejoiced. "David, please come quickly."

Around the same time, our company donated 330 wild acres on a nearby mountain to the Lehigh Valley Conservancy, an organization which preserves open space. On the property, there was a dilapidated 200-year-old stone bank house at the very end of a desolate half-mile lane. What would we do with the house? Bob said, "Now that David is coming home, do you think he would want to fix up the house and live there?"

I thought only about the painful experience of his isolated winter in Provincetown. I couldn't help remembering all the times, after talking with him on the telephone, that I got down on my knees and prayed, "Oh, God, please watch over David and keep him in your protective arms. He doesn't want my protective Umbrella, but maybe he will accept yours."

I told Maria what Bob had suggested, and expressed my concerns. She shouted happily, "Oh, Mom, David would love it! He always dreamed of being able to live there." She was right. David shivered with anticipation. The plans for the renovations would be up to him. He could implement all his innovative ideas, plus the things he would later learn about building while working for Rodale's *New Shelter* magazine, one of our magazines whose theme was home energy conservation.

For David, life became a grind of working for *New Shelter* during the day and working on his new house evenings and weekends, while living at the New Farm 20 miles away.

David threw himself into the demolition with his full physical force, then gradually started to rebuild the old place. He did the bedroom first, so in October he was able to move into the house—but there was no inside bathroom and no kitchen. David weathered the winter there, spending some time at our house during periodic bouts with intestinal problems. With these crazy living arrangements, I thought he needed his mom's good food, and besides, it was good to have him near. After a harried day at work, while I prepared dinner for whoever would be here, David's soft piano music was a balm for my wearied spirit. Peace entered my mind and I had renewed strength to finish the day. These extended visits from David helped to speed the winter away.

In the spring of 1982, our spirits were high as we prepared for Heidi and Charlie's wedding, scheduled for Memorial Day weekend. Our whole family would be together again. How lucky Bob and I were to have our children all around us. So many other families were scattered all over the country, with at least one family member likely to be missing from any major celebration.

After the wedding, David became ill repeatedly and went to the doctor often. His illness was finally diagnosed as shingles. Fortunately, David's old friend Jesse came from New York to support him and help to nurse him back to health. In one of our publications, David read about the use of vitamin B_6 in large doses as therapy for the itch accompanying shingles. He insisted that his doctor try it. "Well, if you really want it," the doctor said, "but I don't see where it will help." But it did help, and David was soon well again!

Through that entire year, turning the old house into a master-piece became an obsession with David. Here was a project whose prospects were so dismal to begin with that its completion threatened to take a lifetime. But David persisted.

I was relieved to see that the frantic need to work all over the place at the same time subsided. Now the seasons began to dictate projects for the outside and the inside. David bought two goats, Amelia and Amaranthe, to help with the tremendous job of controlling the poison ivy. They just devoured it! He also bought Obie's nephew Murphy as his companion on the mountain. A large fenced-in area next to the barn was constructed for the goats, so they could get out of the weather at will.

The finishing touches on the house were completed the weekend before Christmas. That night it was just starting to snow, and the lights of Emmaus were visible from the mountain. He described it to me. "You know, Mom, as I was leading the goats in, I caught myself humming 'Away in the Manger.' It was all such a beautiful sight." Each goat received a bell and a red collar for Christmas.

David had a job change. He began doing computer networking at the Press, helping Bob explore new innovations for possible expansion. I could feel that Bob and David were accepting each other more as equals now, instead of only relating as parent and child. To David, that change in their relationship was a dream come true.

In the summer of 1984, David met Mark. They were both artists who appreciated each other's talents. David cooked, Mark cleaned up. They worked together on the house—building walls, planting gardens and bulbs as they anticipated the beauty of each new season.

David felt that he finally had utopia in sight: He had found Mark to love, he was finding fulfillment in his work, and he had paradise in his beloved mountain. He could sit on his wraparound porches to see the sun rise and set. He could see deer romping in the meadow of tall pampas grass. He could hear the water gurgling up from the many springs and flowing into the pond. There was *so* much here, *so* much to appreciate. It was breathtaking. And David had a lifetime of dreams still to be fulfilled.

Both family and friends enjoyed going to the mountain house. We all sensed the peace that was there. In fact, we began to spend more time with Mark and David as a way to settle down ourselves.

David and Mark had perfect parties. The guests all accepting each other in a wonderful mix, sharing good food, the good humor, and the tremendous mental energy that characterized those gatherings. Each one of us there seemed to be in quest of life's answers.

The grandkids dominated my own once-a-week family dinners. But their presence wasn't conducive to sharing feelings and ideas at a meal as David liked to do. He wanted to talk about all the exciting things that were going on in the company, and that wasn't possible on such occasions. As a compromise I started to separate family dinners, having different groups of people at different times. Periodically, David and I would have lunch together, just to keep in touch with what we were doing and where we were headed.

To get everybody together in a freer atmosphere, we planned a family reunion with my side of the family for Labor Day weekend that year. David and Mark volunteered to have it on the mountain–and it was perfect. All my brothers and sisters, nieces and nephews, cousins and their children were together. Heather organized games for the little ones, and we all ended the day in fond reminiscence around a campfire, singing old camp songs. Something magical took place between the old and the young. Mark's father sang Pennsylvania Dutch songs, and my brother Jim answered him in dialect. We all mellowed, repairing relationships and renewing some lost dreams. The wonderful photos of the event show David looking trim–but thinner.

Sometime in October, I invited just Mark and David to come for a spaghetti dinner and David said, "It's been a long time, Mom."

"I know, David," I replied, "I'll make it up. Take care of that cough."

"Yeah, Mom."

I am an early Christmas shopper, and that night I asked David what he would like for Christmas. He smiled, thought for a moment, and said, "I'm not sure, but I find I don't want all the gadgets I used to love anymore."

I promised to give him money for Christmas, as a contribution toward kitchen cabinets for his house. That made him so happy. The house was almost in order. The magnificent view from his mountain represented an ocean of serenity for David. The tumult was over at last!

David had really left my Umbrella of Protection long ago. He just darted back now and then for a hug he knew was always there for him.

As I finish writing this chapter, the radio plays, "There is someone walking behind you . . . Turn around, look at me." ("Turn Around, Look at Me" by Jerry Capehart. © 1961 WARNER-TAMERLANE PUBLISHING CORP. All rights reserved. Used by permission.) I will leave David's chapter for now. But the story is not finished.

CHAPTER 6

How do you solve a problem like Maria?
How do you hold a moonbeam in your hand?

Oscar Hammerstein, *The Sound of Music*

In many ways, Maria was born grown up. She fit right in with the established family and other adults. Very often my mother would say to me, "For heavens' sake! Let her be a child." Maria would be what she wanted to be.

When Maria was not in her adult world, her life was filled with wonderful and exciting experiences. Her imaginary friends, Coke, Candles, Birdie-Birdie, and Ice Cube, traveled with her on her wanderings around the farm every day. They ate with us at the table and were her constant companions until she was 3½. Then we went on vacation and she decided that the time had come to part with these good friends; they would stay in Savannah when we went home on the train. For Maria, fingers were better eating utensils than spoons and forks. Her room was always a mess, with her favorite toys strewn about.

As she grew older, books were a favorite pastime. When Maria was in first grade, the creative stories she wrote were memorable. If her pencil wasn't busy, her crayons and watercolors were splashing pictures of what her active mind was feeling. She went to art school and dabbled in clay; she also learned to play the piano reasonably well.

Maria seemed so self-assured that sometimes I wondered if she needed me at all. This was bound to be an easy child to bring up feeling safe and secure about herself.

She was named after Maria von Trapp, the real-life character in *The Sound of Music.* And many times I thought about the words from the song that seemed so much as though it were written for our Maria: *How do you solve a problem like Maria?*

Maria's Great-grandmother Lessig was called *Huchal,* which means "wild pony" in Pennsylvania Dutch. I have always thought that Maria inherited her great-grandmother's spirit.

When Maria reached age 13, I suddenly realized life didn't hold that magical mirage of a child easy to handle. Like most children that age, Maria had tremendous drive to fit in with the rest of the crowd. Her rebellion against anyone who interfered with that aim came full force. When she came out from under the protective Umbrella, Maria deliberately rushed into the rain, the wind, the snow, and the sleet.

Junior high school opened a whole new world for Maria. When she was in grade school, she had to be transported to and from home by a parent because our home was located in a remote country setting. Now her school was right in town. All the stores and hangouts were within walking distance of the building. We knew it could spell trouble for Maria, so at 13 years of age she began an after-school job at our company.

Maria's peer group in school was part of the party scene we didn't approve of. But it was impossible to ban her from all entertainment, so I drove her to parties and picked her up at her curfew time. I hoped I had trust in Maria, but I know I didn't trust some of her friends. She was aware of my feelings on this point, and it became a constant source of friction between us.

I continually racked my brain, asking myself, How can I keep from alienating this strong-willed child? I prayed hard, and I tried to work out some kind of understanding in my own mind. I was really fearful for Maria and for myself. I stayed under my Umbrella hiding from alarming situations and the potentially dangerous experiences she faced, which I knew nothing about.

It's no use to tell a young person that being an individual with your own set of values and creative ideas is far more desirable than quashing that creative spirit just to fit in with the crowd. No child can believe it. Yet I remembered the unhappiness I brought on myself by trying to fit the mold of what I thought it took to be accepted. I opened myself up to rejection: "Here I am, I have arrived. May I come in?"

Like Maria, I was accepted on the fringes, but never into the real inner circle all young people seem to yearn for so strongly.

As you try for acceptance, you have to sacrifice some of yourself to conform. First of all, Maria began to smoke. All of her close girlfriends came from homes where smoking was the norm. Bob could not believe that a daughter of his would even try smoking! Our family teaching and philosophy shunned the very idea of cigarettes.

No punishment worked in trying to get her to stop. We tried forbidding TV; she had enough to do without it. We tried keeping her home from the Youth Center—and that hurt, but it didn't accomplish anything, except to fire even more belligerence. We took away *all* her peer fun; no use. Maria would stop when—and if—she alone decided to do so.

During this period, I was teaching Couples and Singles class at Sunday school, as I had for many years, and though my children refused to go to their own classes at church, they did come to mine. I was eager to have this continue, just to keep another line of communication with my kids open, both with me and with the other members of the class. In some ways, it helped Maria to realize that she was not alone; others had problems too.

Because we lived on a farm, all of our children learned to drive before they were 16. Each one could hardly wait to get that license. Characteristically, Maria didn't wait, as we discovered several years later. At 15—when she was supposed to be taking care of Anthony for the evening—they would pile in the car and travel down the highway to the store for some adventure. Anthony remembers the rides today. "Boy, did I hold on tight!" I couldn't believe Maria would dare do that. But that was Maria.

We kept urging Maria to bring her friends home. We wanted to meet them. Her response: "Mom, you wouldn't understand. You wouldn't fit in." In effect, I was shut out!

The other children never locked their bedroom doors. Maria took to locking hers. She did not respond to my knock when I came to say goodnight. No wonder—Maria had taken to smoking pot.

The communication between us broke down often, so we took to writing notes to one another. At least, this kept some kind of dialogue going.

Maria,

> *I really appreciate your letters. I want to be close to you . . . and somehow I feel you don't want me there. I'm not so bad and so lacking in understanding. Love your family a little more and the genuine feeling will be returned.*

Her language went from good to bad to worse, and my heart was wrenched as I looked for answers.

Dear Maria,

Two men looked out from the prison walls . . . one saw mud and the other saw stars. . . . If you would only realize the importance of lifting yourself to the stars . . . to use your whole potential! Never in my growing up did I ever lose track of reaching for the stars. Never did I use such base language. Never did I try not to present my best self instead of my base self.

You have so much going for you . . . not only because of your own loving family, but because of your own intellect and talent . . . and right now, I'm blasted mad!

Love, Mom

As children go through those adolescent years, they are seldom willing to hear about other people's problems and the solutions to them. Until young people have some basis for comparison, they are not really capable of sorting out the good from the bad and storing that information for future reference. Sometimes they have to hit bottom before they are willing to listen. I tried to remember if I knew enough to care at that age. What did it take to get me to listen? I couldn't recall.

In the agony of looking for answers, I cried out, Who is a kindred spirit? Who understands, or wants to? I am in pain with no outlet, except for my thoughts and my writing.

A letter came to me:

To: Mother Dear
From: Maria Dear
Subject: Children

Your children are not your children.
They are the sons and daughters of Life's longing for itself.
They come through you but not from you,
And though they are with you yet they belong not to you.
You may give them your love but not your thoughts.
For they have their own thoughts.
You may house their bodies—but not their souls,
For their souls dwell in the house of tomorrow which
you cannot visit, not even in your dreams.

You may strive to be like them, but seek not to make
them like you.
For life goes not backward nor tarries with yesterday.
You are the bows from which your children as living
arrows are sent forth.
The archer sees the mark upon the path of the
infinite, and He bends you with His might
that His arrows may go swift and far.
Let your bending in the archer's hand be for gladness;
For even as he loves the arrow that flies, so
He loves also the bow that is stable.

Kahlil Gibran

Bob and I decided that we needed a change. We made reservations for a trip to Alaska with Maria and Anthony. We sailed from Vancouver, British Columbia, up the inland waterway to Alaska and back. We were inspired as we viewed the glaciers with awe, saw turquoise icebergs, watched porpoises playfully leaping in the air. There was time to think about all this beauty and to try to determine where we were headed in life.

For all of us, it was sad to see young Alaskan Indians drunk and being sick; sadder yet to realize their lives had no direction and, worst of all, little hope. For our family there was lots of hope and fun, and we were so glad to have Maria, our wonderful daughter, who was fresh and excited and happy, back with us for that time. Among our friends on the ship and at dinner parties, Maria was always her interested, delightful self.

With the reopening of school in the fall, we fell right back into the old set of peer problems with Maria. This time the school added to them by instituting an early dismissal policy. Now Maria had *so* much loose time on her hands that we made her take a job in the company again. It was a valuable recourse in more ways than one. Each time Maria changed departments, she met new people and learned a new skill.

Relations with Maria were still strained. As the time for my work period in England approached, one evening Maria said to me, "Oh, Mom, I need a change. Won't you take me with you to England?" After carefully considering the pros and cons of granting her request, I agreed. The time together might be good for both of us. She was 15 years old, going on 20.

We worked it out with her teachers that for the remaining two months before we left, Maria had to have at least a B in every course. Each teacher would report regularly on Maria's progress and the final decision would not be made until the day before we were scheduled to leave.

I also laid out rules for Maria's behavior on the trip. There would be no wandering around London on her own, and she had to come to work with me every day. Our free time would be spent together. (This would include two wonderful side trips–one to Bath, to see all the ancient ruins; the other to Brighton at the seaside where, in November, Maria rolled up her jeans and waded in the icy water.)

We went to plays, met lots of good people, and we dealt with each other adult to adult. Again we were amazed at how well we got along, talking and laughing together. It was a delight to see England through the enchanted eyes of my 15-year-old daughter, as she was enlightened and challenged by the history and the majesty of the country. One Sunday, we went to St. Paul's Cathedral and as we marched down the long aisle, the resounding of the massive organ seemed to shake the huge structure. It was soul-shivering. Amidst the thundering sound, I heard a voice beside me exclaim, "Holy shit!" Irreverent, to be sure. But I had to love the spontaneity of Maria's reaction–so in character.

If only our relationship could have remained so understanding and accepting! But as soon as we came home, we fell into real tussles almost immediately and the mother and daughter roles were back in full force. What was wrong?

"Mom, you don't seem to be listening to me! You are cramping me. I want to be in the center of things, not just observing from the peanut gallery. I've got to find out about life by myself!"

I was willing to bend and to stretch in an effort to understand, but I didn't want this child to be hurt and have her life ruined.

A few months after Maria and I returned from England, Bob, Anthony, Maria, and I went on an exciting adventure to Austria for the Junior World Bicycling Championship competition. Because the World Championship would be ridden on our track in Trexlertown the following summer, it was important to see how this event was conducted. Maria and Anthony knew many of the riders from seeing them ride at home, and they went with us to parties where they had the opportunity to meet the promoters from other countries.

It was a perfect time together. We roamed through museums and shopped between going to the races.

When the competition ended, we met with an old friend of Bob's, an Austrian named Ernst Winter, and his wife, Johanna von Trapp, the youngest daughter of the famous von Trapp family who were portrayed in *The Sound of Music.* The five of us spent a memorable day traveling by van to see solar windmills and picturesque farms, eating our meals at the wine caves we passed along the way.

In the afternoon, we sat for a while in the courtyard of a very old farm near the Hungarian border, and I noticed that Johanna was eyeing Maria. I said, "Maria was named for your mother."

"I thought as much," she replied. "Very often, people grow up to reflect the person they were named for, even though they have no personal connection. She has the same spirit my mother had!"

We never gave our children middle names; that way they could choose their own when they found a name they liked. Soon after we got home from Austria, Maria started writing her name with a flourishing style, *Maria Johanna Rodale.* I wrote to Johanna to tell her about Maria's choice, and she wrote back to say that tears had filled her eyes as she read my letter.

At wonderful times like those we experienced while traveling and when we entertained at home, I saw glimmers of hope that Maria and I were not beyond understanding one another.

Maria continued with her jobs at Rodale Press after school, as a buffer against getting into trouble. Often, when I happened to pass her friends' hangout in town, I saw them smoking pot. It upset me so much that one day I wrote to one of Maria's special friends, telling the girl of my concern about what she was doing. Could I help? I asked. I signed the note with love. The letter backfired. It ruined the girl's friendship with Maria. "Mom, why do have to stick your nose in other people's business?" Maria shouted at me. Maria and I were both miserable.

Finally, at the beginning of her junior year in high school, Maria said to me, "Mom, something has to change!"

"I know, Maria. Maybe another school is the answer."

We looked into this possibility, and by February, Maria was enrolled at Lawrence Academy in Groton, Massachusetts, for next fall's term.

When her last term in her Emmaus school ended, Maria celebrated with a party at our home. She accepted my insistence that I be present *some* of the time. We were making progress!

After the party was over, I couldn't sleep. At times like this, if it's a clear night, I often do the wash as I sort out my thoughts—like clothes. While I waited through the cycles, I wrote:

Dear Maria,

I'm glad your party was a success. I'm glad, too, that I had the opportunity to meet some of your friends and acquaintances. Some were really nice.

I sit here in the dark . . . watching the last two of the torch lights at the pool expend their lives. They started out as two bright stars . . . and now one flickers in a struggle for existence.

I have many things on my mind. I'm thinking of persons I talked to tonight. I'm thinking of my daughter in her glory.

In you, I see a lot of myself . . . only at different time spaces. I've seen us react as equals in England. Thought a bit of being the mother . . . but a friendly one!

Sometimes, like tonight, I am scared for you. I see (sometimes as an old sage) many paths you might follow. My heart cries out to you!

Love . . . but with specialness! Don't ever sell yourself cheap . . . just for the moment. The consequences are not worth the risk!

I know how young people are . . . they want to find out for themselves. I feel that the most important thing in life is to strive for a feeling of worth . . . not only in yourself, but as your life affects others.

I could pick out the people tonight who felt that way . . . I could see others striving so hard for acceptance . . . I could see those who had mixed-up objectives and I felt sad . . . but I still saw each one as a special person.

What else do I want to say . . . there's not much time left as the second torch is fighting for its life. I think I want to say, "You are unique in my sight, and maybe I should have more faith. I care so much what happens to you." Karl said you were meant for special things. . . . Don't ever sell yourself short!

The torch has gone out, so I guess I'll go hang up the wash! 3:00 A.M.

Love ya! Mom

Two years later, Maria graduated from Lawrence Academy. During her stay there, I saw a big change. She had many good challenges and she rose to each one. The teachers were so very caring and they became Maria's good friends. Her school work expanded, as did the potential it offered for new experiences. With a group from school, Maria went sailing on a schooner in the Virgin Islands. Another trip took her to live in a castle in Scotland, overlooking the North Sea, in the middle of March. She never did take off her long underwear the whole time there!

Maria enjoyed being known and liked for herself; that was the criteria she used for friendship. She stood alone, a single self on the beach, using no props to make friends. She had herself to offer.

At graduation, Maria received the art award and the headmaster's award. Best of all, she had forged friendships that would continue far beyond the walls of Lawrence Academy.

Maria decided to wait a year before starting college. She wanted to try living alone and she moved to the house at our New Farm. She worked for the summer as a farm laborer, and she dug right in with her pioneer spirit to do a good job. Her desire for freedom and for being her very own person grew stronger. Lawrence Academy had nurtured in her the urge to release her creative self once more.

That summer she wrote:

* * * * * * * * * *

I am a woman
and I like delicate flowers
that spring up from cracks between rocks,
Lace that hangs in doorways,
The scent of patchouli in dusty rooms,
and the contented aroma of the earth after it
rains.

I am a woman
I have worked side by side with men
in fields where hands are muddied
and boots worn thin.
I have tasted sunsets with them.

I am a woman
and I speak in silences
that sometimes sparkle
and sometimes fall discarded to the floor
like dirty clothes after a long hard chore
I have words and visions in my head dancing
like children on a snowy morning
all laughing and bundled up warm.

I am a woman.
I believe in love.
I walk the streets
my boots shouting softly
each step my declaration.

* * * * * * * * * *

After that good summer, Maria moved in with Heidi at a house on the main street in Emmaus. She took a job at our company as a technical artist. Maria worked with Karl Manahan, a 90-year-old artist who had been with our company for many years. Maria was always a favorite of his. Not only had they worked side by side, but they had known each other all of Maria's life. Perhaps you could call this wise, kind old man her mentor. Maria went to his house for discussions on astrology, reincarnation, and general philosophy one evening every week. She had a tremendous need to learn as much as she could from this man, who amazed everyone with his energy, arriving at the office every day and working full steam. He was a strong force in helping Maria to develop what was truth for her.

After our family dinner on the cold, snowy Christmas Eve of 1981, Maria became restless, anxious to leave the merriment for her regular discussion with Karl. I told her to call Karl and tell him she would come another night. "He won't mind if you don't come tonight," I said. I was worried about her traveling over the icy roads.

But she insisted, "No, no! I must go!" And the need seemed so urgent that I didn't argue anymore.

Later that night, as she was ready to leave Karl, he hugged her and said, "Oh, Maria—I hate to leave you."

It was her last session with him. Karl died in his sleep within the week.

The yen to go back to school flickered and then took fire in Maria. We were glad that she decided to go to college in the fall. Maria was short two courses for admission, so she enrolled in Cornell's summer program. She left for school (a drive of about four hours) on Tuesday, and, inexplicably, she came home for the first weekend. I couldn't understand why she would travel so far, so soon, for one short weekend.

Maria returned to school and called me on Monday. "Hello, Mom. I came home this weekend to see the doctor. I have something to tell you. I'm pregnant. I am going to have a baby in March."

"Maria, how could you do this?" I raged. "I can't believe you. I'm so upset I can't talk!" I screamed at her. I said some bad things I was very sorry for later. I also insisted that she go to Planned Parenthood for counseling.

"Mom, I know what I am doing," she said. "I can't give this baby up. It would set me too far back in the long way I have come through my life. I've given up smoking cigarettes and pot. I'll go for counseling to make you happy, but I know already what I am going to do. I will keep this baby."

The counselor was convinced that Maria was thinking straight and that she was mature enough to handle the situation. She gave up drinking any alcohol whatsoever for her whole pregnancy. Like everyone, Maria wanted a perfect child.

I was a mess. First I called my friends, Ellie and Guy, whose daughter was in the same situation. All the things we had often talked about doing *if* . . . were not going to work. Ellie said, "Ardie, we just have to pray a lot and have faith that it will all work out."

People were shocked. I read that most cases of child abuse occurred among young single mothers who couldn't cope. I cried at work and at home at the drop of a hat. Finally, after three weeks of painful concern, Bob said to me one morning, "Well, I don't know about you, but I have a job to do." I looked at him and said, "Dammit! So do I!"

From then on, we started to prepare. I made arrangements to spend the next weekend with Maria in Ithaca. We walked through the beautiful parks, we toured the countryside, we ate in nice places—and we talked, talked, talked, and hugged and cried. By the time I was ready to leave for home, I was at peace and I was ready to *stand behind my daughter* who would become a mother at 20.

I couldn't help being sad when I thought about all the trials that Maria would have to face alone. The reaction of the family and friends to the news never crossed my mind. A handful of them rejected Maria because of her situation, and my ire over their intolerance and narrowmindedness surfaced for all to see. This was not a time to condemn, but to help build on what was there. We treated Maria as a daughter we were proud of—and we were! She willingly opened herself to the unknown—hardships if they must be, but also potential joys.

Maria's brothers and sisters all stood behind her. David said, "The baby might not have a father she knows, but there will be lots of uncles and aunts to give a lot of love. We'll all help." And they did.

We transformed the carport and the garage of the house where Maria had lived with Heidi into a cozy apartment big enough for Maria and her child. Maria went back to work at the Press and the many friends she worked with there were wonderfully supportive.

As her due data approached, I got more and more nervous. One day I shouted at Maria in exasperation, "Get yourself together! Who will be your coach through the delivery?" I was terrified that I might have to be the one, and I felt that I simply could not handle it.

Very calmly, she replied, "Heidi volunteered."

How I cried! Heidi's action showed a deep love toward her sister; it also showed strength that I as a mother did not have. Wonderful reassurances and love pour from those who are close to us when life's trials come so unexpectedly. I never cease to be amazed at the "angels" waiting in the wings to step forward in kindness when the right cue comes.

When Maria went to the hospital, Heidi had to explain that she was the coach each time she wanted to go into the labor room. There was confusion each time. This was new. "Usually only fathers are allowed in there," she was told time after time.

Maya, wonderful and perfect, was born to Maria March 10, 1982. She is truly a magical child, for she has brought joy and healing and so much extra love to all of our lives. Life without her is inconceivable now. We would have missed so much! She has given us the opportunity to look at life in a new way. In the midst of our ordered lives, it's so easy to forget about the wonder a child can bring to us.

The first Mother's Day after Maya's birth, Maria wrote a poem and sent it to me:

> All of a sudden
> I feel like a mother . . .
> Apron on
> dishes in the sink
> Child sleeping soundly
> Resting worn, clean hands
> Competent, loving
> And all that wild energy
> That once made me young and free
> is now nestled in the folds of my skirt
> Ah memories . . . so far away!

Love, Maria

Maria returned to college locally, worked part-time, and took care of her child. Upon graduation, she had a double major in art and communication, and was within a tenth of a point of graduating cum laude. Before she even finished school in December, Maria had a job lined up with a public relations company in Washington, D.C. She also had an apartment and had chosen a day care school for Maya. She was all set to go—and then David left. . . .

Bob pleaded with Maria to stay for a while, instead of going to Washington. She was sad about David, of course, but she had already made her commitment, and she felt she had to stick to it for at least a year. How hard it was to see Maria and her child leave in the beginning of January. There was a deep hole in my heart, and now, without their sunshine near, the hole was harder to repair.

While Maria and her daughter were in Washington, they combed the museums every weekend. "Mommie, just one more museum, please," became Maya's plea.

Maria is now back in Emmaus and working for Bob. I'm proud of this daughter who caused us heartaches, and forced us to grow up by throwing us new curves. She is a talented, creative, original-thinking person who is not afraid to lift her face to life!

When I asked Maria about her life as she grew up, she shared these thoughts:

"David and I often talked about how lonely we were in our growing-up years. No one listened to us to learn who we were as persons. Our background was always the most important thing. We wanted to fit in, but no one wanted us. We were set apart.

"Going away to school helped me tremendously. I could get to know people there and have them accept me just for myself."

Of all the experiences Maria threw herself into, the greatest was having someone to love. Her direction in life now has focus. She has developed a critical mind and eye that affects her art, her writing, and her outlook on life. She has challenged herself and survived.

The person comes through when we are finished *shloshing* around. It's like discovering a treasure in the ancient tombs—it lies hidden deep beyond the surface.

We are all so very thankful that we never gave up the love lines of communication and faith and hope and prayer!

CHAPTER 7

Heather
A Blossom Unfolds

I see you, child
a joy that lies
beyond mere form:
incarnate wonder, delight, amusement, and
surprise.
You are a child-bud!
Folded under
familiar features that we know,
the thousand petaled heart of you
grows toward maturity
in much the way that flowers do.
Let me be patient in my trust,
remembering that time and room
are needed, that the lightest touch
of love can make a flower bloom.

R. H. Grenville

"Mom, as the eldest child, where did I stand under your Umbrella of Protection?" Heather asked me.

"You stood next to me. You never left," I replied.

"No, I guess I didn't," Heather said thoughtfully. "I was so scared for much of my life that I couldn't leave. But I'm not scared now."

Bob and I were so thrilled with our first child that we couldn't believe she was really ours. I would tiptoe into her room, carefully pick her up and hold her close, feeling her warmth. I was thrilled to be a mother.

During the first three months, the early evenings were trying. If it wasn't colic, it was visitors who insisted on waking Heather. When the crying started, they left, and I was often left, too—in tears. Bob and I soon learned that the best way to calm Heather was to drive her around the block in the car until she fell asleep, and I did that often.

As soon as Heather was able to talk, Nana insisted that she take elocution lessons. Heather dutifully memorized her little poems. She was so shy we were not sure if she would recite them in front of others. I couldn't understand why she wasn't more forward. Certainly Heather had plenty of neighborhood children to play with at the time. But she and David would often cling to my skirt and peer out from behind.

As Bob's parents had done with him, we sent Heather to private school for kindergarten, so she could enter the first grade at age five. Sometimes parents choose life situations for their children in good faith, hoping the decision is the right one. It's taking a chance. Heather was so nervous for the first several weeks that she threw up almost every day on the school bus. The headmistress would call, "Well, she did it again!" As the months went by, Heather became used to the routine.

When Heather was in first grade, I became the art teacher at the school she attended. All the students seemed to enjoy our time together and we did many fun projects. It was a good time for everyone.

Heather began to have trouble in second grade. When I peeped in on her other classes in my free moments, Heather was obviously dreaming in some far-off world. Her mind simply was not on the class work. I thought starting her early in school must be the reason. Her short attention span didn't allow Heather to keep up with the older children in the class. When the year ended, we enrolled Heather in a public school to repeat the second grade. The work appeared all new to her—different books, different subject material—but she managed.

Heather's eyes were a beautiful piercing blue. Though she complained occasionally about her eyesight, we never took her seriously. In third grade, her eyes were tested in school and we discovered that she did indeed need glasses. We acted at once. With glasses, a whole new world opened for Heather. She was able to see things she had never seen before: "Mom, the trees aren't just green; they have lots of green leaves!" This might have had something to do with Heather's poor concentration in the first and second grades.

Heather held reservoirs of deep thoughts and knowledge well beyond her early age. She was my real friend. When I was sad, I could tell her how I felt and something of why I felt that way. Her sensitivity was amazing and her simple words of comfort were just what I needed to pick me up and start me on the path to feeling good again.

Every day, for most of the day, Heather was around me, helping me in the kitchen, helping me with chores, then helping me with the other children. I got to rely on her as my other hand. She was dutiful and I can't remember her ever turning down a request for help.

Though Heather worked hard at school, she only received average grades. However, when the time came to choose her high school curriculum, she chose college prep with my approval. The guidance counselor, a friend of ours, called me at home one day and said, "Ardie, you know, of course, that Heather signed up for college prep. I'm sorry to tell you that I don't think she's college material."

I'm sure annoyance showed in my voice as I indignantly replied, "I want her in college prep!"

"It's your choice," Gertrude said, "but I cannot take the responsibility for your decision."

Over the years, I relished bringing Heather's many accomplishments and successes to Gertrude's attention. I wonder how many other guidance counselors discourage students that way, pushing them into lives that offer too little challenge? Encouragement from teachers and parents is the fuel that propels young people to explore the challenges and excitement that lead to success.

Anthony was born about this time in 1965, and I was suffering through a serious depression. I relied on Heather tremendously, and I don't know what I would have done without her help. Maybe I expected too much of her? But if Heather was short on confidence about her schoolwork, she was secure about her ability concerning the ins and outs of running a house, caring for children, and cooking. This is still a strong part of her life today.

There was a lot of carousing among the children and me. If two of the children were wrestling on the floor and it looked like fun, I joined in. Then sometimes another child would get into it, and the two who had started wrestling each other often ended up wrestling against the others. And there were wonderful pillow fights too. Usually, we ended up laughing so hard that the tears came to our eyes. These sessions always ended with all of us the best of friends, banishing any tensions that might have existed during the day. They were fun times. But there was one occasion when the chasing and wrestling ended on a serious and painful note.

Heather and David were teenagers and their chasing and wrestling probably should have been limited to the outdoors, but it was wintertime and cold out. As they played, David tried to stop Heather from coming through the swinging door from the kitchen to the dining room. David stood behind the door next to the hutch, and Heather pushed the door from the other side. David braced himself against the top of the hutch, not realizing that it wasn't fastened to the base cabinet. With one heave, the hutch top slid off the base and crashed to the floor like thunder. It barely missed Anthony, who was standing nearby, "taking lessons" for this type of play. Thank God, no one was hurt.

We all came running, to find almost total destruction. Broken glass and smashed antique dishes and statuary covered the floor. We all cried, but Heather was hysterical; she felt it was all her fault. There was no reason to punish anyone; the loss was punishment enough. We all picked up the pieces, salvaging a few things, but forced to throw away many material memories that had become important in our lives. Strange to say, I can remember only a few of the items that were lost—beautiful antique delft plates, Grandma's petal sherbets, and some Wedgwood. It all seemed so vital at the time, and now it's all but forgotten. New memories have taken the place of things we thought we couldn't live without.

When the older children were in their teens and Maria and Anthony were in grade school, travel to faraway places with the whole family was impossible. But I wanted to expose the family to people of other countries as an aid to better understanding, and I found a way. We began to welcome exchange students from overseas into our home.

The first one to come for a lengthy stay was Chuck, a young man from England. Chuck's father was the famous Commander Whitehead, the majestic man with a long white beard who was once the spokesman for Schweppe's tonic on TV. The commander, a friend of Bob's, had asked if his son could come to Emmaus for a summer, to work and learn about organic gardening. Of course we had agreed to this new experience for us.

Chuck's smiling face was an advertisement for his positive view of life. He had attended progressive schools and had sorted out for himself what was important to him in life. I remember one incident that demonstrated how mature his outlook was. Drugs were beginning to take hold in our local high school and our children were curious—and afraid—about this new wave. Chuck was about 20, three years older than Heather, and all the children looked up to him because he seemed to have it all together. Heather and Heidi asked Chuck if he ever took drugs. He smiled and simply answered, "No."

"Why not?" they questioned earnestly.

"Because I feel I don't need it in my life."

His answer was enough. Both girls realized that they didn't need drugs in their lives either.

After Chuck's stay, Lisa Lotte came from Sweden. We all loved her, and Heather had a new, very close sister. We did lots of things together, including many parties at the house. Several times a week, Heather, Heidi, David, Lotte, and I would get up early in the morning, throw on some clothes and go jogging. We'd look for signs of spring, listen to the birds, and breathe in the good fresh air. We came back invigorated, ready for breakfast, and ready to face whatever the day might have to offer. Lisa Lotte shared some Swedish recipes with us. And in our house, at least, the poles of understanding between the U.S. and Sweden became very close.

What a wonderful treat it was to see our surroundings through Lisa Lotte's eyes! Everything seemed so fresh. Old experiences suddenly had a new charm.

One day, when Heather and Lisa Lotte had all their girlfriends here for the day, I invited them on a tasting and smelling tour of the farm. Even the local girls had never smelled some of the flowers or tasted the delicious, aromatic herbs or eaten vegetables right out of the garden. It was a simple but wonderful day we all remember still!

When the time came for Lisa Lotte to leave, Maria cried as though her heart would break. It is a fact that our lives go through little deaths when we say goodbye to a friend, go to a new school, or leave a job to move on. We experience a real grieving process, and we can't brush these partings over. They need to be given their due.

The following summer, Lisa Lotte invited Heather and Heidi to visit her home in Alvsbyn, a town 50 miles south of the Arctic Circle. I saw to it that they went—and what a memorable time they had! Living in Lisa Lotte's home with her family was a delight, and the experiences the girls had there could never have been arranged by a travel agent. Staying up all night celebrating Midsummer's Day with many friends at the summer house was a day the girls would never forget. (In America, few people are even aware of that celebration.) Then there was a trip to Lapland and Finland, where the reindeer were so close you could almost touch them.

A teacher who was special to Heidi at Carnegie Mellon made arrangements for the girls to visit some friends of his in Narvik, Norway, when they left Alvsbyn. They took a train through some of the most spectacular scenery they had ever seen. At the end of the eight-hour ride north, Heidi and Heather were greeted by the Bloomsoys, who gave them a memorable taste of Norwegian culture and who have since become lifelong friends. In fact, it was our joy to have the Bloomsoys come to us at a later time, so they could get to know Bob and me and our other children.

Henri, from Cherbourg, France, spent a summer with us through the Le Grand Exchange program sponsored by the Rotary International. The following summer, Heather was invited to visit Henri's family in France for three weeks.

It was important to me that the cultures of others be woven into the fabric of my children's daily experience. The blend of enrichment and understanding enhanced the lives of all involved.

Over the years we had 15 exchange students. They came from Sweden, France, Belgium, Chile, England, Israel, Mexico, Norway, and Switzerland. They learned from us, shared with us—and taught us, too.

Each place Heather went, she stepped out from under my Umbrella only briefly, to stand under that of another secure mother. Now she would have to try her own wings.

Heather pleaded not to go when it came time for college. She had been miserable in high school and she was sure she was destined to get only average marks forever. Somehow, I talked her into trying a junior college just for two years.

Harcum Junior College gave Heather time, understanding, and, above all, the confidence she needed to succeed. Through the encouragement she received there, Heather discovered that she *could* learn, and very well, too. Heather dearly loved children, so she majored in elementary education. Her experience here was comparable to the treasured benefits Maria and Anthony reaped during their student days at Lawrence Academy.

Heather's introspection and her sensitivity to life led her to write some very fine poetry as a way to express her innermost thoughts. An outlet for releasing pent-up feelings can keep one sane in the middle of the maddening frustrations and storms of living.

More and more I was away from the house. If Heather were home, responsibility for running things during my absences fell on her shoulders. She held my Umbrella over the younger children in our family. She had some experiences similar to mine and she told me that they helped her to understand a little of how I felt.

Here is a typical example: After the children began to drive, I always waited up for them when they went out. Occasionally their deadline came and went and I would become angry, telling myself that I would take stern measures when that door opened. I would watch out the window as the cars drove by the house, sure, time after time, that the next car would turn into the driveway. My anger was transformed into prayer as the time marched on. "Please, God, even if she is late, just bring her home safely."

When the door finally opened, I would try to sound calm. "Hi! How was your time? I'm glad you're home." Inwardly I prayed, Thanks, God!

In time I stopped waiting up–but I always left the hall light on. The last child to return would switch the light off–then Mom would know that all was well. I always kept an eye on that light shining under my closed bedroom door and barely did I sleep while it was still on. This happened to Heather, too, as she waited for Heidi and David to get home. One day, she brought me one of her poems.

✳ ✳ ✳ ✳ ✳ ✳ ✳ ✳ ✳ ✳

THE NIGHT BEACON

There's a light down the hall,
The beams of light
fall softly in
through the crack in my door.
As I rest in darkness
uncertainty pumps through
my quiet body.
There's a light down the hall,
A light that seems to warm
my room
Such a gentle light
Can only seem to warm
My body—getting colder
There's a light down the hall
Where a room is so light
Everything is vivid and certain.
There's a light down the hall
A light of comfort, warmth
and certainty,
Except for me.
When the light beacon goes out,
I know you are here!

✳ ✳ ✳ ✳ ✳ ✳ ✳ ✳ ✳ ✳

With love, I knew she understood how a mother feels. The intuitive sensitivity she developed at an early age was still there and growing.

Heather graduated from Harcum as salutatorian and went on to Lehigh University for a B.A. in journalism. Then she earned a Master's degree in elementary education. This was the child a guidance counselor considered doubtful as college material.

What amazes me as I write this book is how often I was wrong in the way I perceived my children even though I thought I was really close to them and gave them a lot of time!

Heather, as helper, friend, and ally, was often near. We had many mother-to-daughter discussions about whatever was important to us. One time in Sunday school, we discussed growing and being forced out of our niche even though we don't want to change. Change means taking risks and being open to pain. We can't always avoid the pain.

Later, I wrote to her concerning the discussion we had alone after Sunday school:

> *Two episodes that concern Dad stand out in my mind. I don't tell you this to show fault. The situations began unpleasantly but turned out to be tremendous growing experiences for me. The two episodes also concerned you.*
>
> *When you were an infant I was a real clinging vine in some ways. At certain times in my life, I was probably afraid of my own shadow. I had once been threatened with a gun and I was scared to death about life!*
>
> *Once when you woke up in the middle of the night, crying in your crib, I got out of bed and came to console you. There was no way. You wanted a bottle. I was petrified of going downstairs to the kitchen in the dark. I woke Dad and asked him if he would go downstairs to get it for you.*
>
> *"Look, if you think I'm going to spoil you to that extent, you're mistaken," he said. "You go!" I'm sure he was just angry at being wakened out of a deep sleep.*
>
> *In tears, shaking like a leaf, I went downstairs because it was the only way you would get your bottle and stop crying. I overcame that fear! The first step is always the hardest.*
>
> *Some years later, we had you and Heidi and David, and we traveled around on weekends to the shoots with Dad. I always had my eye out for places where your education could be expanded and we could have fun, too. I expected that Dad would take part in the sightseeing, and in the beginning, he did. But on one trip, I came up with a huge agenda for sightseeing activities after reading the tourist information. He became angry and said, "Look, I came here to shoot. If you want to do all this, you rent the car, you be the tour director. But don't count on me!"*

I cried. How could he do this to me? Then I got mad and said to myself, "OK, I will handle it all!" And I did.

I am not sorry about these experiences, even though they caused a lot of pain at the time. They forced me to be ready for growth and I'm still looking for new ways to grow. Traumatic at the time? My God, you better believe it! But the benefits of accepting new challenges far exceed the security of staying the same.

Heidi and David were stretching their wings, facing life head-on, and a couple of times I asked Heather when she planned to leave home to be on her own. Earnestly, with real determination, she replied, "Don't push me, Mom. I'll go when I am ready!"

I often wondered why Heather didn't leave my Umbrella. Now the answer is clear: At that time she wasn't a risk taker.

Heather made me realize that rebellion isn't a necessary part of growing up for everybody. If a parent and child listen to each other, and exchange new ideas, both can grow. It's different from the kind of maturity that grows like a pearl in an oyster—through irritation and pain. We need to find our own ways of learning about life, and we can't always predict what that way will be. Heather's was a gentler way.

When Heather and Tom, a Ph.D. in microbiology, found each other, Heather knew it was time to leave the Umbrella and marry. She also became a valued first-grade teacher and a mother to the dozens of little children in her classes who adored her.

After a few years, Tom and Heather became the parents of a beautiful baby girl. She was the first of three girls in their delightful family. Now Heather is a full-time mother of four whose days are devoted to helping them grow.

Just the other day, Heather told me what every mother lives to hear: "Mom, now I am really happy." Her own Umbrella of Protection is an active place!

I think Heather is more like me than any of my other children. I am so thankful for her, my first child who stood by my side through hard times as we grew together.

STAGE III

Making Progress

I first imagined the Umbrella of Protection as slightly larger than the usual size black umbrella, with me in the middle and my five children clustered around as a close-knit unit.

Today, the Umbrella has been put away. I think about where to stand now — and my mind tells me I am standing under the sky! The concept of the Umbrella still fits, but it no longer describes a confined space.

Instead, the Umbrella is a wide blue cover that has been transformed from Protection to Limitless Love!

I want to explain the circles of influence in my life that got me from a black spot to a vast blue sky. During my years of Climbing Toward the Light, as I protected my children and watched them grow, my own life began to unfold in new patterns.

C H A P T E R 8

The Simmering Pot
The Need
for New Goals

And after all the journeying,
all the pain and the joy,
we may discover that the Transformation
was difficult to grasp, not because
it was so very far away but because
it was so very near.

George Leonard, *The Gift of Awareness*

For a particularly complicated kind of weaving called double weaving, the loom is set up with two sets of warp threads so that the finished weaving shows a different pattern on each side. Sometimes people don't even notice the design on the second side; they don't appreciate how one side helps to create the pattern on the other. Often in life, we only look at the surface, never turning the weaving over to see how our lives are affected by those close to us and by the challenges we face as we go on. You have viewed much of my life through my children—the one side of weaving. Now let's turn the weaving over.

The words Dr. Shaw said to me during my hospital stay in

Rochester kept slipping back into my mind: What are your thoughts? Many people believe that your thoughts can make you sick or well.

Sometimes we aren't aware of our thoughts at a given instant. We need to filter them out, as though we were panning for gold. The roughage goes through a sieve, and with time and work, the golden thoughts come through. I needed to discover what was important and what I believed in, what my goals were, what had made me get sick, what path would lead me to my destiny in this life. Now I wonder why I never verbalized these thoughts. Was I afraid that my desire for some changes in my life would be misunderstood? How could I respond when people asked, "Why aren't you content with the way things are? You're so lucky—don't you know how good you have it?"

Self-help books were scarce then. Terms such as self-esteem and awareness were not part of my vocabulary. But I needed to begin somewhere, and I did, even though the first answers were not always the ones I might have chosen in the end.

This period of wandering and thinking, living and dreaming, internalizing and looking for answers, lasted for six years. At the end of this period, Bob and I were working hard at ways to help Anthony deal with his hyperactivity. Heidi's problems were beginning. David was very busy with music and drama in high school. Heather was at college discovering her potential. And Maria was just being creative Maria.

My first birthday after my hospitalization was a touching one. Though Bob was away, my children decided to make this a memorable day for me. They invited some of my good friends to the house for a surprise party, and they placed me in a distinctive high-backed chair in the living room, with a footstool under my feet and a handmade crown adorning my head. It was a welcome and wonderful expression of my family's affection.

A well-known artist, Sascha Lautman, came to the farm about this time to paint a portrait of my father-in-law, J. I. Rodale. While he was here, Sascha persuaded Bob to have my portrait painted.

Sascha and his wife, Bea, the stylist, came to the house. First we had to choose the clothes that I would wear. We looked all through my closet and Bea said, "Oh, my, you have nothing that will make you look special." This upset me at first; then as I considered my clothes through someone else's eyes, I knew Bea was right.

Bea went to the fabric store and bought some wonderful turquoise brocade. Then, just by draping and pinning, Bea created a wonderful gown for me to wear. While Sascha worked, Bea told me stories about other people Sascha had painted. Several of the women had come back after many years to tell him how their portraits had influenced their lives.

When the picture was completed, Sascha wanted to hang it in the place of honor in the living room. "No, no!" we all exclaimed. The painting already there was one the whole family dearly loved. Besides, my portrait didn't fit in that place. We finally hung my portrait in our bedroom, facing the bed. And it's true, over the years, the portrait has influenced my thoughts greatly. To this day I sometimes ask myself, Is that really me? The Ardie in the portrait is, above all, a lady who has dignity, vision, dreams, serenity. Is that what I am becoming? I want those traits for my life, and whenever I get off track, the painting reminds me of what I want to be.

Our basement was always a busy haven for all kinds of crafts and artwork. As I had since childhood, I continued to make Christmas presents for my special friends every year, taking care to use a different kind of craft for each year's gifts. I liked the challenge of making older types of crafts as well as looking to new horizons.

I did this craft work not only for myself, but to teach my children what I knew. They became curious and were soon busy painting designs, weaving, sewing, etching and cutting stained glass for projects. Occasionally, Heather, Heidi, David, and I took our easels out on the back porch, set up a still life and painted the same subject—each from his or her own perspective, each in his or her own style. My children were my best friends; they are my pride and my joy!

Bob continued shooting every weekend, from May to October. As a member of the U.S. shooting team he went to Egypt, where the team won the gold medal over the Russians. Over Bob's career, he represented the United States 14 times. The family tagged along for some of the national shoots each year. The skeet shooters, their wives, and the children had their own society, like a club. The children were always included in fancy parties we attended, and we all looked forward to those times.

Bob and I gave one very special party every other year. It took weeks to prepare for these parties. Each one had its own theme and every invitation was handmade by me. For example, the Teahouse of the August Moon had a teahouse bedecked with handmade cherry blossom trees, and we sat at low Chinese-type tables on grass mats. The family had inherited a dance floor, and we booked a wonderful band to complement the event.

For our Gypsy Lantern party, a "caravan" occupied one side of the dance floor with tables topped by red checkered cloths placed around the other three sides. For that one, everything was all set up by late afternoon, so the family went to a diner for a snack and some relaxation before the party started.

Then the hail came! The *Farmer's Almanac* had predicted hail, but we hadn't really believed it would come. It was June! We rushed home, swabbed up the dance floor, and put everything in order. Somehow, the party for 160 guests began on time. The music was wonderful, but the rains came again, and the band finally ended up playing in an upstairs bedroom where we pushed the beds aside so the dancing could continue. Would you believe this party was a grand success?

The three older children helped to plan and decorate for these memorable events. In time they would have their own theme parties. Then *they* would direct and I would help, just as they helped me. It has pleased me to see it all happen in reverse.

The last exchange student came to us from a family Bob and his mother had met on a mountain in Switzerland. Bob had assured the family that I would love to have their daughter Corinne come and live with us to learn English. "She's been a mother to many students," Bob had told them. For the first three weeks after she arrived, Corinne followed us everywhere. She would not let us out of her sight! Finally, in desperation, I asked her, "Why do you do this? What is wrong?"

Her reply amazed us all. "My mother heard so many bad things about the United States that she was afraid I would be killed. She made me promise that I would never leave your house unless accompanied by a family member." This included going into the yard! I was annoyed with her mother. She had limited my own activities by giving such an absurd directive to her daughter!

It took some time until we understood each other and Corinne became her independent self. Then she became active in her church and signed up to do volunteer work at the nearby hospital. Corinne's hospital experience was particularly influential, for she attended nursing school when she went home.

After Corinne returned to Switzerland, I wrote a letter to her mother. "Corinne is not the same girl you sent to us. She has gained strength and independence. Now she is her own person."

I never heard from her mother, but Corinne kept in touch with us. She is a caring, compassionate woman and her letters to us demonstrated these qualities in reporting her nursing experiences. Eventually, Corinne went to England to train as a hospice nurse. Her tender ways with these needful people showed that Corinne was a person of great love and inner strength.

Corrine's visit was our final exchange student experience. As I told Bob, "I have done my duty for students. There are other things I want to do now, other directions I want to take, and I must find those pursuits that will be personally satisfying for me."

We were becoming more and more frustrated by the unrealized projects waiting their turn at the Rodale Experimental Farm, where we lived. Space was sorely lacking and the city was beginning to crowd in. The time had come to look to new places for our organic gardening and farming experiments.

One of my jobs was to start the search. We looked at a number of farms, but they were all too small for our purposes. Then one day, I went with Jim Foote, our farm manager, to look at a new prospect. This time, the place was larger than we thought we needed. It included three houses, two barns, numerous sheds, and an old school house. It encompassed a whole valley with rolling hills. It was an area utterly unspoiled, a place that looked as though time had stood still there for well over a hundred years.

The houses were in reasonably good shape; they had been renovated in the 1960s with an eye toward historical preservation. Still, as I looked at the place, I figured it would take a lifetime to get it in shape—then I thought about the breathtaking view from the top of the hill down over the valley. My mind flashed to images of people who must have lived there over the centuries.

This was a valley that held the dreams of hundreds of people long before Revolutionary times. It must have been hard for the early settlers to survive. Then each generation built on the dreams of those who went before. I had a feeling that this was one place that love had built. Now we had an opportunity to perpetuate that love by caring for the environment and people by means of the research center we would create here.

After weighing these and many other considerations, we bought the place! This purchase was to have a very significant meaning for my life, and for that of my family.

In those days, whenever I had enough time in the afternoon, I spent long hours dreaming about a life change. I vicariously lived the various possibilities in my mind, and when the dream was over, I went back to being who I had always been. Many people are like I was. Perhaps it's the reason TV and movies are so popular. As we watch, we can become that person on the screen for just a little while. Our real life becomes more tolerable until the next show, when we can live in new dreams.

The problem lies in transferring the person we want to be to our true life. We are hampered by such thoughts as, I would like to, but I can't. What would others say? I don't have the nerve! All the "what ifs" surface to crowd out the possible reality of the dream. The parent in us won't give us permission to change the pattern of our life.

I stayed in this limbo for a long time. I was to learn later that I didn't need to maintain this status. But at that time of my life I felt guilty. I had so much. So why was I so increasingly restless? Why did I spend so much time in a fantasy world? Clearly, I must be ungrateful for all my blessings. I still believed, like Snow White, that if I had faith, all my dreams would someday come true. If I worked hard enough, loved strong enough, and never lost hope, everything I wanted would come to pass.

In fact, I began to realize that I was no longer able to control everything in my life. Things kept "slip-sliding away." The old dreams and goals had largely been achieved, and the children already had their own views and goals.

With each successive family trip the experience became less rewarding. Trying to direct the family show left me frustrated and more exhausted than I was before the "vacation." I didn't need this struggle anymore. (I'm told now that the family remembers these times as something quite wonderful.)

When school time rolled around in the fall, I got really depressed as I looked at the surroundings. My order was nowhere to be found. Like most children, mine largely ignored my messages about being responsible for their own things. Family belongings were strewn around the house, like palms to the Hosannah—and I was left to clean up the debris after the parade!

I felt like a puppet, with everyone in the family pulling my strings at will. Then, in later years, I questioned whether I had been trying to manipulate the strings on my children's lives.

The decorating and renovating work I did for the company facilities was increasingly demanding and took more and more of my time. I began to question my value as a *person*—Ardie.

Sometimes I look back on myself in those days as a kind of computer where all the information was being fed—and I was supposed to come up with the right answers. But I was not a machine. I was a human being who was being pulled in too many directions. I was on the rack, and, oh, how it hurt!

Many of my dreams were of drowning. Were the waves of other people's needs and desires swallowing up my identity? My arms thrashed about to save myself from going under!

The time was fast approaching for another reevaluation.

> Where was Ardie?
> Where was I going?
> What time was it in my life?
> What else did I want to do?
> Who was I anyway?

But I did have dreams! And these dreams needed to be realized.

The simmering pot was beginning to boil and bubble. I was not satisfied with my life. How could I inflate my balloon so it could take off in new directions, wherever the wind would blow?

C H A P T E R   9

The Big Step
My Will to Change

Oh what love can do!
Enabling me to see when I look,
Hear when I listen, feel when I touch,
Allowing me to wake up and live
when the world is with me too much.

Maggie Finefrock

I remember the day: September 23, 1972. I remember that day so clearly because it marked the start of my personal change and the beginning of my struggle to climb toward my own light. Previously my thoughts and aims were directed at changing what was going on around me. I was always trying to create an environmental explosion. I believed that if I could change these outside factors, my frustration and boredom would disappear and my life would be better. On that day in September, I realized that a new dream really was possible.

I had been working very hard with other staff members to plan a big field day at our old Farm. Advertisers and the news media were coming by bus from New York to see what organic gardening was all about. They would be touring the gardens and the fields, viewing the condition of the crops and observing new developments. Our harvest was already fantastically abundant and the produce was perfect.

I worked with some of the women at the Press—our sewing machines flying!—to make gold, green, and lavender net bags that would be filled with fruits of the earth for our city visitors to take home. To make this an elegant event, I set the table with my silver service and finest of tablecloths for the reception that would follow the speeches. The enormous table, laden with baskets of fruits and vegetables and flowers, became the focal point under a tent where the speeches were given. We were all glad to be shielded from the heat of the day and the blinding sunlight.

As I sat, exhausted, listening to the speeches, my mind began to wander over the fields of the farm. My eyes slowly passed over all the people who sat with me under the tent, listening with interest, and I felt a strange stirring deep inside of me that I had never experienced before. Was this uneasiness the next stage of the simmering pot that was to boil over? For the first time, the idea came to me that if I wanted to change my life, I had to change the inside of me! I made a declaration to myself that I would begin to grow toward my own light instead of growing toward the light of others.

It was a momentous declaration! I didn't know all that it would entail. I would have to take many risks. I would have to stop trying to appease everyone else before myself. I would find that sometimes other people would be unhappy with me in my growth. I would find that sometimes my growth would come in tremendous spurts and at other times it would seem barely alive. I would find also that growth can be very painful when my crises would peak at the same time as those of my children. Sometimes I would have to postpone my own growth experiences to help the family with theirs. But I would never again lose sight of my own goals for growth.

Personal change is hard work. You must read continually, throw yourself into the paths of new situations, study, ask questions, search your soul. It means remembering what you see straight ahead of you, what you see sideways and behind. It means that you have to tune in on what you see, what you feel, all that you experience—and what you love.

My implosion had begun, and I was on the way to discovery. The implosion had become necessary for my survival.

One of my first thoughts was that life should be more vibrant and exciting than mine was. I couldn't sit in the backseat of life any longer. From now on I was a front seat driver in full command of Ardie! I needed to free my pent-up feelings. How? I thought about Anthony's tendency when he was frustrated: run, run, run! That's what I would do for release—I would run!

I'm a very early morning person, so it was a perfect activity for me. Oftentimes I ran over the fields of the farm in my nightgown. It was fun and I felt free! As I ran, I would call loudly to the trees and the plants, "I love you, world!" I'm sure the plants felt the positive vibrations I gave off. As I passed the violets, the roses, and all the other flowers through the garden, I exhorted them to "Grow! Grow! Grow!" The birds and the chickens answered my singing.

I looked at the trees carefully, trying to correlate their lives to ours. At first, I looked upon the straight, even-growing trees as neat and beautiful. Then I wondered: By pruning our trees to help them grow, did we prune away some unknown opportunity as well? The old crooked trees became my favorites. Like the many limbs on a tree, our life can lead to new paths of discovery—some glorious, some commonplace, some dangerous. The choice of which path to follow is ours.

I was on a natural high. Spring was in my heart. "Wake up! Wake up!" I called to the owl I passed. I wanted to rediscover the world as a happy surprise—like a flower in the snow or an oasis in the desert.

One early morning, I opened my eyes to see the most beautiful moon through my window. I heard God say to me, "Wake up! Realize that along with love, there's other beauty in this world."

I said, "But, God, without love one cannot see beauty." I prayed that I might never forget all the good that was here.

To me, God is a very real being. He is the friend I can talk to when no one is there. Through the many trials of life, I have felt Him at my side and urging me onward. Usually, when I talk to God, it is like talking to my best friend, not at all like a formal prayer. I think of my Friend as a polestar who could keep me from losing my direction. I knew my pathway would be clouded at times.

Like the seasons, life never stays the same; life cannot remain on a high forever. I learned that Climbing Toward the Light happens by steps. Sometimes we climb fast and sometimes we rest. And sometimes our feet slip.

One day when I happened to be in a slipping stage and feeling sorry for myself, my son David, then age 15, came into the bedroom. When he saw me, he asked why I was sad. "David, I don't know what's wrong," I said. "I'm in a slump and I just can't seem to pull myself out of it. I wish I could go away for a while."

"Why don't you? You really should. Where would you like to go?" he asked. We started to brainstorm.

"I have always wanted to go to Hawaii," I confessed. "Since Dad is in China, and since he can come home by way of Hawaii, maybe this is my chance."

"Then do it!" David shouted.

We planned together how to make this happen. A big concern for me was that a trip to Hawaii meant flying. I had always refused to fly because I worried about who would look after the children if something happened to me. But now our eldest daughter, Heather, was old enough to be in charge of the family. And she was a very good assistant mother. I packed with enthusiasm. In several days, I was off to Hawaii on my own. This was new excitement for me.

I planned to have several days by myself in Hawaii before Bob joined me. Bob had many speeches scheduled for when he returned to Emmaus, and a stopover in Hawaii would give him time to have his pictures developed and get his speeches in order. As I waited for Bob to arrive, my free days were wonderfully fulfilling. I had chosen a hotel with several restaurants, so I had a variety of eating places to try. I knew I wouldn't get bored. The beach was heaven; the rainbows after the rain were enthralling; and the amazing discoveries in the shops were exciting. This was just what the doctor ordered for getting me back on track.

Bob landed in Hawaii after spending 30 days in China. He is not a beach person, so 4 or 5 days in Hawaii held little appeal for him. He was anxious to get home after his long trip. I, on the other hand, still had all kinds of plans. On the third day I came back to the room at noon, my face all aglow with the pleasure and excitement I found in each new excursion. Bob said, "Hurry up and pack. We're leaving for the airport in an hour. We're going home."

"No, no, I'm not finished with this place," I cried. "I don't want to go!" But, dutifully, I threw the clothes in the suitcases and we left.

En route, Bob kept changing the flights to advance the time of our arrival at home. The luggage didn't keep up with us, of course. When the bags were finally delivered a day or two later, they were minus the gold earrings I had bought as presents for my daughters to wear in their newly pierced ears.

I felt angry for a long time. As I calmed down, I saw Bob's side. Maybe I had tried to manipulate him into staying. But I had my side, too. He had manipulated me into going home. I was still the dutiful child; I bowed to what Bob wanted.

Today, the scenario would be different. If Bob wanted to go home, I would say go ahead. I would come later—when I was ready!

CHAPTER 10

Looking at Life through New Glasses

Learning to Solve Problems

We often stand in our shadows. We have to learn to turn around and face the sun.

Ardie

A wounded spirit can be just as painful as a wounded body, but we don't take care of a spiritual wound the way we do a hurt we can see. Unless we treat these wounds with kindness and understanding, they can leave deep scars inside. With age, we accumulate many such scars from unresolved hurts and troubles, and they often color later decisions we make in life. Through Gestalt, I found a way to treat these wounds of the spirit so my life could go on happily.

When Heidi learned about Gestalt in college, it showed her that our relationship was the root of many of her problems. My goals for her were not her goals, so Heidi felt stifled, held back. She was determined to find a way to get on with her own agenda for life.

I never realized that I was doing anything wrong. If Heidi felt this way because of Gestalt, I wanted to know more. I tried to find a nearby college that offered a course in Gestalt, but not one of the five in the area could satisfy my hunger for this knowledge.

Several months later, a friend called to tell me that a local pastoral institute would be offering a course in Transactional Analysis and Gestalt. I was 1 of 20 in the class, 6 of whom were clergy.

For the first six months, the sessions were basically class/lecture work. Then our leader, Fred, announced that a new class would be starting, in which we would work on our life scripts in depth. The class would be smaller and I was invited to join it. I laughed to myself, thinking I didn't have anything to work on—no real problems. But I decided to join because I might learn something. As it turned out, I learned a lot that has helped me to help myself. My newfound knowledge made a big difference in my view of life.

At one of the first sessions the group was divided into partners, one continually and rapidly asking the other, "Who are you? Who are you?" This continued until the answerer exhausted all possible responses. The roles were then reversed and the answerer became the questioner. All responses were recorded. The idea was to see how we perceived ourselves.

Try it yourself. Allow two minutes for the exercise. After each answer you write down, ask yourself the question again, Who are you? Do it rapidly. Now consider what you have written about yourself.

This is the list I made in answer to "Who are you?"

Mother of five children	*Guide to children*
Wife	*Helper to others*
Working for the company	*Lots of imagination*
Person with energy to do a lot	*Artist*
Questioner of ideas	*Drive to keep on growing*
Sunday school teacher	*Love life*
Love to be out-of-doors	*Have sense of humor*
Independent person	*Instigator of trouble*
Hard worker	*Sensitive*
Like to be inspired	*Can't tolerate being overrun*

Most of us answered first, I am a wife, a mother, a priest, and so on. Few of us started with our name and that we were a person. Most of us perceived ourselves as helpers to others; we did not answer who we really were. Then each of us worked on a statement of who we were. After much laborious thinking I wrote my statement on pink paper in large print, and attached it to the refrigerator. Imagine my family's response when they read the following declaration.

I am responsible for myself
I will respond
I'm here if you want me
But don't hem me in
I Am Myself!

Feathers flew. Bob and the children looked at me with suspicion. I could feel them thinking, This means trouble! What's she up to now? Whoa! How is this going to affect me? They were not interested in the personal changes I was experiencing.

Sometimes we grab the sword by the blade instead of the handle. I learned how to avoid doing that, how to dialogue in a conflict without raising the other person's hostility. If one person talks down to the other, as a parent might reprimand a child, anger flares easily and guilt feelings follow. If I were to say to you, "How could you be so stupid! Just look at what you've done!" of course you would feel resentful. But if I were to say, "I feel sad because this situation occurred. Let's discuss it as adults, talking together on the same level to see what can be done to improve things," each person feels like an equal and there are no putdowns.

I started to talk this way with my family and our relationships rapidly improved. It was particularly effective in my dealings with the two younger children whom I treated as equals–friends, rather than parent and child.

Give it a voice–that was another important lesson I learned. If we talk about our problems with someone, or write them down, they often cease to exist! Whenever I experienced frustrations in my own life, I started to write about them in my diary. After a while, I noticed that this simple activity helped me to feel better–and it was a very effective form of therapy. I started to find some answers. I talked about this with my assistant Bonnie, who has started to do it too. She said, "You know, Ardie, it is almost like looking in a mirror. What you write down comes staring back at you. You find solutions." It's true!

We also learned a technique for resolving a conflict with another person. Three chairs are placed in the room–one for the observer, the other two for you, the person trying to resolve a conflict. You place the image of the person you are at odds with in the vacant chair opposite yours. You state the problem, explain how you feel, and why you are angry. Next, you become the person you are at odds with, sitting in his chair. You articulate the answers you think he might give in response to the reasons for your anger.

The dialogue continues back and forth until you feel that the problem is resolved. This therapy helps one to see the other person's point of view, so often overlooked in a conflict. I did this exercise in the class using the conflict I still felt with my father, even though he had died many years before. My conversation went like this:

Ardie: You know, Daddy, I don't think I ever knew who you were as a person. My view was that I was a second-class citizen in your eyes. Your work at Mack Trucks and your friends always came first. I wanted to feel special in your eyes. I was your child!

You only talked to me when I needed a reprimand. I saw other children having fun with their fathers, but I always felt that I was held at a distance. I couldn't get close to you. When I came up with a new or creative idea, you always put me down. I felt that you were embarrassed by my wanting to be different. You seemed to want me in a mold, just like everyone else. Why did you treat me this way? I'm angry and hurt. I wonder if you loved me.

Daddy: (shaking his head tensely) I worked hard. I was always trying to prove myself. I wanted people at work to acknowledge that I was doing a good job. The people with a college education got the advancements. Couldn't you see that I had so many cares? I didn't need any more problems. You were hard to handle.

Ardie: Why did you treat me as if I weren't important?

Daddy: I enjoyed my friends. They helped me relax and forget my worries about work and tight money. I had to make an impression on my friends–to let them know that I was some-body too. Your mother went to college. She was the articulate one. I never had her opportunities. The family was just another responsibility for me. Maybe I didn't know you felt that way.

Ardie: There were so many things left unsaid. We just didn't communicate in the best way. Sometimes when I asked for things and you answered me so sharply with a "No!", maybe it would have been good to tell me why. For instance, when I wanted that car for my teaching job, if you had told me that the money just wasn't there, I could have tried to understand.

(Silence)

Maybe I wouldn't have been hard to handle if I had felt that I was wanted. You know, I often came to kiss you goodnight before I went to bed, but I don't remember that you ever looked up from your paper. It would have been nice for you to return that kiss sometimes. I feel sad. . . .

Daddy: Ardie, I didn't mean to hurt you. I guess it's true, we didn't talk much. That's the way I was brought up. In my *family, we didn't talk about how we felt. I thought if I could be a good provider, that would be enough. Your mother was the one who could do the other things I couldn't do.*

Ardie: *Daddy, when I saw you on the bed at Rockport and you were crying, that was the first time I ever felt any compassion for you. I really did see the child in you, and not the disciplinarian that I knew. I felt sorry that it was almost the end of your life and that over all those years we had missed so much!*

Daddy: *I'm sorry. I should have done more. It's too late.*

Ardie: *No, it's not too late. Do you think we can hug each other in spirit?*

Daddy: *OK.*

Ardie: *It feels good. Thanks.*

Finally, I was able to see that Daddy was a loving person. He did the best he could in his light. All the anger left me. I was able to forgive him and release my hurt. I was able to close the circle, to heal the spiritual wound that I had harbored for too long.

There was an interesting side effect concerning the way I perceived my relationships with older men. The men with whom I got along best were usually younger than I. (My husband, Bob, was a younger man.) Before this experience, I always felt as though I were a child, waiting for a reprimand, or for orders of some kind, from the older men I knew. Afterward, this feeling disappeared and I was able to talk with older men on an equal level, adult to adult.

Even today, when I feel conflict with someone, I practice this imaginary conversation method in private, using two chairs. Then I can usually understand the problem much better.

The singular experiences shared by two other people in the class had a big impact on my outlook on life. The first was Martha, whose mother continually put her down. No matter how hard Martha tried to please, nothing she did was right. Eventually, her mother refused to have anything to do with Martha, who felt angry and deeply saddened by her mother's rejection. The whole situation was grim, and finally, when it appeared that there were no answers, Fred asked Martha, "Why do you want your mother's love when she always makes you feel so bad? You can't change other people; you can only change yourself. There are other nourishing people who can provide the love you want from your mother, and it can be just as rewarding."

This left a deep impression on me. It made me recall my high school years, when I had wanted certain people as friends but they just hadn't accepted me. They had made me feel like the kid from the other side of the tracks. I had to make my mark. If someone didn't like me, my strong will said, I'll *make* her like me! The harder I tried to *push* my way in, going the extra mile, the less successful I was. I needed to look for other friends who could fulfill my need for acceptance. I needed to discover that the socially elite were not necessarily the best people, that there were many other wonderful, truly sincere people out there. Had I been accepted by the "crowd," I'm sure my life would have been different. For one thing, I doubt that I would have turned as often to my inner resources in trying to make my life better. That would have been a loss for me.

Jane, the second person in the class whose experience impacted on my life, was in the throes of a divorce, preceded by the death of one of her children. One day Jane came to the session in deep despair. Her anguish was felt by all of us. In her dialogue, she cried, "If only I could get away. . . . I would feel so much better. But there is no escape. I'm stuck." Fred asked Jane where she would like to go. She replied, "I have always wanted to go to England, but it is out of the question."

What happened next was a revelation—a directed visual dream of a trip to England that Jane could take just by closing her eyes and imagining she was there! She chose the places she had always wanted to visit and Fred directed her through them, so she could describe what she was seeing and how she was feeling as the beautiful trip unfolded. The session was long. It went on until Jane had "been to" all the places she really wanted to see, and was ready to come home. Afterward, Jane said she felt refreshed and better able to cope.

I looked back to that time in my life when I had spent much time daydreaming, and I could relate to what Jane had just experienced. Dreams and visions offer an oasis of temporary relief when we feel battered by our daily lives.

The class members were very supportive of each other. There was a real loyalty among the group; we were all searching for ways to make our lives healthier. When I felt I was well on my way to that goal, I knew the time had come for me to drop out of the class.

Fred continued as the leader for a while, then he decided the time had come to move on and he went to California. I felt safe while Fred was still in the area even though I was no longer in the class. I knew if I needed help, he was there. Both current and former class members felt a sense of loss in Fred's leaving, thinking if we need help, whom do we turn to?

We needed to *learn our own strength*. We had to put all our lessons into practice. And many of us found that we had been taught well.

As we achieve each goal, we must reevaluate our life and move to a higher level—another step on the Climb Toward the Light.

CHAPTER 11

Learning and Growing Together
Teaching Others

TEACHING

Only the man who understands and appreciates what it is to grow, who understands and tries to satisfy his own needs for growth, can properly understand and appreciate growth in another.

Milton Mayeroff

Epigraph from ON CARING by Milton Mayeroff.
Copyright © 1971 by Milton Mayeroff. Reprinted by
permission of Harper & Row, Publishers, Inc.

One of my life's strongest influences for growth came through a class I taught in Sunday school for over 20 years. Because I didn't like the traditional Sunday school lessons supplied by the church, I found more appealing material on my own. The membership in my class rose steadily. I was never questioned by the church authorities, so I continued to spread the Word in my own way. I didn't dwell on Bible history; rather, I concentrated on how we as individuals who cared about our fellowmen could become better people. All of our lessons were discussion-oriented; we sat in an informal circle rather than lecture style.

Our class became known as the Couples and Singles Revolutionaries. Toward the end of my time there, sons and daughters of the original Couples and Singles were joining the group. The excited faces around me on a Sunday morning were proof that something good was happening. I was to realize later how important this discipline of learning and sharing was in my life. My mind was being changed to new and broader views. It was as though I were a flower, opening petal by petal.

When I first began my Sunday school classes, I had doubts about whether it was right for me to direct these people. I didn't think of myself as being all that generous; in fact, I was selfish sometimes. I wanted to keep all the sunshine I was feeling inside, and hold it tight, to be sure I wouldn't lose it. I prayed:

> *God, why is it that we sometimes try to build walls around ourselves? Are we afraid to risk hurt in our lives? Please forgive us when we shrink from sharing our feelings with others, afraid that they see the human failings in our hearts. When we don't measure up to your expectations, I wonder how often you say to us, "I still love you."*

Faithfully and eagerly, my students came to class every week and I, as the shepherd, was sometimes imperfect, often revolutionary, but always caring.

I shared what I learned about Transactional Analysis and Gestalt in the counseling sessions with members of the class. Like me, they needed to get a handle on problem solving and dealing with pent-up anger.

We talked about learning responsibility, standing on your own two feet. The message was: Don't continue to do for others what they can do for themselves. Smothering with love can be a disservice. By being oversolicitous you can rob a person of his initiative. We must learn to sense when enough help is enough.

We tried to determine the most effective way to help others, and arrived at a surprising conclusion: To be effective we must make sure that we ourselves are healthy—emotionally, physically and spiritually —so we have the right direction in helping others.

When we talked about setting personal goals, each person was given a paper and an envelope, and instructed to write down what he or she planned to accomplish in the next six months. Then the papers were sealed in the self-addressed envelopes which I collected and filed at home. Six months later, each class member received his or her envelope in the mail. Imagine the stimulating class we had the following Sunday!

Most people had forgotten we had done this exercise, and wondered about the envelope when it came. "That's my handwriting. When did I write a letter to myself? And why?" Some class members found that they had accomplished a lot; others were still unfocused.

Let's think of our heart as a house with many rooms, I suggested on another Sunday. Take a look at what some of the rooms in our hearts might look like–damp basement, narrow hallways, cramped spaces, tight closets, shuttered windows, drawn blinds, padlocked doors. Perhaps we needed to fling open the doors of our hearts to look out the windows to wider horizons, to light the fires that warm the hearth in large airy rooms!

The more we love, the more we become aware of the huge expansive rooms in our hearts–and the larger our hearts grow. Embracing new experiences and sharing love unlocks the doors to the rooms in our hearts, freeing us to love as God created us to love.

Our session on guilt emphasized the necessity of self-forgiveness regarding personal weaknesses. It's important to know that even though we don't always live up to expectations, we are lovable and have worth in God's eyes.

Sometimes I used symbols in my teaching. One such idea came from a magazine, where I read about Forgiveness Cups given as engagement and wedding gifts. For Christmas that year I gave an antique cut glass cordial cup or a new crystal cordial glass to each couple. Every cup was different. This message accompanied the gift:

> *Each cup is unique, just like a person. This gift to you is called the Forgiveness Cup. Sometimes in our relationships with people close to us it is hard to resolve conflict. We find it hard to say "I'm sorry!"*
>
> *The Forgiveness Cup is the "bridge over troubled waters." If you face such an impasse, fill the cup with wine and hand it to your partner, signifying, It's OK. It's all right. I love you!*

Another year, the symbol I chose for my gift was a glass bluebird. This also makes a wonderful little wedding gift. The inspiration came from the beautiful story called *The Bluebird* by Maurice Maeterlinck. Here is the message:

The bluebird is a symbol of happiness. True happiness results from allowing each person the freedom to be himself. The joy comes when other people respond to us not out of duty but out of true love. Then we have found the Bluebird of Happiness.

Over the years, some members of our class became terminally ill and the class became a support team for those people and their families. One class member, Marie, became ill during a springtime that was one of the most beautiful I could remember. I wondered what went through her mind as her time became shorter. Did she look upon each beautiful sunrise and sunset as an experience she wanted to hold close forever? How did she feel about leaving her family behind? Did it hurt her? Did she even think about it? We all supported Marie in love and concern. I know we were important to her. We were there for her, however she wanted us to be.

One day Ellis, a street person, came through the doors of our church, which was in downtown Allentown. I think he originally came to get in out of the cold. Perhaps he knew we served coffee and cake. Whatever the reason, he kept coming back. I tried to bring Ellis into the conversation, and sometimes, in his simple faith, the answers he gave were just what we needed to hear. One Sunday, I asked him to read and he replied, "Oh, no. I never learned to read . . . but I can sing." I asked Ellis if he would sing for us and he sang with such vibrancy and conviction that it touched our hearts, and there were tears. Over time, Ellis taught us a lot about acceptance and caring.

Our class members were trying to become better people themselves, and help to make the church better as well. While we were considered revolutionaries by some of the congregation, when a church social event took place our class was right out there doing most of the work—preparing the food and cleaning up afterward. Members of the class were involved in the local food bank and in other social ministry projects. We were active and visible. We wanted the best for the people and the church.

Unfortunately the pastor was not strong. We felt our church was in trouble. The minister's lack of organization was particularly upsetting. We loved our church, but we objected to the disorganized way it was being run. I became the spokesperson for a committee to replace the minister and my life suddenly became a frantic whirlwind of crises and activity. I was soon worn thin with the aggravation of this struggle. It was too much to bear, and eventually my anger and disappointment over the church situation came to a head. I wrote to my Sunday school class:

> I've looked at all the years of where we have been together. I've looked at our growth . . . our pains . . . and our joys. We've learned a lot, we've shared a lot; we've laughed, we've cried. We've been sensitive to one another's needs. . . . We've cared.
> I have a couple of friends with whom I've spent long hours in the past because they needed someone at that time. Then we

kind of drifted apart and we occasionally talked, but those lines of communication are always open. They know that if the need was there, I'd be there to help, night or day. Sometimes we don't talk for months, but when the phone rings, it's instant connection. Know that I will always be there for you in whatever way I can help, as a friend or a supporter. I think you realize that we have established those caring lifelines throughout our years together.

I find myself in a catch 22, so, with regret, I'm resigning as Sunday school teacher immediately. This is one of the hardest decisions I've had to make . . . but remember I'm out there as your friend.

Love, Ardie

My cut was clean and I didn't go back. There was great guilt and suffering on my part. I sensed anger from some of the members of the class, an unspoken message that said, How could you do this to us after all these years? You were always here when we needed you!

The feelings were the same as those we had when Fred, our counselor in Transactional Analysis and Gestalt, left us to go to California. The time had come for the class members to use their own strength, to try their own wings. Many of them grew tremendously.

About a year later, Betty, who had taken over the class, called in the name of the group to invite Bob and me to a dinner at a local restaurant. After the meal each member told about his or her activities during the past year, and what the class had meant to them personally over the years. It was fun, but above all it was touching and nourishing for each of us. My silent questions about what was happening to the lives I had touched through all those years had answers now. There was a real pride within these people as they told of their newfound strength, soaring high on their own wings.

As the evening ended, we hugged each other and sensed a genuine care. That evening finished another circle of Gestalt for me. It saw the healing of an open wound for all of us; the message of "love one another" was sincere.

I felt overwhelmed when I heard how much the years had meant to these dear friends. To know that I was a vehicle for spreading God's care and peace was humbling. And these dear friends were all there for me later in a sorrow yet to come.

As the years rolled by I became clearer in my mind about what I taught and what I believed, and I worked out the following statement of what I tried to teach.

♥ ♥ ♥ ♥ ♥ ♥ ♥ ♥ ♥ ♥ ♥ ♥ ♥ ♥ ♥ ♥

God Created Us in His Own Image. *Therefore, it is our right to be happy, healthy, whole and alive!*

Only Good Comes from God. *He loves us even though we don't always measure up. This love never fails. He always forgives us when we fall short. This is the grace of God. Because only good comes from God, He doesn't punish; He loves and forgives. Through Him, we have this power to love and forgive ourselves.*

God Cares for Us with a Nourishing Love. *It is our right in His world to be all that we wish to be. He wants us to be our best self but we must allow it to happen. We decide. His nourishing love gives sunlight to the unfolding flower in us. We can make the flower bloom more beautifully or let it wilt. The choice is ours.*

God's Love Is Unconditional. *He loves us no matter what we do. We are energized by His love, and we share it by showing our caring and concern for others.*

God Is Our Best Friend. *He is always there when we need Him, constant and faithful. We cannot lose when we have the best to cheer us on. We feel the love of God, not the fear of God.*

For myself, I worked out a code of personal belief and behavior that I follow every day. Because I have been blessed with life, I will act in this way:

♥ ♥ ♥ ♥ ♥ ♥ ♥ ♥ ♥ ♥ ♥ ♥ ♥ ♥ ♥ ♥

I will see each life situation as a learning experience.
I will neither condemn myself nor others—we are all still learning.
I will respect the right of each individual to create his or her own symphony.
Through God, I have the power to make my symphony of life beautiful or discordant.
I will strive for awareness of all aspects of beauty, love, caring, and needing. I will respond to these feelings in a positive way.
I will nourish my curiosity about life and try to discover all it has to offer.

God says, "Keep on. You have the opportunity to make life even better. Just keep growing in a more beautiful way than the day before. By sharing your joy with others you make the world a better place."

CHAPTER 12

Spreading Wings
Taking Risks

I made a statement to myself: I want independence and dignity, I want to be something more than a wife and mother who also works for the family company.

I thought about Henrik Ibsen's *A Doll's House,* in which Nora, the heroine, asks her husband, "What do you consider my most sacred duty?"

His immediate answer: "Your duty is to your husband and your children."

Nora takes exception. "I have another duty, just as sacred . . . my duty to myself. I believe before anything else, I'm a human being . . . just as you are . . . or, at any rate I shall try to become one. I can't be satisfied any longer with what most people say, and with what's in books. I must think things out for myself and try to understand them."

The first thing I needed was space, space to grow and think—plus the opportunity to make a road map for my new journey.

To begin, I announced to the family that one day a week I would be off on my own. I would go shopping and I would be back when I was ready—probably, after dinner. I soon got to know all the shopping areas within a radius of 50 miles. I learned to enjoy dinner alone, and my mealtime entertainment lay in observing my fellow diners and their habits. I noticed some who were very uncomfortable in being alone. Those people would sit facing the wall in a restaurant instead of facing out toward the other diners. Often they brought reading material, and looked up from it only to speak to the waiter. Others sat looking out to the crowd and were aware of the other diners. They were alone in a positive way, not lonely. That was how I wanted to be.

I needed to take risks and to be ready to handle complaints from the family about the times I was absent. Some of the children wondered, Why doesn't she want to be with us all the time when *we're* available?

The family needed to know that there were times I would not be at their beck and call, that they must learn to make some of their own decisions and to do more for themselves. I thought I might be appreciated more if I weren't always there. Above all, they had to know this: Just as they needed freedom, I needed it, too.

Of course, the family made me feel guilty. And this was something I needed to work on. There was a private place I went to when these feelings came and I wanted to be by myself to think. It was a beautiful grove of pine trees at the side of our home. The thick carpet of pine needles helped to muffle the sounds of the outside world. The scent of the pine filled my senses, and the world was transformed into a spiritual cathedral. Here I could be alone with my thoughts and I could talk to myself out loud about my feelings. Here I could talk myself into having a positive attitude again.

The only way for me to stop feeling guilty was to tell My Friend, God, about it. "Please help me to forgive my own weakness. I will wash and bleach this old guilt, Father. Then I will hang it in the clean air and the sunshine. I'll fold it neatly and put it in a box to toss away." This was not a once-and-done situation. I had to talk to myself like this many times.

The most rewarding way to get in touch with my inner self was to spend some time at the New Farm in Maxatawny. The place speaks utter beauty and contentment and one feels the world become hushed as though this land were hallowed ground. It was the Indians who settled on this spot, and it was here that my son Anthony learned to quiet his thoughts and to develop his perception of the best in nature.

Bob and I shared ownership of the New Farm jointly with the company, Rodale Press. I had a real stock in this place, and it became my retreat. One of the houses on it was to be used for conferences. This was the perfect place to utilize my talents as a do-it-yourselfer and a perfect excuse for me to escape. I began by painting the walls of the very large farm kitchen, then the rest of the first floor.

One day Bob said, "What are we going to use the other rooms for?" I told him I had no idea. Then he said very slowly, "How about putting bedroom furniture in those rooms? Then when there are no conferences, we might want to stay here ourselves." Great!

As I worked hard, painting and papering, I used the time for personal reflection. New ideals and goals began to take form. This place became a haven where I could get in touch with my feelings. I spent hours walking the fields or just looking over the land and dreaming. One spring day, I wrote in my journal:

Today is Appreciation Day! It's good to be alive and happy. As I sit on the back steps at the New Farm, I notice that since last year someone has planted a lot of daffodils for me. It's a lovely surprise, and they are now gently swaying in the breeze. The heads look like the speaker on the old-style telephone. It tells me to appreciate gifts.

As I look around, I notice that the red tulips are also new. Their petals are like arms that reach upward and out. It reminds me of reaching out to give to others, and, at the same time, of being like an empty cup—eager to receive life. I appreciate that, too.

The birds are gaily chattering to one another. I can't see any, but I hear at least five different songs. I love the sounds of today!

I see the rippling water, the green sprouting trees, the clear blue sky. And now I want to touch that brown earth. How warm it is on the surface! Like the sands of time, the soil runs through my fingers. I feel its softness and its occasional pebble. I notice the temperature change of that earth directly below the surface. It feels so good to touch. I am at peace. I feel love.

I believe our capacity for love is related to our ability to appreciate life. I think that's the way it was meant to be. The secret is not necessarily to be *awakened* to love, but to keep love's inspiration vitally alive—each experience becoming more meaningful and more beautiful. People who do this don't have to ask, How can I become more aware? Awareness comes out of the freedom to be yourself, expressed in a love you accept as it happens.

It takes a tremendous commitment to grow—it's not just a matter of preserving your dreams, it's continuing to make them *better.* The question is, Do I want it that much? I made my decision. I was ready to go. I looked out at the farm and saw the ducks having a field day in the flooded stream as they bathed, ate, ruffled their feathers, and waddled around, poking here and there, eager to make new discoveries. I felt like the ducks. Transactional Analysis calls this the "Free Child." I was ready.

As my awareness of being the Free Child expanded, I began to question how that "child" develops. I concluded that it was the same as being at a railroad crossing: stop, look, and listen.

♥　♥　♥　♥　♥　♥　♥　♥　♥　♥　♥　♥　♥　♥　♥　♥

Stop means we have to pause, perhaps to change direction, abandon habits, rest, and regroup.

Look means we must train our eyes to see in every direction, to be ready for the unexpected. We have to look for signs of beauty, tenderness, love, care, and, yes, even danger.

Listen means we must hear what others are really saying and feeling. Often we are so caught up in our own thoughts that we miss the subtle nuances that could contribute to our good. Listen in every direction, and be a total receptor of life's miracles.

As life opened up for me, I began to invite all my senses into more concentrated action. Once my mind and body woke to the wonders out there in the world, I was bursting with the need to share all that was going on inside me and around me. Not everyone wanted to hear. The family wondered: What was happening to Mom?

During a vacation with Bob in Mexico I had a momentous experience in exploring my feelings. One night Bob was very quiet throughout dinner and I just couldn't engage him in conversation. Frustrated, I fumed inside until we had finished dinner. Then I went down to the pool to find someone else to talk with, but no one was there. I thought about how important talk is. Many times you can measure your thoughts against what others say, and that might serve to reinforce what you believe.

Suddenly, I looked at the reflection in the pool and saw my whole thought pattern there! The pool was in a courtyard open to the sky, surrounded by the very old buildings of the hotel, which had once been an abbey. The buildings were reflected in the pool. The water elongated the reflection so that the buildings seemed two-thirds larger than they really were. This is just like life, I thought. One-third of life is clear and apparent, but the other two-thirds is deep in the pool of our thoughts. Unless you dialogue enough with someone–or thoroughly explore an idea yourself–the submerged thoughts never surface and remain forever a mystery.

As I looked deeper into the reflection of the buildings in the water, I saw all kinds of arches and beautiful doorways that I hadn't noticed before. They were much more beautiful reflected in the water. It reminded me that there are doorways inside of us that we don't ordinarily see. They are there to be opened–new experiences, new horizons.

I could hardly wait to share these new insights with my friends in a letter. But I also needed someone to talk with about these new ideas I was getting. When I returned home I found that someone–by accident.

Our company had a food co-op, and we had discovered a source for fresh organic produce for it that was only 20 miles away. Since I had the station wagon, I had volunteered to pick up the food every Tuesday morning. I left early to choose the fresh food for the co-op to sell later in the day. It was fun to go through the aisles and pick out the best. After my order was filled I had to wait about half an hour while the goods were packed into the car and the bill was tallied.

Every week during this half-hour wait, I talked with Guy, the head of the company. He became my sounding board for all these new thoughts. He took the time to listen while others were busy with their own thoughts and their own lives. He pushed me far beyond what I thought I could do in my search for awareness. Guy was a friend to whom I could tell both the good and the bad. And it was a revelation for me to discover that he didn't judge me. Guy was still a friend no matter what I told him. He gave me something nobody else had given me. And to this day, I cherish that gift–the gift of accepting me for who I am. It came at a time when I needed it most.

In retrospect, I wonder why I didn't reveal my new thoughts to those at home. Maybe Bob wasn't ready to listen then, and my children thought they had listened enough. Perhaps it was because I didn't know Guy very well that I took a chance and bounced these ideas off him. He had no preconceived ideas of who I was.

This story reminds me of another friend to whom I will always be grateful. In our conversations, Peggy often told me about how she and Pete laughed over this and that. "We may not have a lot of money, but we sure can laugh," she said. I thought a lot about that, and wondered why Bob and I didn't laugh more, why we took life so seriously. I would ask Bob about it. This situation needed to be turned around. Life was meant to be enjoyed and I began an earnest search for new ways to lift the spirit.

One great example of getting in touch with joyous feelings stands out in my memory. Bob was away on a business trip, so I took Maria and Anthony out to dinner, planning to spend the night at the New Farm. The meal was wonderful, and afterward we sat on the back porch of our house. We noticed that the stream had been newly dredged—there was a bank of mud on each side of it. So we followed an impulse and took off our shoes and stomped in the mud to see how it would feel. We sank in mud up to our knees. Soon the people in the apartment above heard us laughing in our excitement and came down barefooted to join us. In very short order, the couples in the other two farmhouses saw our utter delight and hurried to get in on the merriment.

You can imagine what we all looked like, flopping around in the mud! We were almost at the point of exhaustion when we came out, but the evening was still young. Everyone went home to clean up and returned quickly with some food. Someone also brought a guitar. We shared each other's hospitality and friendship, and closed this memorable evening by dreaming our thoughts to the sky.

Many undreamed-of rewards come with the decision to take risks. I began to feel that it was worth the pain to grow so I could participate in all that was going on in life!

Now, as I walk through the halls at work, people often say, "Ardie, what's happening to you? You have a glow. You're so alive!" I can tell that my "growing old" spirit has changed. I am becoming young in heart. My wings have spread, and I have taken a flying leap in my Climb Toward the Light.

CHAPTER 13

The Emerging Woman
Striving for Acceptance

Thus, the appearance of things changes according to the emotions, and thus we see magic and beauty in them, while magic and beauty are really in ourselves.

Kahlil Gibran

Reprinted from BROKEN WINGS, by Kahlil Gibran, by permission of Lyle Stuart, Inc.

I knew where I had been and I knew that, as a woman, I wanted equality in a world where all people respected the dignity of each person. That was a large order. The goals my family and society had set for me were not really my goals, so the biggest challenge was to change from the person I was expected to be to the person I wanted to be. In the eyes of my family I was growing really fast, perhaps too fast. But personally, I was afraid and unsure, still playing old tapes of my childhood, some of which echoed Daddy's words: *"When you grow up, you can choose first. . . . You've got to prove yourself. . . . We'll listen when you can pay your own bills."*

I was always a person of simple faith and optimism, who often forgot that there were valleys to go through in life. When hard times did come along I was able to view them as I did childbirth: I could forget the pain and remember only the joy of reaching the mountain peak. But now, when I encountered these valleys, I felt depressed and trapped.

Maria said something to me one day that changed my thinking. "There's a rainbow out there for you, but only you can find it!" So it wasn't other people who caused my pain; it came from the way I perceived myself.

I needed to stand back, let my mind slip out of my house, and take a look at me from far off. I needed to see myself as an artist might when he checks the perspective in his work. I needed to look at myself in a full-length, three-way mirror to see every side.

I knew that the counseling classes had taught me a lot and I had learned a lot more from teaching my class. Now I needed to apply that knowledge to my personal growth; I had to take stock of what I had to work with. One day I got a startling picture of how I really felt as I worked through my usual errands. It was cold outside, so I had slacks on. Throughout the day I had been striding like a man, bending like a man, crossing my legs like a man. Wait! I said to myself, I'm a woman; I want to be feminine! I came home and washed my hair, carefully applied my makeup, and put on a skirt. I felt so much better! I had taken the first small step in my self-evaluation. I realized I was proud to be a woman!

Now I wanted to houseclean. When I houseclean, I literally remove everything from the room, and after the walls and floors are sparkling clean I bring back what is necessary. I ask myself, What is important? What do I need? I might bring everything back, or get rid of certain things that are useless now. All things must be removed from the room before I can decide what to keep.

Like rooms, our minds can become crowded with useless junk. "Mind cleaning" provides the opportunity to get rid of old worn-out thoughts, old ideas, and old habits. I had to cleanse my mind just as I cleansed my house, at least twice a year. Call it spring and fall mind cleaning!

One immediate result of my mind cleaning was the realization that I wanted to be appreciated and recognized as more than a wife and a mother. Since I was working hard for the company, I decided I should be paid for it.

When I told Bob, he said, "Ardie, I don't want a wife who works." I was devastated. I felt undervalued. I had a need to feel some dignity and self-worth. I knew that noisy rebellion would never work with

Bob in winning my point. Instead, one night I slept in another bed in the house. Bob found me the next morning. "What is the matter? Why did you sleep here last night?" I told him how I felt, and how sad it made me to think that my work and my life had such little value in the eyes of others. After he thought for a while, Bob said, "Well, if you feel that strongly about it, OK. You'll be on salary next week." At last, I would be a working woman whose efforts were worth paying for! Since I was already doing the job, there was no change in my work habits. There was no announcement in the company either, but I was put on an hourly rate and I worked with fresh purpose.

Bob was still doing a lot of competitive shooting, so he was often out of town on weekends because of it. If we were invited to social events I would respond, "I'm really sorry that Bob will be away shooting, but if you don't mind, I'll come by myself." People were taken aback with my response at first, but in time they just assumed that I would come alone if Bob had to be away. I felt a victory for myself. I was sure Bob didn't mind. It gave him the freedom to shoot or travel for the company without worrying about me, and I could enjoy myself too.

At one party, I had a conversation with the president of Muhlenberg, a local college, and we spoke about the things I had learned in the counseling sessions. I said, "You know, this is just what all young people should be learning. They need to know how to solve life's problems and how to feel good about themselves." I made an appointment to discuss this idea in depth and arrived at the office loaded down with an armful of books on the subject for him to read.

Shortly after our meeting, he invited me to be a candidate for membership on the college's board of trustees. Oh, I'm not knowledgeable enough for that, I thought, I'm not good enough. Then a friend who did a lot of brainstorming with me said, "You're fine. Of course you can do it. You will!" I did!

I was the second of two women on the board at that time, and I held the position for nine years. It gave me a chance to work for the cause of equality. I stressed that the students were young *men* and *women*, not kids, *not children*. And the two *women* on the Board were to be treated as *persons of equal stature*, not girls.

I took my position on the Muhlenberg Board of Trustees very seriously. It was important for me to get to know students, to find out how they felt about life at the college. I wanted to know how we could help them in their relations with the college and the community. With this in mind, I invited various groups of students, five or six at a time, to join me and my family for dinner at home. The young people were always glad for a home-cooked meal, and it was fun for me, too. The conversation was always stimulating for all of us, with the exchange of ideas about college life, the working world, and the family.

While I was on the board, the student council, backed by many teachers, petitioned the college to remove the president. It was assumed that the board's vote to support the president and reaffirm their confidence in him would be unanimous. But I sided with the students. I stood my ground and I abstained from the vote.

The local newspaper covered my abstention. I was quoted as saying, "I couldn't honestly vote for the board's position. I didn't feel good about it. The students I know were sincere. They did what they did in good faith.

"The President had many good qualities as a hard worker and excellent fund-raiser who works for the community, too. But because of turmoil on the campus—unrest among the students and faculty; court cases opened and closed; and upheaval in the community—the college needs a 'Good Shepherd,' a healer, a nurturing parent as president. We need the Christian principle practiced here. We need to show genuine love and caring and openness. This is what it means to me to be part of a church-related college."

I stood up for what I believed in. Many students and faculty wrote to say they appreciated my support.

Some time later, plans were submitted to the board for the new Sports Life Center at the college. As the plans were being presented, I could barely keep quiet. When I got my chance, I got up and said I thought the plans were wrong. The pool was on the north side of the building with no consideration given to using the solar heat as a hedge against heating costs. My statement was greeted with silence. However, at the next board meeting, plans were presented again. They had been changed to incorporate my suggestions. My ideas were taken seriously! Now the pool was located to the south, and a whole solar corridor had been added. As the meeting ended, the board member who gave the presentation commented, "I don't know why we didn't think of this in the first place."

When it came time for me to leave the board of trustees, I still cared very much about what happened in the college community. I felt close to many of the faculty, the students, and the board members. They were wonderful, sincere, understanding friends. Our lives still keep circling back, renewing each other and helping each other to grow in new light.

Now years later, I still meet young men and women who say to me, "You probably don't remember me, but when I was at Muhlenberg you invited me to dinner at your house." And their faces tell me that the experience was important to them. Friends we make along the way in life can return to surprise and nourish us in other times!

Another trait I wanted for myself as an emerging woman was independence. Here is the story of one step I took to get it.

I passed a well-kept house on Main Street in Emmaus every day on my way to the Press, and I enjoyed watching the owner, Emma Schuller, at work. I realized that this 90-year-old woman had some lessons to teach me about working. She was extremely active and had a way of orchestrating what she did—a little weeding, a little raking, a little planting, before going on to the next section of her garden. Mrs. Schuller never seemed to tire because she used all parts of her body as she varied her chores in the garden. My way would have been to do all the weeding, then all the raking, then all the planting—and I would have been all worn out. I thought a lot about Mrs. Schuller's work habits and they influenced the way I proceeded with my own life's chores. I grew to be sentimental about her and her house. Even though I only observed her actions and never spoke to her, I often wondered many times what other lessons she could have taught me.

After Mrs. Schuller died, I had the opportunity to purchase her house. To be a land owner on my own was a big step for me. It was up to me to buy the house, get my own mortgage, and renovate the place to make it into a good income source—and I didn't know *anything* about finances and investments. I vowed I would learn what I needed to know on my own, and I did! With that experience I asserted my independence and added "good business woman" to my résumé as I strove to become my own person.

As a part of defining goals and knowing where you are going, I find it is important to read, to look for new ideas, and to learn by participating in projects with other people. I decided to attend a workshop called Taking Responsibility for Your Own Life.

Rollo May, a leading psychotherapist, was the main speaker. Here is one thing he said that was important to me: As you inhale and exhale, there is a pause between. It is during the pauses of life that insight comes. This is where one learns to take charge of one's own life. If this is true, then it is vitally important to fill life with more pauses so we can use them to discover for ourselves how to make our lives better.

Gerald Piaget, who wrote *Barriers to Change*, was another speaker who made me think. He stressed the value of humor in the process of change. He also stressed the great need for focused time. He commented that too often people give no prime time to family and loved ones; they usually get unreserved "left-over time." But for me, the whole conference's most important concept was this question: "When can I start doing what I want to?" and its answer: "Now!... Just as soon as you take responsibility for your own life." I realized that I was starting to do that.

In our home, each child's birthday was an all-out event. I have always put tremendous effort into making these days special. Even after my children left home, they presumed that Mom would still do the birthday celebration—the child choosing a favorite menu and a favorite homemade cake. But for all the effort I put into "their day," my birthday was often minimized, if not forgotten, by most family members. My birthdate became a dismal day for me because I set myself up for disappointment every time.

The situation had to be changed. During one of those pauses Dr. May described, I decided on a plan: Since I had to travel to England for our company once a year, I made up my mind to go there over my birthday. Instead of being disappointed at home, I would make it a "nothing day" in England. I felt really good about this decision. As it turned out, the next birthday was one of the most significant ones of my life.

I went down to dinner at my London hotel on the night before the birthday and fell into conversation with a man at the next table. I told him that tomorrow would be my fiftieth birthday, and I had chosen to come to England at this time partly because of it. I said it would be a nothing day. The next morning there was a note in my mailbox. "Best wishes for much happiness on your special day, from the man who sat next to you at dinner." The day started with a smile.

In many thoughtful, quiet ways my English friends at work made the day very special indeed. I received cards, and one friend gave me a beautiful little book on Chinese philosophy; flowers came from other meaningful friends. I cherished that caring feeling. Even the family rallied and sent me flowers. Some even said I was missed. As I looked at home from far off, I realized that I had set myself up for my miserable birthdays in other years by *expecting* people to act in a certain way. By being away from home and experiencing all these kindnesses, I found the value in the *unexpected*. It was an important lesson. I realized that only *I* could allow myself to be manipulated by my expectations. I had control of my own airplane as I flew through life.

After that birthday, as I organized my thoughts and actions for living the good life, I realized that I did have my own limelight. I was my own person. I felt I was really living and I had a true zest for life. The adrenaline flowed and I never felt healthier. I laughed hard... worked hard... loved hard... and sometimes cried hard. Somehow they all purified each other. I made some new and valuable discoveries.

♥ ♥ ♥ ♥ ♥ ♥ ♥ ♥ ♥ ♥ ♥ ♥ ♥ ♥ ♥ ♥

I learned that some things in life can't be changed. It's like owning a wonderful art object that has a mark on it. You want to erase the mark, but sometimes polish doesn't work. You try to get to the root of the problem, and maybe the mark can be removed with the proper cleaner. But sometimes it can't be removed and the mark remains. You have to learn to live with it as an imperfect but lovable object.

I learned that worrying about all the possible consequences of my every action allowed guilt and fear to take control of me and inhibit me. As long as my actions didn't hurt someone else, I simply had to act in my own best interest.

I learned the importance of keeping optimistic and happy. As tensions were released, I began opening up my fists. I stopped clenching my teeth and I felt my jagged tongue become smooth again.

I learned the importance of loving. It has got to go deep if it will survive. Love is feeling the mist in your heart and the inspiration of the elements in your mind, a unification with the universe. To have that love continue, it must be shared. It cannot be locked away in a box for safe-keeping. Only when you give it away do you get it back in greater measure.

I learned that our experiences mold us into who we finally become. The farther our horizons expand, the faster we develop ideas of our larger self.

I learned the value of looking into each soul to find its essence; and to keep on loving, never judge, just find the beauty by reaching a little higher and loving a little more.

I felt like wearing party clothes more often. Life was turning into a celebration. I could even get along without approval now. "Thanks, you did a good job" wasn't necessary. I didn't need it. I knew in my own heart I had done my best. It was my approval of myself, my own satisfaction that was important.

I like to recall that magical night when I walked around the farm in my nightgown. I stood on the edge of the moonlit pool and I slipped out of my clothes, plunging into the refreshing water. I was happy. I was alone and free and was finally coming to peace with myself. I no longer resembled the piano player who plays all the correct notes, but never looks up from the keyboard to see the effect his music is having or to see what else is happening around him. Now I was observing the relationship of the earth and the sky and the elements and marveling at the mystery of it all. I tingled with new feelings. I looked at each new day as though it were a Christmas stocking with hidden surprises.

CHAPTER 14

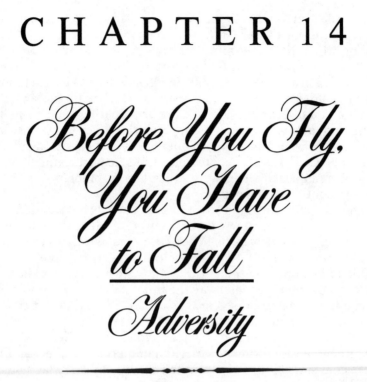

Before You Fly, You Have to Fall

Adversity

---

*Every now and then, go away, have a little relaxation, for when
you come back to your work your judgment will be surer; since
to remain constantly at your work will cause you to lose power of
judgment.*

Leonardo da Vinci

"Hello! I am adversity! Sometimes I come by accident, but most
often I am forced to visit when you are tired, discouraged, and over-
worked. Sometimes you forget that your body is your temple. When
your temple walls are in need of repair physically, mentally, and
spiritually, they must have time for healing. When you look at my
face, you might think I am ugly, but when you look at me as I leave,
you may be able to see my angel's wings."

As I write this, much pain comes back, but a lot of healing, too. I
am able to look back and see how adversity has helped me to overcome difficulties and to become a better person than I was before.

I'm sure my childhood ailments were related to a multitude of
fears and frustrations I had then. Later, when I had myocarditis at 37,
followed by spinal meningitis, I'm sure it was because my resistance

was low due to emotional depression. The way we treat our bodies can have repercussions that last through most of our lives.

For a long time, my mind told me to slow down. Where was I racing to? I was so busy taking care of everyone else that I was neglecting to treat myself with care and respect. I was tough; I thought I could handle anything. But I couldn't deal with the anger and frustration I was feeling inside. Maria was preparing herself for single-parenthood, and we were arranging a place for her to live. I worried about how she would manage without the family support. David, living up on Cape Cod, was a constant concern as he went through terrible spells of loneliness. There were other family problems, and I was worried about friends who were ill.

I needed to shout among the trees as I used to, but I couldn't seem to find the time to go out to where they were. I felt as though life were closing in, and where was the hope? I didn't realize that I was a prime target for physical adversity to come knocking at my door.

Major foot problems emerged. First there was a very painful heel spur. Physical therapy took away the inflammation on the sole of the foot, but the pain had caused me to shift my gait and I tore tendons in the ankle. That called for more physical therapy. Then knee problems and hip problems developed. My toes had always curled under, but I didn't know the condition was called hammertoes. My feet and body were in constant pain; still I continued on with my everyday schedule. I felt old, worn out, and so tired.

My feet continued to get worse. I wondered if I would end up crippled and have to give up dancing—a very dear love of my life!

One day, a woman who worked for Bob came to the house. "My mother had your problem," she said. "Those toes can be fixed surgically right in the doctor's office. My mother had it done and she can dance again!" I didn't know there was such an alternative. Hope began to fill my thoughts. I was anticipating a new birth—new feet.

I had the operation and unrealistically expected to be wearing high heels within a few weeks. After three weeks, I was merely hobbling. I returned to my craft work. Using leftover material I made 11 outfits for the grandkids and a friend. In the evenings, I sat with my feet propped up, doing creative stitchery. I was still sewing away with anger and impatience.

During the day I felt the need to exercise. Since walking was hard, I took to tree trimming and worked with the same energy and determination as I did with other chores. Then bursitis took over my arms. First the feet and then the arms! That meant a lot more physical therapy and a lot more healing time. But I know now that I was fighting the healing.

In the fall of 1986, Heidi went to Canyon Ranch Spa and came back with a glowing report. "Oh, Mom, you should go there. It would do you a world of good."

In spring, when I couldn't take it any longer, I decided to follow Heidi's suggestion. I called her to say, "I did it. I leave for Canyon Ranch this Friday." I wondered if I'd have the strength to make it to the plane.

I thought the exercise at the Ranch would clear all ills. Unfortunately, my blood pressure was sky-high, so I was placed on a limited activities schedule. Looking into the mirror, I could see that my face reflected all the past pain, and I looked as though I were ready to cry at any moment. Something had to be done. Probably what I needed most was someone to talk to. There were counseling sessions available and I made an appointment. As I spoke to the counselor, the tears and the sadness and all the anger came out in a rush. I had someone there to care and to listen and to hug.

The experience of that whole week was one of nourishment. I felt the beginning of letting go all my cares, and I felt, at last, that healing my spirit and body was really possible. I felt I had found Shangri-la. Time stood still and I wanted to stay there forever, sheltered from life's storms.

I had forgotten the message in Dr. Shaw's words at the hospital in Rochester, "Some people believe that thoughts can make us sick or healthy. What are your thoughts?" After you abuse your body for years you can't expect instant recovery. Habits and outlooks have to change. But now, at least I had started looking at life from a new angle—toward hope and happiness. I was learning to lead again.

I'm sure that all these problems were the result of my being rebellious and insensitive to my life's needs. It was necessary for me to take a strong look at life's priorities and reevaluate them. I needed to learn to discover again, to feel the pulse of life, to take time to enjoy, to touch, to taste, to live.

Maria's baby daughter helped bring healing and laughter back to me. And David decided to come back to our town to live, and I sighed with relief that I didn't have to worry about him any longer. He was coming home!

Yes, I was beginning to see the angel wings of adversity and what it taught me about learning to live and care for myself as well as others.

I keep remembering that life gets to be down when there are too few "highs" in it. The highs are laughter, fun, activity, and involvement with others. Even people who cannot dance with their feet can dance with their heart and mind. Give yourself gifts—plant seeds, grow flowers, take a walk, sing, or dream. This is the real spiritual/physical therapy we need for well-being. Learning this was a big, hard step on my upward Climb!

CHAPTER 15

Caring and Sharing
Finding Fulfillment at Work

The world is so empty
if one thinks only of mountains, rivers, and cities;
but to know someone here and there
who thinks and feels with us,
and who, though distant, is close to us in spirit,
this makes the earth an inhabited garden.

Goethe

Through the years, I have often asked myself, Why do I work? The answer has always been the same: Because I love it.

I love the challenge, the excitement, the opportunity to meet a wide variety of interesting people, the satisfaction of doing a good job. Work makes me a more interesting partner and mother; it gives me a feeling of personal worth and opens up wider horizons. I would be bored beyond reason if I stayed home all day long. I feel a constant need to find new ways in which to grow, and to share what I have learned in helping others.

When I was growing up (in a safer time), my friends and I often walked to choir practice and Girl Scouts after dark. I became a window snooper, looking into the lighted houses as we passed. My goodness, some people live in such drab places, I thought. A home should look happy. I made up my mind that if I ever got the chance, I'd do something for people who lived in surroundings such as those. I dreamed of creating living spaces that would sing.

My wish became reality. Today, as director of environmental resources for Rodale Press, I am responsible for the total physical environment of our company—the plans, the design, the renovation, the rehabilitation of some old office buildings, and the historic preservation of the company's research center—right down to the furniture and to the artwork that adorns the office walls. This mandate involves more than a thousand employees in 15 different buildings.

I try to plan work spaces so that people who need to work together are near each other, always keeping the company's growth potential in mind. I take great pride in the comfortable, cheerful, efficient surroundings our company provides for the employees. I have been doing this job—and loving it—for some 30 years. And as the company grew and changed, so did the job.

It all began in the late fifties when our company was planning to move out of an old silk mill into a new space built to house up to 100 employees. As we discussed this new space, I told Bob that I wanted the job of coordinating and decorating all the offices, and he said OK.

None of my women friends worked at that time. This job was strictly volunteer work. I was satisfied. I could arrange my hours so that I was always home when the children were dropped off from school.

I worked at home and out of my car. The artwork that would be hung on the walls of each office was stored in the basement of our house. (Both Bob's family and mine were interested in art, so we had collected many paintings that could be used in decorating the building —and many of these pictures had been painted by family members.)

In the beginning my budget was very limited. I had to use old, unmatched furniture in any decorating I did. My solution to this puzzling problem was simple and inexpensive. I put bright paint on the walls. If people were distracted by the wall color, I thought, they might pay less attention to furniture.

As the company grew, we added on to the main building and then branched out, buying clusters of buildings around Emmaus. In 1979 we built a new passive solar building which would house 150 of our 300 employees. This was a new experience for us, since employees had rarely changed office space before that time.

I worried a lot about the relocation. Would the workers be happy and would their new work spaces allow for maximum efficiency and productivity? Now I began working with architects and engineers and tradespeople. My education as an art teacher helped me in unexpected ways. I was able to read mechanical drawings–and make them!–and I knew how to handle and care for tools.

The challenge was to plan the move for minimal disruption in the work force. We hired a moving company to help. I color-coded every department and briefed all the people involved concerning their roles. The whole move was accomplished over a single weekend. By Monday most of the employees were set up in their new spaces and ready to work.

For the first time there was room for an office for me. Work was no longer a hobby, but a full-time occupation. My car and the dining room just didn't provide enough space for me to do my job. Also, I was getting tired of being asked by friends, "Exactly what is it that you do?" Many of them thought that I didn't really work, since I didn't have an office.

Most of a person's day is spent in the workplace. My first office did not have a window. I often lost touch with what was going on outside the door. I know, from that experience, that people at work need some contact with nature–the sun and the rain and the wind and the flowers.

I decided that all interior offices would have operable windows. If daylight wasn't available, at least I tried to create the illusion of daylight. Employees help to decide how to adorn the windows for their spaces–from the usual blinds, drapes, or shutters, to lace curtains and window boxes with live plants. I try to avoid the feeling of little cubbyhole offices by providing this illusion of space.

The sense of freedom in the workplace carries over into the mind. The surroundings for people at our company are conducive to expansive thoughts. We foster this sense by using glass-paned French doors on the offices, both interior and exterior ones; skylights show the blue of the sky and we hear the pelt of the rain on the glass. The light shining down from the ceiling is God's daylight. In some of our conference rooms, light filters through glass-block walls and spills its charm into corridors. Here and there I place stained glass surprises.

I see to it that employees have a say in the decor of their personal workplaces–the wall colors they feel best with, and artwork they like as a decoration. A mutual respect grows between the employees and me as we work together. They know that I want them to be happy where they work.

Of course, it doesn't always work smoothly. I'm thinking of two women who decided on lavender walls for the room they shared. After the room was painted, they were thrilled with their choice. Then they heard comments like, "I feel so sorry for them—imagine working in a room with that color!" The women were so upset that they tacked paper over the window in the door so no one could see inside.

When I asked what was going on, they replied, "Oh, Ardie, we think we made a mistake. Everyone who comes by says how awful the color is. We are so upset."

"Just wait till the room is finished," I said.

When it was done, there were *ohs* and *ahs* of admiration from all who saw it. The two women were happy again, and I overheard the other employees say, "Gee, now that I see it all together, I wish we had been more daring about our office color!"

Architects and engineers usually figure the technical requisites for artificial lighting precisely, but the people who work under the light have to be consulted, too. It's amazing to learn how diverse the need for light really is among individuals. Some need a lot, and others can stand only minimal brightness. I have found that employees must be satisfied with the light level of their surroundings if they are to do their best work. No wonder we try to meet individual requirements for comfort whenever possible.

Even the placement of office furniture is done with a purpose. My courses on self-actualization and learning to be the best you can be taught me that strength comes from within a person, not from outside forces. So instead of having the desk face outward toward the door, I try to place the desk facing toward a wall hung with something beautiful to look at. This way, a visitor sits beside the desk, not on the other side of it, and the conversation takes place on an equal level. Psychologists say defenses automatically arise when a desk is positioned between two people. Further, concentration is so much greater without the distraction of seeing people go by the doorway.

Sometimes I think of myself as conductor of an "ambience symphony," where all instruments/people are needed for the full sound, and all parts play in harmony. My goal is to have that symphony played to perfection every day at Rodale Press.

In our company offices I try to emulate the example of our pediatrician, Dr. Moyer, whose waiting room displayed all kinds of arts and crafts he and his wife had acquired in their travels. This helped viewers to become aware of other people and other places. So, wherever we travel, I try to return with arts and crafts to be hung in the corridors, as a changing exhibit in the various buildings. I feel excited as I travel, looking for cultural souvenirs to share with those at home.

Presently, I am working on a show from Scandinavia which has wall hangings, fine cutwork weaving, decorative ironwork, two pieces of creative stitchery, some photographs of everyday life there, and a wonderful child's dress from Lapland. I love to anticipate the reaction the people will have to the display.

Creative stitchery is my hobby; it stills my soul when I need quiet time. I do a lot of this work and enjoy sharing my output with those at the office. I created four changing exhibits; after they were displayed at each building, the individual works were available for hanging in various offices.

I shop flea markets for stained glass and handcrafted wrought iron that can be used to decorate our buildings. Years ago, when I would ask an employee to choose a piece of art for his or her office, the usual reply was "Anything will be fine. Pick something for me." Today, perhaps due to their exposure to so many kinds of art, the answer is different. Most employees know what they want. Recently a longtime employee sent me a note: "Thank you for surrounding my life with beauty all these years."

To foster a consciousness of fellow employees in the workplace, I conduct building meetings every month. A representative comes from each department in the building. This provides a chance for people to meet and to voice their concerns. I always follow up with a memo to summarize the meeting, and I conclude it with an inspirational message—perhaps a poem, a quote, or sometimes a little message of my own. Just a few words that might bring a little lift to someone who needs encouragement.

I have a whole network of friends to whom I send books of inspiration. In turn they share them with their friends. As the years go by, I find more and more occasions to give someone a hug or to lend a shoulder to lean on. We share in giving each other gifts of flowers or special foods to provide an unexpected lift. I'm there to participate in the sad times as well as the happy ones. Through talking with these people and being a listening ear, my message is "I'm talking with you . . . not at you."

As I get older, I am convinced that the amount of love we have in life determines our understanding and compassion in our home life, at work, and in our community. Even when another's view differs from our own, there is still room for understanding. We are all children of God—loved unconditionally and fully—accepted in His sight for our own uniqueness.

I do love my work and the people I work with and for. I am grateful I can help make life easier for them in some way.

CHAPTER 16

Contemplation Leads to Revelation

The most visible joy can only reveal itself to us when we've transformed it, within.

Rainer Maria Rilke

Jesus went up to the mountain because He needed space, contemplation time. I was slow to realize the need for it in my own life. It took me even longer to claim it as a necessity for living.

Kahlil Gibran said, "Let there be spaces in your togetherness."

The spaces are those quiet times when you stop to listen to that still, small voice within. Sometimes my need for these quiet times comes in clusters, or I might go for days without the need. That inspiration of quiet time seems to come from a well that sometimes runs dry, and it can take a lot of pumping to get the water flowing again. Then I drink the cool refreshment and it brings back strength and vigor for daily life.

When there is confusion, when I am surrounded by too many voices, I can't think straight and I begin to make mistakes. That is the time I visit my well of contemplation. Sometimes I just have to sit quietly and look back over my life. I wonder about how well I am doing and if I am headed in the right direction. The biggest growth I've seen is in solving my life's frustrations by channeling the energy of my rebelliousness and belligerence to an energy of tenderness. I feel as though I were a free child given permission to love in a new way. I often wanted to stand on the high Alps and yell out loud and clear, "I love you, world!" and another mountain would echo back and there would be unending reverberations . . . "I love you, world! . . . I love you, world!" I feel alive with freedom and willing to accept life as it happens. No more the nagging fear of the unknown.

I often talked about life's problems with a farmer named Jim who used to work for us. He said, "Ardie, the best advice for anyone when life seems to crowd in is to get out in that garden and dig." His words have stayed with me. I often go out with the shovel and dig with a vengeance. Gradually, my mind calms and my body relaxes. Then the anger leaves me.

What joy it is to feel the warmth of the earth, to touch the delicate flowers, and to examine the root structure as I pull the weeds. Their strength comes from a whole network, not just one source, and this is how it is with each of us. The wider our experiences, the stronger our nourishment from life. We need to reach and stretch continually to face the future.

I love the Canon in D Major by Johann Pachelbel; I never tire of hearing it. It brings me peace when my nerves are rattled.

One night my son Anthony said to me, "Why do you listen to that music all the time? How *can* you?" I asked myself, Why do I? Why has this music survived? What does Pachelbel, a seventeenth-century musician, have to say to me today? I think I need to hear the old message he imparts again. Pachelbel takes me on a life-walk, and tells me that traditional values are good for all ages. Each life must have grace, dignity, beauty, harmony, order, and inspirational strength. Pachelbel's music says, Be strong and know that each person, like each note of music, is an important part of the beautiful whole. He inspires me to expand life's horizons, to play more beautiful music with notes of my life.

I visit my well of contemplation when I do my needlework. It's hard to recapture the relaxation if I have been away from the work for a while. My mind must be freed from what I had been doing to become receptive to new creativity. I look at my work and see only the basic colors at first. Then after a while, as if my lenses are adjusting, I begin to see many shades of colors that I can choose from. Before, all these shades had evaded my eyes. In life situations, we must look at the total picture first, then we can focus in depth. Our choices become clearer, then we can pick the direction that makes life most harmonious.

I woke very early on one Easter morning, and my restless mind needed some release. So I went down to the craft room to work on a new design for a felt appliqué picture with a Pennsylvania Dutch motif. First, I cut out felt symbols without making a pattern, then I tried to fit them into place—turning, adjusting, discarding. This time I started with a large red heart and added green leaves. At the top of the design, I placed a yellow circle. I had no idea about the final design.

As I worked, the radio played softly in the background and suddenly the strains of Handel's "Hallelujah Chorus" poured forth. My mind surged with excitement and my fingers danced swiftly, and as I worked, I realized that my design was an interpretation of Easter— of hope and life! The revelation resounded loud and clear: Every day is an opening and a closing, a death and an awakening. Every day can be an opportunity for new ideas, new inspiration, and new starts as we lay aside old worn-out ideas and frustrations to face fresh challenges.

I had a similar revelation on another Easter morning. We had stayed overnight at the New Farm. I had never been up to the old cemetery on the hill beyond the house, but this particular morning my walk up the road and across the furrowed field led me there. As I pushed the creaking gate open, I was filled with peace. Bluebells and daffodils swayed all around, and the barely legible German script tombstones stood majestically in this silent place. The sun was just beginning to rise above the horizon. I wondered about the people who were buried here these many years. I thought about death and how the symbol of looking for new life was carried out even here, for all the tombstones were faced east to greet the sun and the new day for anticipating life in heaven.

Once a year in the fall it happens. I look out of the sunlit window at breakfast and say to Bob, "Look, today is the day for the leaves to fall!" After a heavy frost, when there is no wind and the sun is brightly shining, the two English walnut trees in our yard defoliate almost completely in one day.

"This time I think I'll pull up a chair under the tree to see what it feels like to be in the midst of the falling leaves," I said.

I had to go. What a beautiful sight to see the leaves fall all around you. And to *hear* them fall. It sounded like heavy rain! They were soon piled all around my feet and the cool fresh air of the day made my face feel wonderful and refreshed. With my eyes closed as I enjoyed the moments—the touch, the sounds, the smells—time passed. My mind was filled with peace and happiness and the joy of being alive.

Time flew for me as though it were only a minute. But as I turned to go back to the house, I glanced at my watch and was amazed to discover that I had been there well over an hour.

Sometimes I find myself contemplating as I drive. One morning I drove to the New Farm in Maxatawny. The day was an odd one. Everyone was expecting a snowstorm, and the sun was only a hazy fuzz ball barely visible in a bland sky. My eyes were suddenly alerted to a floating black ribbon in the sky. What looked like the tail of a kite turned out to be a flock of geese fluttering across the sky!

Soon the sky was alive with ribbons of geese. I exclaimed, "Wow! Fantastic!" As fast as one flock disappeared over my head, two more appeared in the distance. I had never seen anything like it! I had to stop the car and roll down the windows to enjoy it all. The call of the Canada goose is a beautiful sound. I wonder if the honking helps them to fly, or is it a call to others to join the crowd?

Gracefully, the geese swooped and looped through the sky, sometimes bearing left and sometimes right. These maneuvers seemed to give the stray birds time to catch up to the throng.

Are there any leaders in a flock of geese? As I watched, I could see that they were all leaders—and followers—each one taking a turn. Alternately leading and following created a perfect rhythm in the flight that made it like a work of art.

It made me think that we all have the opportunity to be leaders and followers in life; the art of it is to know when to lead in confidence and when to step back to let other people provide us with renewed strength and wisdom to move ahead. This was a momentous day to remember, the day when I saw Nature with its brush paint the sky—with *geese!*

Like most Libras, I love opals—our birthstone. What makes opals so remarkable is the wonderful colors in them. They make me think of rainbows. Often I sit in my favorite chair, and as the sun enters the room I try to create rainbows. I play with the light as it strikes the diamond in my engagement ring. I do this particularly when I'm yearning for happy thoughts. And, sure enough, my thoughts soon dance like rainbows in the room!

On one such afternoon I contemplated how the rainbow starts at a low point, surges up and returns to another low point. What would happen if the rainbow of life were inverted? It would start at a high point and whisk down and up again, ending in another high point. This is what we need in life—more high points!

Now and then my reverie takes me back to my early teaching days. I let my mind wander through the classrooms, recalling a young face, a quick exchange, a talented pupil, and sometimes, a sense of reward.

When I was teaching in New Jersey before I was married, one of my students was quite a promising little artist named Janet. We became good friends and still correspond. I cherish this letter she sent:

I felt the urge to talk to you of circles—the circles of influence in people's lives. When I was in fifth grade and you were my art teacher, I don't know what made me feel close to you. Why did I stay in touch with you and none of my other art teachers? My later visit to you in your house in Emmaus is still vivid in my mind.

I went on to be an art teacher, too. Years ago, before my children were born, I had a student who became close to me. We corresponded through her college years and still stay in touch. She was young and wealthy and, as a young adult, was guilt-stricken over the fact that she never needed to work a day in her life to support herself. She now lives in another state where she is aware of much financial poverty. My letters pointed out the unique opportunity that her situation gave her—the freedom to lead a creative and productive life unconcerned with her own life support.

For the past years she has been setting up preschool nurseries, organizing recorder groups, establishing art and photography classes, and she has opened a gallery.

I wanted you to know how your life has been expanded through mine and my students. My husband and I are still teaching. We don't know who else is being influenced by us. Aren't we lucky?

I keep this letter in a very secure place. A feeling of humility comes over me when I think that what we do can be a positive influence for another human being. And most of the time we don't even know that it's happening!

That makes me recall one cold night when Bob was on a business trip. I had gone to bed early. I was startled to hear the door bell ringing frantically in the middle of the night. I peered out of the window and a man yelled, "Quick, call the police. There has been a bad accident!"

I called the police at once, dashed to change my clothes, and rushed out to the highway, where a car lay upside down, the roof smashed way in. A group of people stood close by. "Oh, my God!" I cried. "No one could get out of there alive. Is the person still inside?"

A golden-haired young man, with some cuts on his face, shivering in shock, said, "No, I'm here." I went over to him, wrapped him in the folds of my cape, and held him tightly to help control his tremors. It seemed to take forever for the police to arrive. Finally I said, "I'm going right in the house to get a blanket for you."

"There's one sticking out from the car," he said, "but I guess we can't get it." I crawled under the car and pulled the blanket out and wrapped him tightly. As I did this, he looked at me quizzically and said, "Who are you?"

I told him that I lived just across the street, and he said to me, in a very soft way, "You must be somebody's mother."

Yes, as the mother of five, I was only doing for this young man what I hoped someone would do for my children if they were in a similar situation.

We all need quiet contemplation space in our lives to reflect on how we are treating others, what their lives mean to us, what we can do better. These times have unmeasurable value when we are able to use the insights they provide. I always receive something refreshing and new and wonderful to carry over into my daily existence.

So far, my Climb to the Light has not been an easy one. But I know there are many rewards for the experiences I had along the way. I must keep listening to that still, small voice inside of me, never stop dreaming, and keep climbing.

CHAPTER 17

Widening Circles of Influence

The life of man is a self evolving circle, which from a ring imperceptibly small, rushes on all sides outwards to new and larger circles, and that without end.

The extent to which this generation of circles, wheel without wheel, will go, depends on the force or truth of the individual soul . . .

The heart refuses to be imprisoned; in its first and narrowest pulses, it always tends outward with a vast force, and to immense and innumerable expansions.

Ralph Waldo Emerson

As the concept of the Umbrella has changed for me, so has the concept of the Circles of Influence in my life. I drew a diagram of the intertwined circles representing things that count most in my life (children, marriage, job, independence) with me in the center. As I drew, I thought it was necessary to be meticulous about keeping all the intertwined circles the same size. Then I realized that while all my circles were important, they were seldom equally important. At certain times in life, one circle (job or marriage, for example) might be particularly large because that influence might be uppermost in my mind just then.

I have not even categorized other circles—smaller, but still important—and some unknown circles of influence yet to come may have to be added.

Not along ago, I read an inspiring book by the Reverend Robert Schuller and I realized that his success is largely due to his tremendous storehouse of experience. I thought about how necessary it was to have a good base such as his before all these experiences could be pulled together.

So I see that these circles of influence grow wider and wider, not only because of my own added experience, but because of the new people I bring into them.

I believe these circles have many shades of color, from shimmering gold to mournful black, and that each circle encompasses happiness, sadness, growth, richness, challenge, gratitude—and love.

As I face life squarely and optimistically, I am ready to create new and ever expanding circles that will help me to Climb Toward the Light!

STAGE IV

Life's Unforeseen Circumstances: Falling Down and Getting Up

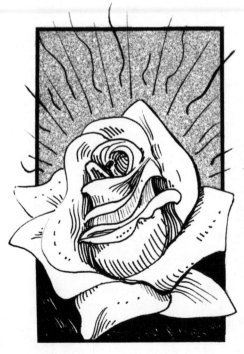

I think about my family a lot. I think about What if? . . . Sometimes life is so matter-of-fact with kids, but you never know. What if my life ended today? As I think about it and spend time with them, I wonder, Do they know all the unsaid things that I want them to know? How is it with them? I'm not sure. I know that I love deeply and that, like the Bluebird of Happiness, those I love need their freedom. So I try to hold them close with open hands, hoping they feel my warmth and my support in every endeavor.

CHAPTER 18

Farewell, My Son

You, my son
Have shown me God.
Your kiss upon my cheek
Has made me feel the gentle touch
Of Him — who leads us on.
The memory of your smile when young
Reveals His Face.

Grace Coolidge (written after the death of her son)

Christmas! The child in me is very active during this season. I sing and I dance as I enjoy the days. Having grandkids has helped me recoup a lot of life's wonder and I am happy. I found a poem that reflects exactly how I feel.

* * * * * * * * * *

WHERE THE WIND SINGS CHRISTMAS

The child skipped ahead of them
up the hill
Sharp against slate sky
she laughed and whirling
tossed her scarf
across December land.
"Listen, it's Christmas,"
she called
Racing, hair wild
she outdistanced cautionary words.

Today, hedged by voices
shrill, unseasonal
I slipped through a door
Abandoned scarf
Deserted adulthood
and ran toward that hill
where the wind sings Christmas.

Beverly Lauderdale

* * * * * * * * * *

I prepared for Christmas 1985 with an unbelievable amount of energy. I could hardly contain my excitement as I went to the attic to bring down the Christmas lights. We hadn't used our outside lights for about six years. So I decorated the shrubbery in front of the picture window, smiling and with a singing heart. I thought to myself, When Anthony gets home from school in California, he'll really be psyched when he sees these lights! I laughed as I anticipated his happiness. I had never felt better in my life. Each day I thanked God for all my strength. I had time to enjoy, to help others, to be quiet. Getting older wasn't so bad. I had a new appreciation of life. Perhaps this was God's way for preparing me.

Two weeks till Christmas! Thursday, December 12th, was David's birthday. When he came to work at the Press, I asked him how it felt to be 30.

"Gee, Mom, it doesn't feel any different."

"David, I can tell you one thing. I'm a lot happier now than I was at 30. Life really gets better."

He laughed and said, "That's good to hear."

I celebrated being David's mom. I took a glorious walk and thought about how lucky I was and how much there was to be thankful for. It was one of the last mild days of fall, and so beautiful!

That evening, as David, his friend Mark, and I sat in the living room together after dinner, David had some respiratory difficulty. He couldn't seem to catch his breath. He decided to go home to lie down. Later he called to say he felt better, and he promised that he would see the doctor the next day. I prayed hard that night.

"Dear God, Make this an easy, solvable problem. For the first time in his life he is truly happy. Everything is a 'Go' for him. It's all coming together at last. From the bottom of my heart I pray. Thank you, Father."

Friday, December 13th, David and Mark went to the airport to pick up Anthony. They brought him to the company Christmas dance that evening. The Rodale Press Christmas dance is usually a great evening. This year, due to a mix-up, the company had to accept an alternate site at the last minute. The place was dark and crowded. Something of the joviality of the night was missing. I wanted to go home early. I saw David and Mark lingering among the crowd. David looked pale. I was worried about his breathing problem of several nights before. I wanted to tell him to go home and get a good night's rest, but I didn't want to sound like a bossy mom, so I said nothing. I felt that somewhere, *right now,* I was missing a step in my dance of life. The rhythm was wrong.

Mark had planned a wonderful surprise birthday party on Saturday, the 14th, for David and many of his friends. Not knowing that the party was for his birthday, David brandished his gourmet cooking skills. (Two of David's specialties, chicken wings and barbecued spareribs, were part of the feast.) His wonderful hors d'oeuvres looked as though a real artist had put them together. The whole evening was a masterpiece. David had a way of doing things with real style. I recall that it had upset me to see him barefooted while he cooked in his kitchen with its concrete floor. This was December!

Sunday, the 15th, I had strength and ambition to spare, so I decided to have a family dinner. It would be a good opportunity for us to give Mark and David their Christmas presents before they left town. This year they planned to visit their great friends Frank and Jean Emerling in Massachusetts for the holidays. We had a quiet buffet supper in the living room in front of the fireplace. David was so happy. For the first time in a long time, he said, he was looking forward to Christmas. With joyful anticipation, he had made all his own Christmas gifts for everyone–a large container of pesto sauce, his special brand of cranberry vinegar, and a nice container of Cajun seasoning for each recipient. We were all thrilled.

On Monday, the 16th, David came to the office to tell me that the doctor's diagnosis concerning the breathing difficulty was "only bronchitis." We hugged each other, both so relieved that it was nothing more serious.

David was working on a very important project for Bob–the first issue of the *Regeneration Newsletter,* typeset on the Macintosh computer using Pagemaker. He worked a very long, hard day on Wednesday, the 18th. That night David had another very bad spell. He had turned blue, Mark told me when he called early in the morning. I immediately called the doctor, telling him this was an emergency. He talked us into waiting to see a respiratory specialist later that day. Against my wishes, David worked on the project while he waited for the appointment. When I came to take him to the doctor, I found him lying on the couch, dripping with perspiration as he put the final touches on the job. He wanted to drive himself to the appointment, so he could go back to the office and print out the newsletter. But Mom was in charge now! It was December 19th.

X rays showed that one lung was more than half-full of fluid and the other lung was nearly half-full–due to pneumonia! It meant immediate admittance to the hospital. I had some telephone calls to make, and when I was through, I found David sitting in the waiting room with tears rolling down his face. He said, "Mom, you know they'll check me for AIDS?"

"I figured," I replied. I put my arms around David and held him till the wheelchair arrived to take him to his room.

As we sat there, I thought of all the articles about AIDS David had given me to read. He was helping a friend compile information through interviews with victims, doctors, funeral directors, and so on. When I had first seen the articles, I had panicked. I hadn't wanted to read them. I had been petrified. I had touched them gingerly, as though I were peeking out of a lace-curtained window to observe a world I knew nothing about. Eventually, I read them, remembering that people are usually scared of what they don't know.

The wheelchair arrived, and as we went down the the corridor, the nurse said to David, "It's easy to see that your body is not getting enough oxygen. Look at your fingernails." They were tinged with blue.

The person in the admitting office asked if we wanted a private room. "Sure," I said. "I hope one is available." It was indeed. We were given a private room with a big *Isolation* sign on the door. Hands had to be washed before and after visits. Surgical gowns had to be worn; masks and gloves were available.

The mom who barely had the strength to come home from the hospital, who had cried enough to make the ocean overflow, prayed: "Oh, God, please give my son another chance! He is so talented and has so much to offer the world. Make him *live!* I thank you, God, for this time to spare at this busy holiday time. You have prepared me for taking care of David."

I awoke on Friday morning, feeling very upset. I wanted to go to a beautiful church where I would find some real peace. I just wanted to sit there and say positive prayers for David. I was on the way there when I suddenly turned around and went to the hospital to be with David until it was time for the biopsy of his lungs. I held his hand and we talked about a lot of good things. As he was wheeled away for the procedure, David said, "Thanks a lot for coming, Mom." I was glad that I was there. I came back again to be with him after he was brought back to the room.

David's wonderful friends from Massachusetts, Jean and Frank Emerling, dropped everything to come to be with David and Mark. This team and our family circled David with love around the clock.

Saturday, the 21st, the phone rang at 7:30 A.M. It was David. He just wanted to talk. I said, "David, is something the matter?"

He said, "No, my nose is just running. Nothing special. Just saying hello."

I went to visit my good friends Peggy and Pete, to deliver their Christmas gift. Then I went to the farmer's market to get some fruit for David. That would cheer him up! The raspberries were perfect and the strawberries big and juicy. I bumped into Bonnie, my doctor's wife, and reported that David was in the hospital. She said encouragingly, "You don't have to worry. Pneumonia isn't that serious these days. He'll be all right."

I went to the hospital and took the elevator to the seventh floor. As the door opened to the waiting room, I saw Jean and Mark holding each other and sobbing. What was wrong? As we all three hugged, Jean blurted out that the doctor had told David early that morning that they were almost certain he had AIDS. There would be a family council at noon. I called the other members of the family.

Dr. Hertz was very kind. He spoke with concern for David and also for us. It was hard for him, too. He told us that David had *pneumocystis,* resulting from AIDS. He also told us that David might not make it. The odds were in his favor, but we must be prepared.

The doctor encouraged us to express our personal feelings. Heather asked, "Is it selfish of me to feel that if anything bad happens to David we will never enjoy Christmas again?"

The doctor said, "No, it is not selfish. It is natural for you to feel that way."

The doctor wanted David to make one major decision for himself immediately. If it became necessary, would David want to go on a life support system? David wouldn't answer.

We no longer wore surgical masks. We knew now that David did not have TB and we could catch nothing from him through the air. It must have been a relief for David to see the full faces of those he loved.

My will for David to live was unbelievably strong. Amid all my tears I tried to think only positive thoughts. It was Saturday night, December 21st. At home, I went to the window where I could see the lights at the hospital where David was. It was a very pleasant view. I wrote in my diary:

> *I'm celebrating all of David's contributions to us. As I look out, I am making a list of his many accomplishments and I pour out my love for him. How do I feel? First of all, my children are my life. I have made sure, over the years, to help them achieve their goals whatever they were. Gladly, I would suffer in their place if I could—I love them all so much.*

I remember how, as David's breathing became harder on each visit, I prayed, "Oh, God, please don't let him suffer!" My heart was still full of hope.

On Sunday, I started by going to a service at a church where I was not a member but where I had many friends. When it came time to pray for those who were ill and in need of support, David's name was lovingly placed on the list. After the service, the salt of our tears intermingled freely as genuine hugs abounded.

This day of December 22nd turned out to be a sadder day. The oxygen had to be stepped up. David had decided against being put on a life support system if it should come to that. "That's not me," he said.

There is a little magazine called the *Daily Word* that never ceases to be an inspiration to me. So often it appears to have been written especially to fit my needs for that day. And so it happened again just when I needed a lift. At dinner that night, I told the family, "We are rejoicing that David has given us so much beauty and love and we have given it back to him, even though he hasn't always seemed to know it. It's hard to see him suffer. I want to tell you what *Daily Word* says for today."

Dear One for Whom I Pray, I Hold Your Hand in Prayer and Place You Safely in God's Care

If loved ones are facing challenges of mind or body or circumstances, we may wonder how we can most effectively help them. The surest way is to remain steadfast in prayer and in our faith.

Whether we live near or far away from family members, loved ones, or friends, we can hold their hands in prayer. As we pray, we can place them safely in God's care, and see them filled with life and vigor.

As we behold their innate potential, we help them to call forth God's mighty, unfailing power to heal.

Whatever the appearance of negation, confusion, or loneliness, we affirm: 'You are God's perfect, beloved child. Nothing can dim your Spirit. You are whole, well and free. You know it and you feel it. With praise and thanksgiving for all that you are, I hold your hand in prayer and place you safely in God's care.'

Pray to me, and I will hear you (Jer. 29:12)

The passage speaks of facing challenges in the mind and body.

It tells us that if we are worried about someone, we can hold that person's hands in prayer. We picture the person surrounded by God's care and filled with health and love. We ask God to use His healing touch.

Knowing that God loves each one of us, we use positive thoughts to see David whole, happy, and free.

We thank you, Father, for your love and care.

At those times when I was in the hospital with David on my night shift (2:00 to 5:00 A.M.), he would hold my hand so tightly—and I his. I didn't want to let go. I wanted to transfer my strength to him. If I were to relax my hold for even one second, he would grasp my hand even harder. Early Monday morning, it seemed OK with him just so long as I was there. I attributed that change to his increased weakness, but maybe it was his way of saying "Release me, Mom."

Bob asked David if he knew he had AIDS before his hospitalization. David replied that he had suspected it for a couple of weeks.

Now Bob took charge of working on a will with David, and David signed it early Monday afternoon. All of the family did a lot more hugging, and Tom, our son-in-law, said, "You know, David taught us all about the love we didn't know we had."

Our oldest daughter, Heather, and Jean Emerling made pads for David's glasses to cushion the oxygen mask and relieve the pressure of its weight on his nose. Heather and Mark massaged David's feet. Our daughter Heidi brought him a painting that she had made and a book she had bought for him for Christmas. She had hesitated to give it to him; it was called *Visions of Paradise*. Maria, our youngest daughter, brought him a big stuffed white puppy that reminded David of Murphy, his great Pyrenees. Anthony, our youngest son, took a picture of the porch at David's wonderful house that morning and delivered it to him at 5:00 P.M., and David said, "Oh, it's so good to see home."

I had been making the meals for David so he would eat better—chicken soup and other foods to help him get well.

As I fed him, he said, "What's new at home?"

"Not a single thing, David."

"Are you ready for Christmas?" he asked.

And I replied, "Yes, all ready."

The support team was getting tired. That night, Sarah Fitz-Hugh, who shared an office with David at the Press, stayed with him while the rest of us had dinner. Sarah and David were very close friends and I was glad she was there. She would be honored to sit with him, she told me.

Other friends in the company and other members of the family also volunteered to sit with David. I asked David how he felt about this. "It's OK," he said, "as long as they don't expect me to entertain them!"

After Sarah arrived, even though David's breathing was harder when we left the hospital, we were all encouraged. His mind was right on target and he had joked with us as we prepared to leave. At dinner, we laughed, and shared good memories. We never got to dessert. The doctor called—"Come at once!"

How can you pack a lifetime into two weeks? It seemed as if the clocks had stopped. When we got back to the hospital, David was gone. I had always had a terrible fear of death, but David looked so peaceful.

I thought, I brought my son into life, he left my body, now I have to touch him, to somehow return this life to me. I rubbed my hand over his soft arm and prayed. "Thanks, God, for releasing my son from his labored struggle—but, oh, how much I wanted him a while longer."

Are any of us ever ready for life's tribulations? Can we ever be ready for the hardest of all, the death of one's own child?

My heart cries out to those who have wrestled with death all alone, in a world we say is full of love. I want to reach out my hand to let them know they are not really alone on their passage. I would like to rock them gently in the cradle of love.

I thought about my son and his life. I tried my best with him. Was my best enough? My only answer was, I did the best that I could do. I had to absolve myself of any guilt. I had to realize that David had become master of his own symphony. I, as the Umbrella of Protection, had to know that David had played his own special music, and that his symphony would never be over so long as my love survived.

CHAPTER 19

The Celebration of David's Life

Now lift me in love

Brunetta E. Winthers

I thought back to a question I had asked myself before. What if life ended today? Now I had the answer: It doesn't end; it keeps right on going through the love we share with others.

After leaving the hospital, the family and Mark, Frank, and Jean all came back to the house. Each of us shared thoughts and experiences related to David that the others didn't know.

Mark talked of how David had enjoyed sitting with him on the porch of their house on the mountain, discussing life and his dreams for the future. It was during one of these conversations that David had told Mark that he would like to have his ashes spread in the meadow in the back of the house when he was no longer here. This was a surprising and important thing for us to know, and it would be done in spring.

We also talked about the service. It would be an uplifting time, an occasion for celebration.

I don't remember sleeping that night. I doubt that I did. Throughout the night I was compiling mental lists of things that needed to be taken care of, and thinking of how *we*, the family, could rally the spirits of our friends in *their* grief. We needed to support one another.

I recalled the service that Paster Tom Reinsel had led when our neighbor Mark died several years before. It had been an affirmation of strong support and love shared. This was the theme I wanted for David. Even though I was not a member of his church, Tom promised to lead the service. Within an hour that morning Bob, Tom, and I had the program pretty well put together.

That night—Christmas Eve—Maria, Anthony, and I went to a candlelight service. It was hard trying to be brave when my heart was in such pain. The tears just kept coming. At the end of the service, many friends crowded around to ask how David was doing. Having to tell them that he left us the night before was devastating. There were many hugs and many more tears.

Somehow we got through Christmas. It seemed unreal, like it was just a bad dream that would vanish when I awoke. But of course it didn't. For some reason, I felt it was necessary that we have the traditional Christmas meal. It lacked the usual wonderful flavor; I even forgot some of the ingredients for my famous potato filling, a dish I thought I could make with my eyes closed.

The notice of David's death did not appear in the paper till the morning of the 26th, the day of the service. I had insisted to the newspaper reporter that the service be listed as a Celebration of David's life—not a memorial service.

At 11:00 A.M. on that morning, over 450 friends and relatives joined in the Celebration. It was truly beautiful. All seats in the church were filled, and the aisles and vestibule virtually overflowed. It touched my heart to see people from the Press who were also members of the church, some whom I knew only slightly, present to be ushers and to help in other ways with the service. Clearly, these people really cared about all of us, and took time from their busy holiday schedules to support us with love.

While our family and Mark greeted friends, the organ music filled the church magnificently. Since he was a master of classical music, these compositions were some of David's favorites: Brahms' Prelude ("O World, I know I now must leave Thee"); Beethoven's "Moonlight Sonata"; Pietro's "Yon-Jesu Bambino"; Knapp's "Blessed Assurance"; Handel's "Hallelujah Chorus" from the *Messiah;* and Bach's "Jesu, Joy of Man's Desiring" from Cantata no. 147. As they were played, even the music seemed to gain in strength. We were surrounded by much of David's artwork–"musicscapes" and weavings that Marian, one of my coworkers, had displayed so beautifully. There was also the church's wonderful wall hanging of the Holy Family surrounded by children from all corners of the world. Masses of poinsettias were ablaze with color. The message was inspiring and strengthening.

Pastor Tom Reinsel said, "We gather with memories of gourmet meals, his music, weaving, art, dancing, singing, acting, directing, producing. What wonderful gifts of God! And his last work of creating in the most modern techniques of computer networking, editing, writing. In all of this, I have learned from the family and from you, his friends, that David was a friend to many. And each of you here told me, "You know, I loved David!" Our God, who made David who he is, is the One to receive him back again!"

The congregation sang my grandmother's favorite hymn:

> There's a wideness in God's mercy,
> Like the wideness of the sea;
> There's a kindness in his justice,
> Which is more than liberty.
> For the love of God is broader
> Than the measures of man's mind,
> And the heart of the Eternal
> Is most wonderfully kind.

Because of David's love for living on the Conservancy land where there is such peace and beauty and inspiration, we sang:

> God who touches earth with beauty,
> Make me lovely, too.
> With thy spirit recreate me,
> Make my heart anew.

> Like the springs and running waters,
> Make me crystal pure,
> Like the rocks of towering grandeur,
> Make me strong and sure.

> Like the dancing waves in sunlight,
> Make me glad and free,
> Like the straightness of the pine trees,
> Let me upright be.

Like the arching of the heavens,
Lift my thoughts above,
Turn my dreams to noble action,
Ministries of love.

God who touches earth with beauty,
Make me lovely, too.
Keep me ever by the spirit,
Pure and strong and true.

My brother, Jim Harter, recited a poem he wrote, dedicated to David, "Please Don't Weep for Me."

The service ended with the triumphant air composed by Johann Sebastian Bach, with words added:

Joyful, joyful we adore thee, God of
glory, Lord of love!
Hearts unfold like flowers before thee,
Praising thee,
their sun above.
Melt the clouds of sin and sadness,
Drive the gloom of doubt
away.
Giver of immortal gladness, Fill us with
light of day.

All thy works with joy surround thee.
Earth and heaven
reflect the rays
Stars and angels sing around thee,
Center of unbroken praise
Field and forest, vale and mountain,
Flow'ry meadow
flashing sea.
Chanting bird and flowing fountain, Call
us to rejoice in
thee.

Thou art giving and forgiving, Ever
blessing, ever blest,

> Wellspring of the joy of living, Ocean
> depth of happy rest!
> You our Father, Christ our brother, All
> who live in love
> are thine!
>
> Teach us how to love each other, Lift us
> to the joy divine!

We greeted more friends. They were all there–from the many old-time Press employees who had known David all through his life, to the newer employees who were among his special group of friends. All our Buttonwood Street neighbors from the first years of our marriage were there, the members of my old Sunday school class, and some childhood friends whom I had not seen for many years. Joe Daddona, the Mayor of Allentown, sent a special citation on behalf of "All our citizens" in memoriam. David's friends were there, many from New York and Washington, and many of our other children's friends came to lend support.

Words that others shared with me came back. Frank Emerling gave me a copy of *The Fall of Freddie the Leaf* by Leo Buscaglia. Frank inscribed the book:

> *In memory of a dear, beloved, brilliantly colored leaf...*
> *one who got swept off his limb in the summer of his life.*
> *Lucky are we that we got to sit next to him on that bough,*
> *share his exuberance, his wit, and his love for life ... David.*

Frank's wife, Jean, told me: "Ardie, you bore for me my very best friend."

Ken: "David found his place–so many never do. You know, he planted so many seeds of vision that have changed our thinking."

Anna: "How often I privately wished that there were more young persons like dear David, so our future would be ensured its bounty of humanists, artists, and individualists–and people of goodness."

Jeff: "David positively touched my life. He turned to me, a virtual stranger, and treated me like a brother and friend. This is what it means, in the truest sense, to be a child of God–a man of goodness. His example of genuine decency, openness, and helpfulness shines like a beacon to me as I encounter new people."

As we hugged and laughed and wiped our eyes, I was amazed that all these people were reaching out to us in our sorrow, letting us know that we mattered in their lives. It was deeply touching. I would never be the same again.

CHAPTER 20

Aftermath

We have not wings, we cannot soar;
But we have feet to scale and climb
By slow degrees, by more and more,
The cloudy summits of our time.

Henry Wadsworth Longfellow

December 27th was a hard day for me. Cards, flowers, visitors, and letters were arriving constantly. The weather was beautiful, and I just had to get out of the house to go for a walk. The tears were an endless ocean. The wind pushed me along gently, as if to say, Come on, I'll help you through these days. Halfway through the walk, the tears stopped and now the wind was pushing me from the front. This time it seemed to be saying, First I'll help you, then you have to help yourself.

I started to breathe deeper and saw this whole experience as a big challenge and an opportunity to grow. The path then led me over virgin snow, and as my feet made fresh imprints, I thought, Why don't we tell people we love them more often? Why do some of us wait so long?

During that first week after David left, the whole family went through all the emotions—pain, suffering, upliftment, denial, anger, and more pain—then acceptance and growing. Each of us prepared to greet the New Year in a different way. The hardest choice for me to handle was Maria's. She had decided that on this New Year's Eve she would sleep in a tent on the side of the hill at the New Farm in below-freezing weather. She said she would be fine, but I had real trouble with the idea. I pleaded with her, "Please don't do this. I just can't deal with it at this time."

Two hours later she called me back and bombarded me with hundreds of *why nots!* I was too worn out to fight. I gave in.

I learned later that every New Year's Eve, Maria chose to meet a special challenge she set for herself. This year in particular, she had a lot to sort out. (Aside from losing David, Maria would be leaving for Washington with her daughter in a few short days, to start a new job and a new life.) The New Farm was a safe and beautiful place to do it. To her it seemed a wonderful way to greet the New Year—alone with her thoughts on an inspiring hillside.

For Heather, David's leaving was also very painful since she had been his assistant mother for many years. She cried, "Mom, every time I look in the mirror, I see David staring back at me. It's so hard." We consoled each other. One day she said in reflection, "You know, Mom, that last day in the hospital, as Jean and I worked on David to make him comfortable, I looked at his wonderful thick curly hair and his beautiful long eyelashes. I felt the hair on his legs and felt his strong arms. I realized he wasn't my little brother anymore. He was a man."

The anguish didn't stop. I never realized how much I would be able to bear. Why was one day so good and the next day so hard? I learned that life continues and we simply have to keep on.

I tried to keep all thoughts positive, recalling all the good that had happened in our lives through David. He had helped us to appreciate beauty—he was always one step ahead of where we were. We kept trying to catch up by pursuing life as we lived it with him.

For example, we send our family Christmas card, which has since become a New Year's card, between mid-January and early February. We started this custom years ago, when it became so hard to get everyone together for the annual picture we include with our card, and now our friends tell me it brightens the post-holiday letdown. Our last picture together had been taken in October. David was in the center of the picture. At the time, I questioned why David's image was so much lighter in the print than all the rest. Could it have been a photographic omen?

So, in the middle of January, our card was mailed, with this insert:

> *Let us celebrate the life of David Evan Rodale—his uniqueness, his sensitivity, his creativity, his deep love and passion for whatever he pursued.*
>
> *Let's celebrate his love of family and friends—and our love for him—his reverence for and revering of the land, to make it produce beauty and continuity.*
>
> *David, Director of Computer Networking for Rodale Press in Emmaus, Pennsylvania, was also a composer, a musician, an artist, a gourmet cook, an actor, a weaver, and a humorist. He gave of himself as he continually shared these many talents with so many of us.*
>
> *This past year, all of his life seemed to be coming together and this was the happiest year of his whole life.*

>

DAVID

December 12, 1955—December 23, 1985

Age 30

>

Always, my purpose in life has been to lift my children up. I have wanted to be the strong and protective wings that could carry them on through life. And yet at the end, David had had his own wings.

I thought about David and all our friends and wondered how life would go on. I wanted to know if the feeling of love among our friends would still be the same, knowing that David had had AIDS.

The title of Carol King's song "Will You Still Love Me Tomorrow?" came to mind. I answered the question for myself: Yes, they will still care. We are children of God contributing and trying to make the world a better place by loving and being loved. What we do with sincerity in life is what matters, and people will still care.

And yes, people still loved David very much. They missed the gentle soul with the genius for myriad creativity and kindness. When the tape of life stops, it doesn't mean it's over. We can still hear the music, but we hear it in a different way. Life continues and augments our recollection, as we, the living, see the reflection of that life.

When I share the story of David with friends, they are stunned: "I can't think what it might be like to lose a child. I can't imagine how I might react. I couldn't face the possibility of letting go."

Before David left, I had felt that way, too. The experience of losing a child is by far the hardest test one can face in life. I think it is harder than facing one's own death. I looked into my heart trying to feel what my "mother love" is like, and I believe it is the closest to how God loves us. It is a love that never lets down, a love filled with trying to understand, a heart filled with compassion, a desire to spare that child's life by replacing it with one's own. I have lived so much of my life—he had so much more to go!

Some days were particularly hard when I was at my desk writing acknowledgments for the many expressions of sympathy. As I sat there, my mind would scream, What am I doing? No! No! Take it all away! It is just a bad dream and I can't stand it for a single second longer. Please make it all disappear! Heaven help us!

When well-meaning but insensitive people would say, "David's dead. He's dead!" I sometimes felt I would become hysterical. How can the special life of one who contributed so much be *dead?* No! He lives on in the contributions he made to life and the way that affects the living. Death of a loved one can be like a butterfly emerging from its cocoon into your own spirit. Then the inspiration and love of this being can expand in a beautiful way inside of you, leading you to help others.

Being at work was particularly hard. I thought I just had to turn around and see David standing in my doorway. "Hi, Mom, good morning!" I couldn't concentrate. In meetings I had trouble making decisions. Was I losing my mind? Did other people understand and would they have patience with me?

I often had to walk away. I felt real anger for those people who expected me to carry on social obligations as if nothing had happened. When I told one woman I was very sad, she said, "To look at you, one would never know. You carry it well."

I think what I was looking for from people was understanding. Those who have not suffered the death of someone really close do not seem to realize that life does not go back to normal in two weeks. We all repair in our own time, in our own way. I didn't expect anything from others, yet when someone said something very kind and loving, I felt it deeply, and the relationship with that person took on a new meaning.

One afternoon I was particularly down, in the very pit of despair. I saw no light in my grief, and my heart wrenched as the tears flowed unceasingly. Then I happened to glance out the window and I saw two little boys coming up my front walk. (This is a rare event when you live in the country.) They rang the doorbell and, as I wiped my tear-stained face with my hand, I opened the door.

"Is Mr. Rodale here?" they asked.

"No," I replied, "he is at work."

"We see him when he is walking the fields with your big white dog. Can we come in?"

"Sure." Why not? I thought. It might help.

Politely, they sat down. They wanted to talk. Chris and Mike were seven years old and lived on the other side of the fields. After a while, I asked them if they would like to see the toys I kept there for my grandkids, and they were all excited. It was, "Wow! Hey, great! Mike, look at this! This is neat!"

Little by little my anguish turned around as I began to look at life through the eyes of these happy and excited little boys who had come to me as "angels unaware." As they left, they called back, "Can we come again?"

"Yes!" I said, with all my heart.

We did not know what a treasure David's friend Jesse had in store for us. David had presented him with a huge package for one of his birthdays. In it was David's autobiography called *DVO My Body*. It was very precious to Jesse. The copy I had made would also be precious to us. As I read the volumes, I laughed and cried, reliving many familiar times, some wonderful, some sad.

There was much I hadn't known. I gained new insight into the experiences of David's life, and many of them made me feel so sad. I was particularly affected by a sense of being alone that had plagued David as he struggled to come to terms with who he was and what his place was in a high profile family heading an international business. If only we all had helped one another more, I thought. How I wished David had tried to work out his frustrations in a relationship of community instead of trying to do it all alone. But then, would that have been David? The thought of his loneliness made me hurt most of all. Though the two of us had shared a lot of prime time together, I could have given him more. Would he have wanted that? I don't know. If only he had shared more of his feelings with me!

I went to the New Farm where David had left half an attic full of things. What would we do with it all? His office at the Press was loaded with much more, not to mention a closet full of his belongings here at home. It would take forever to go through it all. I just couldn't tackle the whole job.

One box fascinated me, however. It was filled with cassettes. Most of these were unmarked. Before any tape could be thrown away, I had to listen to it. I found tapes of him playing the classical music he composed and of his beautiful singing voice. One cassette had him playing the recorder and clowning with the kazoo. The family would pop in at different times as I listened and exclaim, "Why, that's David!"

We thought all this had been lost forever! Now we had a part of David back again.

In the midst of my grieving, I read a book called *Mountaintop Living*, which had one passage that stuck with me: "The buck stops here. The depression and the discouragement stop here. I am stepping out of this ragged suit of mental clothes right now, and I welcome new experiences and life and new blessing today. I am grateful."

There are many lessons to be learned from a painful life-change such as this. Here are some I won't forget:

♥　♥　♥　♥　♥　♥　♥　♥　♥　♥　♥　♥　♥　♥　♥　♥

I am amazed how much love a person holds inside for a child. No matter how much or how often you express your love, somehow it is not enough.

Maybe we feel that we are a pillar of strength, but still it is comforting when others reach out to touch us and we accept their love and concern. I came to realize the tremendous power of hugging–a true comfort and a way for people to show their love. In a hug, you can really feel the concern coming from those who care.

Dwell on all the wonderful contributions of the life that was cut short.

Don't chastise yourself for what might have been. Still the mind, stand tall, take stock of what is still there, and build on that.

Nourish yourself by doing something special just for you. Treat yourself with kindness because you contributed to making that life that was filled with good.

Praise God for letting you share that wonderful life.

Realize that others are in need of care too. Seek those people out and give them your love through a hug, a kiss, a soothing hand, a sympathetic ear, a helpful errand. Only as we begin to get out of ourselves do we start to heal and realize that our mission in life is still not finished.

For years, it's been my custom to send a teardrop prism to friends who have experienced the death of someone close. I never dreamed I would need my own message of comfort someday. Each message that accompanied the prism was slightly different, but this was the idea:

Our lives are represented by the prism. There are many sides, or facets, that make up our total being. We realize that we have both the sunshine and sorrow, tears and laughter, to make us appreciate our days. We grow by the way the pendulum swings through the two extremes. It depends on how we look at life to realize the depth of what we see. We might see only the tear. If we are optimistic, we look through the tear and see the hope that lies beyond.

Place this prism in a window where the sun shines through. At unexpected times you will see rainbows dancing. Let this rainbow be a happy reminder of the wonderful things that happened in your life together. All the warm and special feelings will be released through this energy and give you strength and joy . . . knowing that because your loved one lived, the continuation of that life is through you. And you have the mission to make sure that life continues to live in our hearts.

Anthony and I went to Coral Gables, Florida, a favorite place for the family over the years, to think our lives through for a few days and to try to set the stage for a new road. Many good, nostalgic feelings are generated in this place of peace and we find many beautiful places to walk. This time, the weather was extremely cold–the aftermath of a storm. The two of us felt the need to breathe in the salt air so we went to the State Park Sanctuary Beach at the tip of Key Biscayne, and we walked alone, each at our own pace. It was desolate, not a single soul in sight. Still, the tumult of the ocean and the brightening horizon were beautiful to me. My life was coming out of a storm. I took the shorter walk and sat on the high lifeguard chair to wait for Anthony's return. He climbed up beside me on the chair, and, with our arms around each other, we looked out to sea. We were silent for a long time. Finally, I said to him, "You know, the storms of life are like those big waves out there. All of a sudden, a big one comes along, throws you off balance and you're caught in the undertow. It takes a while to get back on your feet, and then the gentle waves come along to stroke you and to nourish you back to feeling good again."

Sadness comes to all of us in different times and in different ways. It can make us stronger than before. At the same time, it can bring a softening, a deeper feeling of compassion, and a need to reach out to others. This is part of the healing process. Life has lots of endings, but with each one comes an opportunity for new beginnings leading to wider horizons.

One morning, sometime after Anthony and I got back home, I awoke early, just as it was beginning to get light. I opened the door and took a deep breath. The roosters were crowing in the distance. It was very calm and reasonably warm. It was beautiful. As I went to get the newspaper at the end of the driveway, I found myself singing, "Come in from the rain." It was time to begin again.

I have discovered that the spiritual world is a very friendly place. My fingers fly wildly over the typewriter keys because there are lots of messages I want to share.

CHAPTER 21

Messages

Love ever gives,
Forgives, outlives,
And ever stands
With open hands.
And, while it lives,
It gives.
For this is Love's prerogative—
To give and give and give.

John Oxenham

If I had heard a prediction of what is going on in my life this year, I would have said, "That's crazy. That's ridiculous!"

We tend to mistrust and fear the unknown.

One night, about a month after David left, I had an upsetting dream. Yet it didn't seem like a dream. I was actually struggling with two forms, one on either side of my bed, coming closer and closer to me, trying to encompass me. I struggled desperately, first on one side, then the other. It became harder and harder for me to breathe. I was suffocating. I had to fight to live. I got weaker and weaker. Finally, with my last bit of energy, I pushed the form on my right over the edge of the bed and it appeared to slide off, as though it were sinking into the ocean.

I sat up in a cold sweat. I had never experienced anything like this before, and I was confused. What could this experience mean? I told several people about it, but they had no answers. It was my daughter Maria who came up with an explanation: "You know, Karl said that sometimes people who were very close to someone who died could experience that death in a dream."

I'm sure this is what happened. As David's lungs filled more and more with fluid, his struggle for life must have been like this at the last. A strange feeling had filled me, and I had a new appreciation for David's struggle to survive.

About a month later, I had another dream. I dreamed I had died. My body seemed to be lying in David's bed at the hospital, and I was out of my body, looking down at myself.

David appeared at the door, "Hey, Mom, come on."

"Where are we going, David?"

"Just follow me," he said.

We went down the hall to the elevator and he cut his finger as he tried to pry the door open. We got in. "Now, Mom, when we get out, we will get out the opposite side of the elevator." The door opened.

"David, it's dark. I can't see."

"That's OK. Just turn the corner and it will be light." And it was.

He was carrying a transparent gym bag, and he said, "I brought this along for the transition."

He started to take things out of the bag. There was a flowered hat and a dress and black high-heeled shoes for me. I put everything on, and I was grateful that the shoes didn't hurt. The bag also contained an apple and a long string of beads. Standing by David's side was a Great Pyrenees dog. It must have been Obie, the dog that had died three years before. I tried to put the beads around Obie's neck, but they didn't fit. As I took the beads off, we had a good laugh.

David's mood changed and he slowly sat back, kind of reclining on a gradual slope, and exclaimed, "Hey, Mom, look at that!" He pointed to our Pennsylvania Power & Light building, Allentown's skyscraper that looks like an up-ended lighted cigar. It seemed so much bigger than in reality, and it was lit up in the most spectacular way. "Wow! Did you ever see anything like it?" he said.

"Unbelievable!" I agreed.

As we admired the sight, he exclaimed, "And, Mom, look over there!" I turned toward the opposite direction, and there was an unbelievably big orange sun/moon in the sky. It hung just above the horizon line. I sat by David's side and we gazed at all this splendor.

Words were not necessary for us to appreciate the glory and feeling of peace which entered our hearts.

When I awoke, a strange aura filled me again, and I wondered, Am I next? Is David preparing me?

Again, I started to look for answers. Another friend who has strong feelings about the spiritual world said, "No, Ardie, David is telling you he is OK where he is." Together we figured out that David is content to watch Mark, his friend who works for PP&L, grow in his own light. It was neat!

The next experience of this kind was not part of a dream. At work and at home, at unexpected times, I would hear David calling in a very urgent way. "Hello, Mom! Hello, Mom!"

I ignored these calls for about a week, and then one day I stopped and said, "Yes, David, I'm here. Tell me what you want."

Later that day, I said to Bob, "You know, I think David is telling me he doesn't want his ashes at the funeral home anymore. He wants them *home*." We made the arrangements immediately, and Bob took the box up to David's old bedroom, which Bob uses for a study now. He placed the box on the bookcase near a window facing west. The view from where the box was placed was the peaceful landscape of the farm and wide open field. After that, David's voice became silent. I'm sure that was what David had wanted to tell us.

Every month on the 23rd, a fresh rose is placed in a bud vase as a remembrance of David. On one particular night, I placed the vase on the coffee table as I had done in the past, and next to it a bright candle. With this as the only light in the room, I enjoy sitting there listening to soft music as the candle reflects the rose on the white ceiling of the living room. I did the same this night and I closed my eyes. When I opened them, there were reflections of two roses on the ceiling. One was straight and tall and still; the other was smaller, continually pulsating and leaning toward the tall, straight, immobile one. I couldn't believe my eyes. I called Bob to come and see this phenomenon. He said it was "amazing!"

This is how I interpreted it: Geoffrey David, a Korean baby, was due to make his adoptive home with Heather and Tom and their other children. David's message said, "Here I am, silent and tall. There is a new little life that is looking for attention. Work on the living child."

The pain of my loss comes back often, and the grieving starts all over again. Sometimes in this anguish, it is almost as if my hand is directed to write "David, I love you so much. . . . " and I hear David say so clearly: "Mom, I heard it so many times . . . I know . . . But get off my back. I have important work to do . . . and I have to give you so much energy . . . and there are so many others who need it now. I told you

I'm OK and I know you'll be fine . . . now let me get to work . . . you have work to do, too! We'll work together . . . you from there and I from the other side . . . You have to write that book to help people understand!"

Another time, I came home from work absolutely exhausted. I sat down in my white room, I closed my eyes, and I heard myself asking, What are you doing, letting your work control you? I answered myself, I take to heart all the problems. I guess I should take time to sit and be quiet for a while. The answers to the problems will come then, if I don't force the issue. I have to give it time. Wait till all the parts come together in harmony.

Then very clearly, I heard David's voice, "That's what I have been trying to tell you for a long time, Mom! Enjoy some of the wonderful experiences of life. Get off the merry-go-round. So what if you're late? You'll get there and have time to appreciate so much more along the way. Look outside. It's *so* beautiful, and here you are trying to calm down from your race. I care about you. Perhaps I can help you to see things more clearly from the other side."

"David, I'll listen!"

We wanted to do something special for David at church on All Saints' Day. Pastor Tom had suggested wildflowers–but there were no wildflowers in bloom at the end of October. "There's nothing but pampas grass from the meadow," I said.

Tom got all excited. "Great! How about a large, very free arrangement that we can set on the floor right by the baptismal font?"

Friday, before the service, I went to the meadow, slipped off my glasses and placed them deep in my coat pocket as I took off into the meadow. It's like a maze up there and you can easily lose your sense of direction. I picked a huge bouquet and went back to the porch marveling at the fantastic, colorful fall day. Then, ready to go back home, I stuck my hand in the pocket and–the glasses were gone! I trudged back to the meadow and wandered all around, searching, but to no avail. Then I heard David, "You know, Mom, how blind I am without my glasses. I just had to borrow yours because I didn't want to miss this gorgeous, heavenly day." A chuckle filled my heart!

On the last such occasion, I was sitting very quietly, discouraged about the progress of my book. David said to me, "Mom, I'm here. . . ."

"I want to touch you, David."

"I know," he replied, "But Mom, I touch you all the time in unexpected ways. I'm looking for you to help people be more caring and accepting of us. You/I/we have a message that needs to be given to the world. Now don't wait till somebody else does it . . . you know you've always been ahead of the game. . . . Mom, it's urgent! Do it now!"

"Yes, David, I will do it. Maybe I couldn't do your networking on the computer . . . but I can reach out to tell how you felt and how I felt as a mother . . . and that's a start. Oh, David, who said life would be easy? . . . but I accept the challenge."

I mentioned these experiences to many of David's friends, and they all replied, "You don't have to tell me you think this is magic! David talks to me all the time, too!"

With Christmas coming, as much as I wanted to get going again on the book, I didn't. There was so much else to do, and I needed time to be nourished by family and friends. I felt guilty that I was not following through on my challenge.

On Christmas Day, about 1:00 P.M., something in my mind said, Go to the mountain, go to the mountain. . . . It was persistent. So as soon as things quieted down, I made my escape. Without telling anyone where I was going, I went up to David's house. As I drove there, I heard, Go to the meadow . . . go to the meadow. . . . You will find your glasses. I pulled into the driveway and considered going into the house, but I decided to go to the meadow first. I walked up there and thought, I have to keep my eyes fixed on the ground to look—and there they were! The glasses had been there in that meadow for nearly two months. I washed the dirt specks off the plastic lenses, and held them up to the light. They were perfect; not a scratch. To me, this was a special Christmas present. In my mind I heard, "Mom, remember your promise. I give the glasses back to you so that you will start on your writing again. You know how much it means to us. We have to help people to understand!"

In May, there was another lull in my writing. Business took me to San Francisco and then to visit Anthony in Santa Barbara. As I sat in the hotel room one day, I glanced down to the floor and saw a red pencil. I don't need it, I'll just leave it there, I thought . . . but no, I stooped to pick it up, and I turned it over. Imprinted on the side was *David Rodale!* Again David was urging me to get back to work. I don't remember picking up this pencil at home, or putting it in my purse, or dropping it! With care I took it back home and put it in the typing drawer by my typewriter here at home. I used it for editing, then the pencil disappeared again. I have looked hard, but I don't know what happened to it.

Two years after David left, Bob and I went to Coral Gables for a few days. I had been under a lot of pressure before we went away, and when I came back home I was ill with a virus and I was depressed. I couldn't seem to shake either one. One day, the radio played "Somewhere out there, someone's thinking of you". The tears rolled down my face and I was thinking of how I couldn't hear David anymore.

As I cried, I heard the urgent voice, "Hello, Mom! Hello, Mom!" I poured my heart out. I told David how I was being pulled in so many directions and how hard it was. Because of these pressures, I lacked the urgency and direction I needed to work on this book. I cried, "Oh, David, I need your help!"

Then I heard him say so clearly, "Don't let what other people want bother you. Be your own unique self, doing things in your own style. It's important. That's what you taught all of us—to be ourselves. Love pulled us through. Get going now!"

I felt better and I knew this was what I should do. In my heart I knew that if I did this, I would reach those people out there who need help—those with whom I can share my story. I can't be a leaner. A person must be a leader to reach out.

Last Mother's Day, I went up to David's house. I walked into the meadow, and just about where the ashes had been scattered, I spotted a tiny clump of forget-me-nots. I couldn't believe my eyes. This must be a miracle! No, it couldn't be, I thought, there are probably more little clusters up here. I searched and searched but there wasn't a single other one. How did that little bouquet get there? Perhaps a bird lovingly dropped the seed there. I like to think it was David's Mother's Day gift. The tears fell. I held him close in my heart.

CHAPTER 22

The Scattering

You are not enclosed within your bodies, nor
confined to houses or fields.
That which is you dwells above the mountain and
roves with the wind.
It is not a thing that crawls in the sun for
warmth or digs holes into darkness for safety,
But a thing free, a spirit that envelops the
earth and moves in the ether.

Kahlil Gibran

Spring came to David's house on the mountain after the winter of his leaving. All the many bulbs that David and Mark had planted in the fall were in bloom. To the rear of the house is a wonderful meadow filled with pampas grass and wild plants. It is here that David had wanted his ashes to be scattered.

His special friends, Jean and Frank and the Condons, came from Massachusetts for the weekend. Frank suggested having a flutist for the occasion. And together we worked on the music—some of the classical pieces that David had loved, and some show tunes and contemporary songs he had enjoyed so much.

The family gathered at the cemetery where J. I. Rodale, David's grandfather, was buried. It is a beautiful spot overlooking the town of Emmaus and the main building of our company. Papa had been a tremendous influence on David as he grew up, so it seemed right that they be remembered together. The inscription on J. I. Rodale's tombstone reads: "He urged man to live in harmony with the world." David's simple brass plaque, with his name, lay on the breast of Papa's grave. The song being played when David drew his last breaths in the hospital was "We Are the World." So it was appropriate, as we gathered together here, that the single flutist play that song. The message is meaningful for all people everywhere who suffer life's catastrophes, including those special people in our lives who contract AIDS.

For some people gathered here in the cemetery, this was the saddest moment because it spoke to the finality of all that had happened, events we sometimes still thought of as a bad dream that would disappear.

Next, we went up to the mountain that David had loved so much. David had had a live, balled Christmas tree, and after Christmas, Mark and I had taken off the decorations and heeled it in for the winter. Now came the fun part, when all the little nieces and nephews would help to plant the tree. Each one shoveled some ground around the tree. The sounds of laughter filled the air. All the while the beautiful sounds from Elaine's flute, "Dreamers," "My Funny Valentine," "Manhattan," and the music continued with us on our journey up the hill. Elaine played "Yesterday" and, from Vangelis, "Missing."

Next we stopped to view a piece of sculpture we had commissioned from John Knutila. It had been placed on a pedestal in the center of the daylily bed. The sculptor's wife, Jane, wrote of the piece:

> The idea we had while at David's was an object whose beauty was defined by the place and people involved, not by itself alone.
>
> The white square marble sculpture is purposefully simple. It is both a symbol of continuity and wholeness, and a focal point to serve you in an act of silent celebration. Offerings made to David inside the carved circle (a flower, a prayer . . .) complete the sculpture.

We continued our climb upward, striding into the meadow amid the huge clumps of pampas grass. Pastor Tom recited the 95th Psalm and prayed. He ended his part of the service by telling the story that

Betty, a woman in my Sunday school class, had sent in her sympathy note to us:

> *Many had come to bid farewell. As the ship's sails were raised and it slowly moved out to sea, the people sadly said, "There she goes."*
>
> *On the opposite shore, there was a crowd of people milling around with excitement, as if they were waiting for an important event. All of a sudden, the crowd started to cheer as the white sails appeared on the horizon line . . . and they cried with delight, "Here she comes."*

A dozen white balloons were released into the sky as Mark scattered the ashes in the place David had loved so much.

The flutist played "Somewhere" and "The Impossible Dream" and we all hugged each other. Then we proceeded to share a marvelous meal with all those present. David would have loved it!

Seeing Frank and Jean again made it clear to us that the reason their friendship grew with David, and then with Mark, was because they all loved David. They all enjoyed a good time. They challenged each other with their sharp wit and the energy and humor sailed along nonstop. It was this laughter and fun that we had sorely missed these last few months. We needed it back in our lives!

The next day, after Frank and Jean and the Condons left for Falmouth, I drove up to the mountain, and peace filled my heart. I walked around this beautiful, quiet place of David's. I relived all his hard work and his dreams for this mountain paradise. I traveled to the meadow and saw the ashes that had been scattered. It was a surprise to see that it really wasn't ash, but pieces of calcium—hard white fragments gleaming out from the soft brown earth. This was the last physical bit of my David returning to Mother Earth. With tears in my eyes, I turned and walked to the pine tree we had planted the day before. I filled a bucket with water and poured it lovingly onto the freshly turned earth. As the water soaked into the roots of the tree, I cried, and prayed softly, Live! Live! Live!

CHAPTER 23

Life is so generous a giver, but we judging the gifts by their covering, cast them away as ugly or heavy or hard.
Remove the covering and you will find beneath it living splendor, woven of love, by wisdom with power.

Fra Giovanni, A.D. 1513

I keep trying to figure out how all of this could have been avoided. Certainly, if information on AIDS had been available ten years ago, David's life along with the lives of many others would have been spared. He was a very sensitive, gentle, careful, and highly idealistic person.

Today's crisis with AIDS is one reflection of a generation's living through the Sexual Revolution. The message was: Enjoy sex to the fullest. Married or not, we were all curious about how this wonderful part of our lives could be even better. People were encouraged to experiment with the latest ideas. There were suggested positions for having sex that I never heard of before—never even imagined! People throughout the media winked an eye at, even openly approved of, multiple partners.

I was brought up with more Victorian attitudes. The way most of my contemporaries and I got to know someone was by discovering similar interests, ideas, and ideals. Having sex was not a function of getting acquainted as it often is nowadays! If sex isn't good, forget about the relationship, the books advised. "Save yourself for the one you will marry," my mother urged when I was young. I did, and I was respected for that among my friends. That was then, this is now.

With the discovery of the Pill and other methods of birth control, condoms seemed almost obsolete. People always look for new and easier ways to handle everything. Old ways are quickly discarded. But through all this Sexual Revolution, virtually none of the popular books and articles I ever read mentioned anything about health.

Most people, particularly those of the younger generation, were swept off their feet by their peers and other proponents of the New Morality. Our society was led into anguish because we were followers and none of us thought far enough to anticipate this new and extreme devastation called AIDS.

Our emotional and spiritual maturity has not developed at the same rate as our talent for new technologies. So when a tragedy such as AIDS strikes we are at a terrible loss, because in our naïveté we are not prepared for the painful possibilities. We are too nearsighted to foresee the potential consequences of exchanging old-fashioned morality for untested new trends.

When David was twenty, we knew so little about the concept and cause of being gay. Today many researchers and psychologists believe that homosexuality is predetermined before birth, just as being male or female is. This is a new concept to many in our society. What if we could know early on that our adored baby would grow up to be homosexual? Would we love that baby any less, or would we love it unquestioningly for the joy it brought to us? The answer is so obvious when considered on those terms. Why do our hearts change as the child becomes an adult? Does a gay child suddenly become unworthy of love and respect just because he's gay?

God, we have to stop being the judge and embrace life's creative forces wherever we find them. Gay people are often creative people who make a beautiful difference in our world. We can't afford to dam that channel of energy.

(As I write this, I am looking at the sky. I was depressed earlier today and then, as I was typing, a wonderful burst of pink and blue broke through the gray clouds, starting small and expanding across the sunset sky . . . and then it turned to blue . . . and then white light. The significance of uplifting thoughts and new ideas must have a lot to do with sunrises and sunsets . . . so often they happen at the same time.)

I talked with a friend yesterday about his being gay. He said, "You know, Ardie, I came from a deeply religious family. *No way* did I have a choice about being gay. I just was. It would have been so much easier to be like everybody else. I hated myself." (David hated himself too.) "I tried so hard and yet I was so different from my family. I wanted to be part of the group but I never fit in—throughout my life. So I alienated myself from them because I felt they wouldn't understand. I gave up a lot of the family comfort and bonding that I would have enjoyed. If only I had been able to tell them I was different, I wouldn't have missed all that—and it was through David that my family eventually came to understand. They really loved him. They really love me."

Perhaps, if the public had been more understanding of homosexuality, fewer of our beloved friends would have embraced promiscuity so enthusiastically. People who don't feel acceptance tend to strike out against the establishment that rejected them. I remember the rash things I did while growing up that could have had disastrous results. I did things to make people notice me as a way to cope with my feelings of rejection.

David had told me he knew he was different even when he was a young child. I discovered that this was a common experience among many of his gay friends. One of them recalled, "I felt different from my other family members, and, as a child, I would look in the mirror and stick my tongue out at myself." Can you imagine how miserable that little child felt? Can you imagine how an adult feels when he doesn't fit a segment of accepted society?

People tend to judge others by their own standards. Why can't these people be like me? they wonder. Professor Higgins in *My Fair Lady* expressed it when he said of Eliza, "Why can't a woman be more like a man?"

Ridicule and nonacceptance of others is learned. Acceptance comes from understanding and love.

One night, two years before David left, he and Maria and I were having dinner together, reminiscing about our growing-up years. He said, "You know, all during my growing up I looked at myself as being ugly. Now that I have written down my life and put it in chronological order, I see that I have worth after all." (We didn't know that David had already written his autobiography.) I couldn't believe my ears. He always had great value in my eyes, but I knew from my own life that it is how we think of ourselves that really counts.

I wish we could have talked about such feelings earlier in life. I understood what he had gone through. As I grew up, I lived under the critical eye of those who judged me and knew how guilty they could make me feel.

But I have strong hopes for this generation; I see the progress in my own life, in my grandkids' lives. The books I've been reading make a conscientious effort to have adults and children feel comfortable with each other in sharing their feelings on an equal level.

I have often asked myself what alternative there was to giving David the freedom he needed to be himself. I always come up with the same answer: None. It would have meant a life of frustration for all of us. And the worst thing would have been alienating David from our lives. I couldn't have done that. I loved him too much!

Had David been a horse, I might have pulled in the reins, but he was a person—a tremendously creative human being. It was because he had the opportunity to be himself that he was able to contribute so much.

In some parts of his life, David had mood swings—sometimes very happy, sometimes very sad, lonely, and depressed. It was perhaps at these low times that he suffered the biggest conflicts about his own identity. David had counseling during his last several years to help him come to terms with some of the problems on his mind.

I was interested to discover that the composer Rachmaninoff had been given to brooding and introspection. His creativity was blocked by his depression. Rachmaninoff found a doctor who treated him and other musical patients by hypnosis, telling them over and over again that they could do fine quality work and that they would succeed. Rachmaninoff responded to this treatment that provided him with the self-confidence he needed to do his best.

Among David's friends there was a sense of harmony; they all joined in the quest for life's answers and challenges. All had the same high career aspirations, all craved a relationship with someone they could care about. Once such a relationship is found, it's beautiful.

Since David is gone, countless friends of his have told me how much David helped them in accepting themselves as worthy human beings. In one conversation I had with Nana recently, she said, "Not many revolutionaries like David make it, whether they be gay or heterosexual, musicians or artists, scientists or politicians. We are continually growing new revolutionaries, but why must ostracism be the price they pay to pursue new paths?"

David was a revolutionary—not with guns and violence, but with gentleness and concern for all people as equals. It is not appearances or fitting into society's rules that count, but how one feels and treats others in the mutual striving to achieve full potential. We suffer, we grow, but most of all we love because we encourage in each other the potential to grow, each one to his own star.

As I sit here in the living room before a warm fire on a cold and sleeting day, I think about this whole life. Through all of these painful experiences, I can't remember ever saying, Why did this happen to me?

I remember reading some of Elizabeth Taylor's philosophy and I am sure it applies to my life as well. She said she believed that "people, like rocks, are formed by the weather. We're formed by experience, by heartache, by grief, by mistakes, by guilt, by shame. . . ."

I think she would agree with me that we are also formed in important ways by the love we feel in our hearts.

In my life, there is a certain simplicity that takes challenges as they come. When I think about David, my heart wells up with emotion and pride. I say inside of me:

♥ ♥ ♥ ♥ ♥ ♥ ♥ ♥ ♥ ♥ ♥ ♥ ♥ ♥ ♥ ♥

Oh, David, I'm so glad that I was your Mom! I thank God for the chance to bring you into this world, to love you and to watch you grow to be your own person . . . to be with you in your struggles . . . and to be with you in your happiness and to appreciate your uniqueness.

I have shared some of the most beautiful times of my life with you. You lifted me up and made me feel important and worthy at times when I needed it most. We have been helpmates to each other as equals . . . respecting . . . caring for one another . . . sharing ideas, dreams, and talents. I am truly grateful.

CHAPTER 24

Decision
Facing Mother and Memories

God hath not promised
Skies always blue,
Flower-strewn pathways
All our lives through;
God hath not promised
Sun without rain,
Joy without sorrow,
Peace without pain.
But God hath promised
Strength for the day,
Rest for the labor,
Light for the way,
Grace for the trials,
Help from above.
Unfailing sympathy,
Undying love.

Annie Johnson Flint

Wouldn't it be great if we could arrange the order of our lives? From experience, we know this is often not to be.

I was still struggling to overcome David's leaving barely two months before when life dealt me another blow. I had to face this trial (and it was just that) head-on, along with my sister, Joy, and my two brothers, Jim and David. We needed to be caring and loving to our mother and at the same time maintain our own balance.

Mother is a saver. Her home was always her castle, and her keepsakes and collections were her jewels. After we children left home, her four-bedroom house continued to fill up, bulging at the seams. Mother was reasonably content during the many years she lived alone. She never drove a car; she depended on family and friends to transport her, and it seemed to work out.

Mother is also an avid reader. Her life is lived in a spiritual world, where the poetry she loves becomes part of her total being. Her collection of paperweights increased her depths of perception to all of life. Her contemplation of one of these treasures could lead her to a journey of beauty and deep feeling, by way of her wonderful imagination.

For many years, she taught Sunday school and gave many public speeches, always sharing her knowledge and wealth of experience and inspiration for life. Her resource material was all in her home. Her wide library of books and her collections allowed her mind to travel wherever she wished to go. Along with her books and paperweights, she had collections of Madonnas, pitchers, carved animals, bells, semiprecious stones, seashells, donkeys, stained glass, silver for making jewelry, closets of completed and uncompleted needlework, and myriad materials for craft work of all kinds. Mother also lived with stacks of newspapers, *National Geographics*, baskets, and flowerpots.

The Depression years came early in Mother's marriage, a time of great poverty and privation throughout the country. She theorized that she was such a saver because throughout all the years she told herself, Some day I might need it.

In recent years she reluctantly considered moving to a retirement community. She made her down payment, but couldn't make up her mind about when to leave her house. Mother's health began to fail; she couldn't walk very far and it was hard for her to manage alone in her large home. The retirement home finally gave her an ultimatum: "Come within three months or lose your space." She finally decided to go.

It was up to Joy and me to help her sort out what she would take to this beautiful, new blue-and-white apartment. She wanted to take everything! Each item was her jewel, an essential remembrance. My sister and I spent one day a week for three months trying to help her decide what she would part with. She liked having her two daughters near. Of course, the longer she took to decide, the longer we three would be getting together for these all-day sessions.

Moving day finally came, and as the moving van pulled away, we looked around the house in disbelief. The house was as cluttered as it had been before. It seemed as if nothing were missing!

Mother fought the idea of an auction of her things. It would be like exposing her innermost being, her private self, and she simply could not do that. So all that was left had to be sorted out and distributed. Truckloads of items went to charities, such as the AAUW Book Sale, the Rescue Mission, the Girls' Club, and the church. And still there was a mountain of things to portion out to family and friends. Children and grandchildren were invited to choose what they wanted. Then Mother decided she wanted it back. So back some of it came!

The house had been sold, so we were under a deadline to clear it of Mother's belongings. Still Mother couldn't decide what to distribute and what to get rid of. Every time she came back to the house, she took more boxes to her little apartment.

Joy and I were fit to be tied at the end of each day with Mother. It was all so traumatic that we became phobic about accumulating useless items in our own house. We would come home from Mother's house utterly exhausted, take a shower, and then go through our own closets and drawers to throw out—discard, discard, discard! Mother didn't seem to realize that Joy and I were being pushed beyond our limits by this never-ending project, while we tried to take care of our families and the demands of work at the same time.

The deadline for vacating the house crowded in on us, and there was still so much left to dispose of! We just had to call an auctioneer. Mother was made aware of our decision and the sale took place.

After the last item was hauled away, I went to work and people kept asking, "Are you finally finished?" Was I! I got up and did a dance!

I had to regroup. For the first time in 38 years, I planned to take a three-week vacation. Now I began to wonder if I could make it to the plane that next Saturday. Suddenly, everything was too much effort. I felt so ill. I felt angry, abused, and very unloving toward my mother at that moment.

Mother insisted on having the auctioneer slips, which named each object sold and the price paid for it. The last thing I did before boarding the plane was to send her the list and the check. Now I was free.

I hadn't been gone a week when I had a phone call—Mother had been taken to the hospital with a possible heart attack. Somehow I knew something like this would happen. I was still angry inside about the whole ordeal of her moving. I didn't go home. At this point, I felt that I had to save myself from going under, in view of all that had happened since David left. I couldn't go back until I was better myself, both physically and psychologically. The anger I felt had to be resolved, and it would take a lot more than a day's therapy to do it! I needed quiet, ambling walks, sun, exercise, and gentle strokes from those who cared about me. Most of all, I needed to give voice to the anger that was tearing me apart. It would take time.

I bought a book called *Making Peace with Your Parents* and found the exercises in it very helpful in sorting out my feelings. I started to recuperate.

When I returned home, I was finally strong enough emotionally to contact Mother. "You didn't call me," she said by way of greeting. "You don't care that I was sick. How could you do this to me?"

"But Mother, I kept in touch with your progress through the family and I sent you a card. Why did you get sick?"

"I looked at the auctioneer slips and was reminded of the many things I'd forgotten I had," she told me. "There were lots of memories and I wanted them back."

"But Mother, you still have the memories, you don't need the things."

Mother and I talked about what had happened when I had gone with my mother and Grandmother Lessig to help clean out Great-grandma Master's home. None of us will ever forget that experience. Great-grandma Master stood by helplessly as Grandmother Lessig ruthlessly dumped the contents of drawer after drawer and discarded it. All the while, Great-grandma Master watched and cried, "Yes–but–but," all to no avail. Great-grandma Master would be living in her daughter's house and there would be no place for her things. They were tossed out, and that was that!

When it came time for Grandma Lessig to move in with *her* daughter, I was the one elected to help Grandma. When we went to the immaculate attic, Grandma opened the window and just shoved the things out.

Remembering those two episodes, Joy and I tried to be understanding and caring in dealing with Mother, but the frustration level remained very high for us. Through it all, Mother felt that she wasn't given enough time to resolve things her way. What was really lacking was proper organization of the ample time she had at her disposal.

After a while Mother discovered that almost everyone who came to live at the retirement community felt the same deep sense of loss that she felt. Many others had trouble deciding what they wanted to bring with them, and many felt they brought the wrong things.

The retirement apartments Mother moved to provide services the residents need to live independently as long as they are able. However, the jolt of adjusting to this new life, without having her family to fuss over her, made Mother feel abandoned. "I feel as if I died and there was no funeral," she complained.

Older people should have counseling available to them for this type of transition. It would help for them to know in advance that they might have an emotional reaction to relocation. Then it should help to know that one is not alone, that others are in a similar situation.

Finally there are some positives. Mother has adjusted to her new home. She enjoys a large group of interesting friends who live around her—many more than she had when she lived alone. Mother has the peace of her apartment when she wants it, yet companionship and stimulation are readily available through her new society. She can still share her many experiences and creative mind, and she still has the love of her family, even though she thought she had lost it for a while.

As I think about this whole episode in my life, I wonder if my children will ever feel this way about me. I have started to make my list of necessaries for getting older:

♥ ♥ ♥ ♥ ♥ ♥ ♥ ♥ ♥ ♥ ♥ ♥ ♥ ♥ ♥ ♥

Stay flexible.
Be willing to change.
Continually organize your time by making lists.
Remember to do spring and fall cleaning—in your house and in your heart.
Be generous to your family.
Be the one who spreads cheer and love.

When Bob's Aunt Esther died, the rabbi who conducted the service said, "She had her house in order." I think about that a lot and that's the way I want it to be for me. I want to always remember that what is of value to me might not be what my children treasure. And that's OK.

As I look around my house and the room I am in right now, I visualize what is important to me—furniture acquired from relatives that has stood the test of time, my needlework with the many hours of thought in it, my wooden-beaded macramé rosary, six feet long, that hangs on the wall in front of me. I cherish especially the ability to capture the beauty and optimism of the vibrant rainbows that dance around this room on a sunlit afternoon—and the one piece of ash from my son, David.

CHAPTER 25

A Major Healer
The
Little Rainbow

---

*As the clouds of despair
begin to disperse,
you realize that there is hope,
and life, and light,
and truth.
There is goodness
in the universe. . . .*

Coretta Scott King

While our family was recovering from the trauma of David's leaving and my mother's move from her house, a light was generated to bring the joy back into our lives. This light, a healer to our hearts and souls, began to glow first in Korea.

Heather and Tom had three very lively, healthy girls, but in place of having another child of their own, they decided to adopt a child who was in need of a home. Their inquiries to adoption agencies met with resistance. "You have three healthy children of your own," they were told. "You are still young enough to have more children."

Fortunately, Love the Children, an organization from Quakertown, Pennsylvania, was receptive. Infants from Korea were available for adoption, and it made no difference that there were already three children in the house. Because Gillian, the youngest, was only two, Heather and Tom were eligible for an infant. After many tedious forms were filled out and many interviews completed, Heather and Tom were approved and the adoption process put in motion.

In February the good news arrived in the mail, along with a picture of a tiny baby boy in the lap of his foster mother. The child was one month old. He would arrive in the United States in May or June. We gazed at the picture in wonder. We knew we could love this little soul and we eagerly looked forward to him joining our family.

The scattering of David's ashes was planned for the 26th of April. An excited Heather called to say that the Saturday of the 19th would be the day to pick up her new child—a month and a half early. We could barely wait! A new life would come to us just in time to fill the void left by the loss of another!

This is the announcement she sent to friends and relatives concerning her Korean baby boy:

We had just three days' notice that Geoffrey David was on his way. It was difficult to sleep the night of April 18th. The next day, our lives would be changed by a little person we had only seen in pictures. Saturday, April 19th, was a beautiful and warm and sunny day . . . a lovely day to drive to Kennedy Airport.

Northwest Orient Flight #18 was 15 minutes late. There was an additional long customs clearance. Five other families were also waiting for children. We were told not to cry when the children arrived. (Tears of joy are often confused with tears of sorrow by older children).

By this time my emotions were numb. I had many good cries through our total of eight months of waiting. When I first saw our baby, he was clinging to the necklace of his escort . . . not wanting to let go. He then looked at Sarah and Shelbi and smiled. There were no dry eyes.

His Korean name was In Woo Shin. It meant "patient and delightful." He was born to unmarried parents and given a birth certificate of "Orphan . . . Non Person." This would have prevented him from ever getting a good education or a good job. At the age of one day, he was placed in a foster home.

I find my days surprisingly relaxed. Geoffrey and I spend a good deal of time gazing into each other's eyes. It is calming, like watching the waves at the beach. I am reminded that birth is a miracle. Bringing a child halfway around the world to be born in your heart is yet another miracle.

The scattering ceremony would be Geoffrey David's first introduction to the rest of the family. Receiving a child for the first time is exciting, whether it be a newborn or a 4½-month-old baby who already laughs and coos. He seemed to sense that it was his debut, and he put forth tremendous effort to be his best self. He, too, needed acceptance!

Geoffrey David's first Christmas arrived, and Heather wrote to their friends:

'Peace' and 'Joy' have a special meaning for me this holiday. Each season brings more peace in the loss last Christmas of my brother, David. His message to be kind, gentle, and observant of nature's beauty will be with me for always.

Spring brought us one more child to love and for that we are truly rich. Geoffrey David was the "sunshine" we needed after a long winter. We feel he was born just for us and has brought more joy than we ever imagined.

This child is truly "Sunshine." He smiles continually and is very quick with his hands as they manipulate toys with great efficiency. Because he is so light in weight, his sisters carry him around like a doll . . . and when his name is mentioned . . . all the girls' faces light up with happiness . . . Heather and Tom's faces glow.

Love in our lives is here to stay and grows stronger day by day. . . . We have opened the door to our hearts and attached a sign that says, "Welcome . . . little Geoffrey David!"

Our faces still light up when we see him. Yesterday Heidi said to Heather, "Geoffrey is 2½ and he's supposed to be in the terrible twos. Where are they? He's so good." I suppose he has his moments, but he is truly one of God's little rainbows who has come to heal!

STAGE V

Climbing Higher: The Light Gets Brighter

Recently there was a terrible storm. The torrential rains masked the landscape outside. The fierce winds blew. How grateful we felt to be secure inside. Finally the tumult subsided and Bob and I opened the door to see what Nature had done. Huge branches of trees lay scattered on the earth. Several trees were split and some pine trees topped. In Bob's forest of trees, most of them were bent over like weeping willows. A project was started immediately to brace the trees to help them grow tall again. The tree expert was called in. He said some of this work wasn't necessary. "Trees have a wonderful resilience to storms. They heal themselves. They naturally grow to seek the light."

We are like trees.

CHAPTER 26

Beginning Again

Melt my mind
into a glistening new mold.
Heat it, melt it, and strip away
the dark and useless empty parts.
Refine and shape it,
chisel and hammer into me
beautiful, harmonious thoughts
and visions,
a spectrum of sight and sound.
Create in me
a new dimension,
a stark reality, a fresh start
at being.

Barbara Konnert

My role as David's mother was fulfilled. How could I start again?

I thought about the musical *Camelot*. King Arthur, very sad at losing the love of his wife, Guinevere, comes upon a lad singing at the top of his voice. He asks the boy why he sings. "I'm sad," the boy replies.

In *Zorba, the Greek,* there is a bitter lament about all the tragedy one faces in life. "What do you do when you are sad?" someone asks Zorba.

"I dance," he says.

So I began to understand that when sorrow comes, it is wrong to wrap yourself up in a cocoon, trying to be all snug and safe and secure. When sorrow comes, you need a release from the terrible tightness that can grip your heart. Before I could start again, I needed to heal a wound in my spirit that was still open from David leaving us. I wanted to go back to Provincetown. I hoped to experience vibrations David might have felt while he lived there. Perhaps I wanted to recapture some of the good times we had shared. Maybe I could find some peace of mind there, see some reason for this whole tragedy.

David's wonderful friends Frank and Jean went on this pilgrimage with me. Maybe it was important for them, too. We walked the streets and visited the stores David had loved, where he had good friends who missed him still. At the restaurant where he had worked and where he had first met Frank and Jean, we had a wonderful dinner as we renewed touching, healing relationships with people there who were part of David's past. It was a letting go and an awakening to the special caring these friends had for one another.

At sunset, Frank and I went to David's house on the bay. There was a new tenant. As I stood on the deck, I looked at the seascape David had looked at so many times, the same one that many generations of others had enjoyed for hundreds, perhaps even thousands of years. It was an unchanging, unchangeable view. I wondered about all the old dreams and the good and the bad times that had rolled out to sea with the tides. I felt the aloneness David must have experienced during the winter he had lived there. It was there that he had wrestled with the problem of which direction to pursue in life. Through the storms he had weathered in his life, he must have felt like the anchored boats in the harbor, tossed and turned in whichever direction the wind blew. With deep despair I remember talking with David on the phone, then hanging up the receiver and feeling an urgency I could do nothing about, except to get down on my knees and pray, "Oh, dear God, please take care of him!"

It had rained during the night at Provincetown, and I sat at the window in my hotel room, watching the rain clouds break apart. The wind howled wildly. Gradually, the sun reflected its light from behind the clouds and suddenly I thought, I am ready to go home now. I am finished here.

When I arrived home, all these thoughts were in my head. At the same time of day that I had stood on David's deck in Provincetown, I felt the need to go to his house on the mountain. I encountered the season's last burst of blooming perennials as I walked up to the meadow, and the sun cast its fading glint. There two does looked at me inquisitively for a long time, then rollicked off into the woods. The pampas grass swayed. And here, in David's place and among his ashes now absorbed by the earth, I felt the happiness he had felt living here. He had loved the beauty and the peace that surrounded this beautiful home. I felt so much better for making this long trek, because now I realized for myself the happiness he had known here. David is still very much here in spirit, with Mark and me caring for the place, and hosting family get-togethers and retreats here. David would agree, "Why not share Paradise?"

This whole experience was good. I look at each day now as a brand new page of life, with a challenge to reach out to share. The best way for this to happen is to throw yourself into action.

Leo Buscaglia says, "The great bridge that leads to everybody is *your* bridge."

When the oyster rises to action, secreting a fluid to cover a grain of sand that is causing the irritation or pain, the hurt results in a beautiful pearl. Our wounds can become a beautiful pearl too, as we turn our sadness into action. The action of healing takes place in three areas:

♥ ♥ ♥ ♥ ♥ ♥ ♥ ♥ ♥ ♥ ♥ ♥ ♥ ♥ ♥ ♥

First, it must take place inside of you. I found it was necessary to treat myself with love and care, to surround myself with beauty, to give myself love pats and dwell on the positive. Instead of running, I took quiet walks, took time to discover nature, time to sit in a sunlit window and capture the rainbows, time to look around at the beautiful world.

Second, it takes place through the love and caring of people who surround us. The family, Mark, Sarah (who was with David at the end), and I all became the support team for each other. Our friends at work were there for us too, whenever we needed them. We gave each other a fine-tuned listening ear, lots of understanding, plus an extra hug or touch. And our caring for one another deepened.

Third, it is in reaching out to others. Caring goes beyond words. Often, it is only by chance that we find out what it means. I am reminded of a friend from my old Sunday school whose husband was very ill. I went to visit and took along some salad greens from our greenhouse. It was a wonderful visit, but sad to say, he died a week later. We attended the service. I wrote a letter afterward and sent with it prisms for each of the children, and for my old friend. A beautiful note came back telling me how much I had helped the family. I was amazed and gratified that the little I had done seemed to mean so much. I said to Bob, "Maybe I have a gift I am not aware of!"

One of the longtime employees at the Press said to me recently, "You really must have had hard times. There we were, all working for the same company, along beside you, and we were never aware."

The letter I most cherish came from Sarah:

In my house this morning, I started looking around and found myself surrounded by you—by all the wonderful things you have given me. I look up at my bookshelf, and you are there, in the countless helpful books you have passed along to me.

I look at my walls, and you are there, in Heather's lovely quilted star and David's brilliant musicscape.

I look in the room we have set up as an office and you are there, in the typewriter you gave me. (It was David's.)

You are with me every morning of my life as I begin my day reading the Daily Word. Thank you for renewing my subscription. It means a lot to me.

You are here with me at work—thank you for brightening my Monday with the lovely bouquet.

But most of all you are with me in invisible ways, through all the bits of cheer, wisdom of encouragement, and love you have given me from the depth of your soul. You have pulled me through more days than you know—I think to myself, How would Ardie handle this? or, Ardie wouldn't let this get her down, and suddenly the problem doesn't seem so monumental. The good days are even better because I know that you love me.

Thank you, thank you—a million times. I could never repay you or even fully express my gratitude for the countless ways you have touched my life. Instead, I will try to pass along what you have given me. That's the best thing to do with it, isn't it?

Love, Sarah

A friend from New York sent me the *Compassionate Friends* newsletter. It contains many wonderful helps in telling how other people face their sadness. One of the issues describes how a parent feels after the death of her child. A common question is, "Am I still a mother?" The answer is, "Even though your child is gone, you will always be a mother."

Today in "Dear Abby" someone asked the same question. I loved her response: "Yes. You will always be a mother to an angel."

I am astonished at how important the symbols of life are in the healing process. It was as if, subconsciously, I needed to fill in the gap left by David. Life must continue. I had to build, build, build. I decided to throw my efforts into making a new patio on the side of the house, using some of the ideas David had incorporated into his mountain home. It was lots of work, and it gave me a certain satisfaction to know that I was really doing something constructive–making our home more beautiful–to help bring back peace of mind.

Mark and I spend a good deal of time together now up at David's house. We work in the garden, letting the warm soil filter through our fingers, we water the plants and plant new ones to preserve the peaceful beauty of this place. We hope these surroundings will be enjoyed by others who wish to experience that tranquility of the outdoors and gain strength from the stone home built over 200 years ago. I think I hear David in the hum of the wind through the pampas grass in the meadow, telling me he is happy to see his dream alive.

For us, what we do there provides a healing touch that strengthens our hearts and renews our spirits. Mark and I appreciate each other's creativity, thoughts, and philosophy. One day we talked about death. I said, "Many people look at death as the ultimate goal; that at the end of living on this earth, the reward is living with God in Heaven." We decided that each day was important, and that most of life could be heaven on earth. Our challenges can carry us to a higher level of beauty and understanding.

On December 12th, David's birthday, I came home to find a message from Heather. She said, "My kids saw on the calendar that today was David's birthday, so we went to the mountain and decorated his tree with red bows and food for the birds."

It's important to remember these special times when the community comes together to feel that special closeness. On December 23rd, the first year after David was gone, Mark had decorated their house for Christmas, and the family, together with Sarah, all joined in a happy dinner celebration. We talked of the good times we all had shared, and the love we felt for one another.

I mentioned these special times to a friend who lived in an affluent neighborhood of a nearby town. There was an unusually high incidence of deaths among the teenagers in this area, due to automobile accidents on the many curved roads there. The neighbors formed a support group made up of families who had lost a child. That way, no one had to be alone on the major remembrance days. There is strength in being with those who understand and care.

Gratefully accepting help was one of the hardest things for me to do. I was always so sure that I could do everything myself. I was a great giver, but I was a bad receiver. This sorrow changed my attitude. People are waiting to show their love. It isn't weak to accept their help; it's human. We should be eager to support one another through this community of love. Sometimes we are strong, tall trees—and sometimes we have to lean against another tall tree for support.

In our house at the New Farm a beautiful stained glass bird, a cardinal, hangs in the window. On one of my retreats to the farm, I heard a strange pecking noise as I sat reading. It continued for a long time, and I went to investigate. A male cardinal sitting on the outside windowsill was trying in vain to touch the beautiful stained glass bird. How long would the live cardinal continue to reach out without becoming discouraged? It was sad to know that he would never have what he was striving for. On the other hand, he never stopped pursuing his goal. We all need that kind of optimism to pull us through the hard times.

David and Mark were known for their Kentucky Derby parties. Mark and I decided to continue the tradition. The families were invited, plus Jesse and a group of David's friends from New York. Many of Mark and David's friends from work also came. All told, about 60 people joined in the fun.

We made David's favorite recipes for barbequed spare ribs and chicken wings. The table was also laden with wonderful goodies brought by other guests. An accordian player perched on the upstairs porch and his festive music permeated the air. We tried to recapture the spirit of other years—but David was missing. It was fun, but hard. At the end of the evening, everyone left except Sarah, Mark, and me. When all was in order and the place spick-and-span, we hugged and determined to find other reasons for having parties there. We closed the circle of the Kentucky Derby, and as we left we were greeted by the clear, perfect night. "Listen!" The night was electric with the sound of peepers, the first of the season. Maybe this was David singing with happiness at knowing how much he was loved and missed.

Both Bob and I had gone to the Baum Art School in Allentown as children. When the time came, all of our children attended classes there as well. After many years of being harbored in makeshift quarters, the school planned to have a new building of its own. Bob and I were approached to have the gallery dedicated to David in celebration of his life, and we happily agreed. We thought about the influence this school had on our lives and on the lives of thousands of other schoolchildren in this area. It would be a place of inspiration for others in the future.

The school suggested that the first show after the opening celebration be of David's work. We had the musicscapes and the weavings, but what else? I went through the closets and found wonderful photographs of people from all walks of life, photos from David's travels to Mexico and Greece, and I found his humorous illustrated story, "Me in Amsterdam." I threw myself into collecting these things, and my excitement grew as I thought about displaying the work. It was a way to share with others the wide variety of happy creativity that had been a part of David's life. Other young people could use the ideas as a vehicle for stretching their imaginations. The large crowd continually commented, "We didn't know he was so talented. What a loss to our community." David is no longer here, but his life can still inspire. And it did, in many ways I never even imagined.

For example, I was barely aware of David's online activities in computer networking. His essay, "Weekend," which described a visit with his friends Frank and Jean Emerling in Falmouth, Massachusetts, was sent online over the computer network newsletter *The Source,* and it received much acclaim.

After David left, a "Tribute To David" by Lisa Carlson went out online all over the United States. It described his contribution to electronic networking and included an excerpt from "Weekend." Lisa's introduction said in part:

> . . . *David's "Weekend" conference took the medium to a new level as art form. It was participatory theater . . . an interactive short story . . . a "happening" online.*
>
> *David died December 23rd. Although he was only 30 years old, he had already made a mark as a producer, a writer, an artist, and a pioneer in the medium of computer conferencing. When I set out to write this tribute to him I thought about so many examples to cite—his unique graphic style which jazzed up STC's (Source Telecomputing Corporation) weekly newsletter; his talent at dialogue; his contributions to making the online environment seem more like a copy neighborhood.*
>
> *Many who mourn David now never met him outside the online world. But his special quality was an ability to convey himself—a multidimensional, thoughtful, playful, creative self—to us via electronic networks.*
>
> *I think the medium is different because he was here. I know I am. I wish so much that he could have stayed longer. But I can join David's friends and family in celebrating the life he lived—particularly on one very special Weekend.*

At a later date, Ed Yarrish, past president of the Electronic Networking Association, asked our permission to name the first ENA awards in memory of David. We were honored to be at the presentation when Ed spoke:

> *David was the very first "official" ENA member. At the founding meeting in New York City in April 1985 ... there came a point where it was necessary to say, "I am a member and here is my membership to help get ENA started" ... David was the first to make that commitment. By that act he created the organization's sense of membership. A sense that now literally spans the real globe.*
>
> *But more importantly, he was early to recognize the importance of this new medium and to lead the way in creating techniques and processes that make it grow. ...*

The first award was given to establish and recognize creativity in "electronic networking in ways that enriched individuals and enhanced organizations." The second award was given to recognize international online efforts "to build global communities." Each plaque was labeled The David E. Rodale Award, and at the bottom was a quote from David: "We are all figments of each others' imaginations."

At the conference, very informally, people were asked to share stories of David. It was very nourishing and heartwarming. I was so proud of my son. It was a welcome lift in my struggle to restart my engine.

Exercise also played an important part in helping me to start my life again. I discovered a whole buffet of exercise choices to keep me from getting bored, as I worked on my own at home. And the wonderful part of it was that every exercise I did was free. Walking, floor exercises, aerobics, dancing, bicycling at home, and the Nautilus available at work for variety.

Perhaps the exercise I like most is the one I do when I get up before sunrise. I go to the living room and turn on good music. With only the light from a candle, my routine begins. At the end of 40 minutes the sun is rising, my lungs and muscles are stretched, and I am ready to start the day. The exercise routine is usually the same but the music changes, and the varying sunrise is nature's way of introducing me to daybreak. It feels so good!

Together, my dog Bandit and I have an early morning walk. This time renews me as I look for the new changes in the earth, enjoy different smells, and make my "thankful list" for each day. Every day the list is different. It depends who I'm concerned about at the particular time. But mostly, the list has to do with nature's current offerings—the new-fallen snow, the violets in bloom, the trees turning green.

With high anticipation I look for the first raspberry, wineberry, or persimmon of the season. Sometimes my walk takes me through the garden, and I happily taste the dill, the basil, and the parsley. I savor the flavor, and pity those who lack the space to grow these herbs. My thankful list in the morning is filled with whatever the moment dictates. It starts my day in a wonderful, positive way.

I have a different kind of list at the end of the day. This one concerns my family, my job, reactions from caring people, needlework, books, inspiration, grandkids, peace for myself, love of family and friends—and thanks for the free spirit inside me. This list is one of appreciation for the day just passed.

I think about all we have gone through and the experience reminds me of recovering from a heart attack. Healing takes place as other arteries and capillaries take over more of the work load. These smaller vessels reach out, widening to nurture the hurting body. Our spirits can recover from hurt, too, as we reach out.

When Bob and I planned a two-week trip to Scandinavia, people at work stopped me to say I would be missed. Other friends called to say the same, and Maria said, "Oh, Mom, this will be a long two weeks." I was amazed to know my being around made a difference to them. I felt humble and was more eager than ever to reach out to others.

We enjoyed the trip—but it was so good to get back home! The most glorious joy in returning came in the exhilarating morning walk with Bandit. I walked the grassy path between the high tasseled rye grass and the hedgerow, which was heavy with the aroma of honey-suckle and laden with wild multiflora roses. The grass, wet from the rain the day before, made my boots glisten, and every so often I got a whiff of the forest floor.

Even David's goats seemed to sense that I was back. They stood up on their hind legs at the gate until I arrived with my hemlock branch for each as my glad-to-be-home gift for them. Their little tails wagged and they tried to get close enough to be petted.

As I turned around, I looked down and noticed the dandelions. Each one was a sunburst sending its velvet rays outward. It stuck in my mind. The next week, as I walked the fields, the dandelions were different. This week I marveled at the wonder of the white fluff-balls in their stage of glory. I held the mature bloom up to let the light shine through it—and then I blew very softly, and the fluff floated like a starburst. The ripe seeds were ready to be freed and they floated down in all directions.

The seeds of love are like that. Though we blow them to the wind they are not lost. They land in the hearts of others and sprout again to grow and expand our world in more beauty and love.

CHAPTER 27

The Family Together

Keep a few embers
From the fire
That used to burn in your village.
Some day go back
So all can gather again
And rekindle a new flame
For a new life in a changed world.

Dakota Indians

Bob had just turned 21 and I was 22 when we were married. We both came from families with a long history of lasting marriages, even though it sometimes meant working through hard times together. Each of us came into our marriage with insecurities—and we learned to lean on one another. While still in the publishing business, Bob began to search for his own identity. His desire for more time alone as part of his search was frustrating for me because I didn't understand the need he had to expand his creative dreams.

I was often upset when he took his own positions against my wishes. To survive, I had to learn to stand on my own two feet. But once I tasted the thrill of independence and growing in my own light, there was no stopping my drive to be *me, Ardie.* I was 58 before I could verbalize this and realize how lucky I was.

As I look back at the interweaving of our lives, I am amazed at how many of the children's problems peaked in conjunction with problems Bob and I had. And the children were rarely aware that their agenda had to be weighed against ours.

I think my striving for independence was a strong force in teaching our children to be independent themselves. In my initial excitement about self-actualization, I was certain that young people could be saved from life's trials by academic learning. I altered my views as I realized the importance of not missing a step in the experience of growing up.

As the children began to leave home, one message was uppermost in my hopes for them. "Be your own person and grow in your own way. It's not the Me for You I want, but the You for Yourself I love and want you to be." I tried to treat our children as human beings with dignity. The important thing through all these years was to keep love lines open. My mother's life influenced me greatly; I was doing what she had done. She looked for the uplifting and the inspirational in each child. She had faith in us.

My children were going off in different directions—some already married, some living away from home, some away at school—and I continued to keep in touch by letter—one letter duplicated and sent to all. It was a one-way group meeting. Here is one such letter:

I'm thinking about life, and pondering how we have contributed, you and I, to one another's growth. I think Anthony and I started the conversation the other night. He wanted to know how I thought we got along. It was a good conversation, and we agreed with one another.

First of all, growing up, for myself, was to be the best that I could be. I wanted that goal for each one of you as well. It starts with the birth of the family, education in that family unit, and then continues with the extension of yourself. It is amazing to realize that we don't all have the same structure of growth beyond the biological parents. For each one of you, the environment and the education changed as we as parents grew and realized that the same formula does not work for each child. That's why each one in this world is unique. I think that this also means that your growth structures are peaking at different times . . . just like Dad's and mine are. It's not bad . . . and can be accepted as a challenge.

If parents were gods, each kid would be perfect. But as humans (and as life unfolds) we do make mistakes, but we try to overcome our difficulties and keep on looking at life in a new way as a means to become better.

Many times I went through highs in life and thought, My God, this is utopia. Everything was right with the world. It is a fleeting pleasure, for we are not meant to live in Eden. We are meant to live in the real world where there is giving, receiving, sharing, loving, and unexpected challenges that poke us from our complacency into upheaval and change, and then as we sort out our emotional crises we say, "What am I going to do about it?" Then we constructively build.

The other night, I watched Camelot on TV. King Arthur was sad. Someone asked him what he did about it. His reply was, "You learn. You learn why the world wags and what wags it."

One other thought I have is that it is kind of neat to get older because the horizon line can become so much wider. Plans and directions may change . . . but the goal of trying to be the best that I can be has never changed. Looking back, I almost wish I would have plotted out the drawing of a tree as life unfolded. I see the trunk as myself with five main branches. I would like to see what the branch structure would look like for each one of you as you are faced with life choices and problems. One thing I know: The tree would have branches reaching upward optimistically. It would be no weeping willow. Maybe the tree would be oak . . . or walnut. Walnut has the more beautiful grain. Someday maybe I'll draw it.

So, I think that all of you contributed tremendously to my growth, and I to yours, as we face the hard times and the good times. Sometimes my arms waved frantically as I tried to keep my head above water, but I made it.

I am convinced, as I get older, that the amount of love you have in your life determines your understanding, compassion, caring, and action. It determines the understanding of another's efforts and point of view.

In Camelot, Arthur said another important thing: "Love is kind of the seventh day." I did some brainstorming from this statement.

Love is reverence	*Love is a peace*
Love is a change	*Love is a happiness*
Love is a relaxation	*Love is a thanksgiving*
Love is an appreciation	*Love is a celebration*
Love is a sharing	

Let's celebrate life.

Love, Mom

There is a strong togetherness among us and I am constantly grateful for how the family has stuck together and enjoyed each other's company all through the years. We've come a long way. Maria once said, "You know, we all supported one another even though we were far from perfect. My brothers and sisters—we are all best friends."

With David's leaving, it felt as though a right arm were missing and our lives had to adjust to many changes. I asked some of the family what differences they felt since David left.

Maria said:

Most of all, there seems to be a greater proportion of women. Three girls and one boy seems like many more girls than three girls and two boys. I miss David's linking me to the outside world. He was a culture link in terms of new music and new absurdities. Now I feel like I have to take on more of his role as entertainer, party-er, culture queen. We are not satisfied in containment; we need change and action.

In some ways, we are closer as a family. There is a feeling of sensitivity and shared past that I don't like to talk about with other people—especially family—because it trivializes it.

After all, we are the same, only older, which is not a negative thing. We have a great family, close, caring, supportive, friendly. I like that. I really like everyone in our family and I enjoy spending time with them. I feel sorry for people who don't like their families.

Heidi's impressions were deeply positive:

David's death forced me to look at our family and my life differently. I find that I am thinking more good thoughts and appreciating what's good about each person. I don't want to waste my time thinking negative thoughts. It's made me more thankful for what I have and for every day that I'm alive. It's made me want to maximize my time by cutting out time wasters and making good things happen.

I am so thankful for every day I have with my kids. I can appreciate them so much more, since I have learned how precious life is.

Heather shared these thoughts on losing David:

My children have forced me to talk about death, by their endless questions. I had to deal with it as we talked, and that helped us to come to terms with his loss.

Today I feel I'm mending, yet I expect to be scarred forever.

My life is very busy with children and building a new home. I am not sad anymore for David. I can't change what has happened and I focus on the David I knew. In planning my new home and making endless decisions, I often think, David would pick this, or David would have loved this. David's influence is a part of my life and that feels comforting. He had touched us and he is not forgotten. That is my peace.

My life goes on with daily maintenance of a large family and a cluttered house. I have plans this winter to sew a quilt. Life is like a quilt. You work on it bit by bit. Each color, each pattern represents a particular happening. When it's all done you can admire the finished piece and hold the memories in a beautiful masterpiece. Someday my life will end, too, but my quilt made of each part of it will still be here.

It is therapeutic for me to sew. Many of my daily activities— cleaning and washing and household maintenance—need to be done too frequently. When I sew, I see a permanence in a finished project and in my satisfaction that it is well made. I maintain a balance between necessary, disposable chores, and permanent projects that my children and I will enjoy in the future.

David's memories and the things that he made are very dear to me now. Part of his life is gone, yet another part is still here.

Today I look at my family and think how lucky we are. Having a close-knit family hasn't come without hard work. How good it is to have them close and to be able to pick up the phone and say, "Hey, I want to talk with you. I love you . . . I miss you . . . take care, my dear friend!" I thank God each day for each one.

Now, all of a sudden, Bob and I are alone in the house most of the time. While we each had to heal the hurt in our lives for ourselves, we are learning to heal the hurt together. There is much more communication between us, and more love. Knowing what we lost and how precious life is, we hold life tenderly, like a rare jewel.

This all came together for us when we accepted an invitation from Deborah Szekely to be her guest at Rancho La Puerta Spa in Tacata, Mexico, for a weekend, then continue on to her Golden Door Spa in Escondido, California, for Couples Week. In arranging this time together for Bob and me, Deborah gave us a gift beyond measure! We came away truly regenerated in mind, body, and spirit, after what was perhaps the lowest period of our lives.

I think about growing older. One night I said to Bob, "You know,

I've been thinking about Tevye in *Fiddler on the Roof.*"

He and his wife were married for 25 years when all of a sudden he asked her, "Do you love me?"

"You ask me?" she responds incredulously. "I work for you. I give you children. I care for you. I wash your clothes. I cook your food all these years and you ask me, do I love you?"

I asked Bob, "Do you love me?" So much of life is taken for granted that words are important to hear.

"Yes, I love you," he said, as we hugged.

The evening meal together by candlelight has become an important part of the day for Bob and me. We philosophize more about life. Last spring I said to him, "I can't remember a year when our spring garden was more beautiful than it is this year. I bet you didn't even notice."

His reply took me by surprise. "I've been watching the yellow tulips. Every night they close up, but tonight I see that they haven't done that."

"That's because they have lost their resiliency," I said. "They're fast approaching the end of their lives."

Is life like this? Do we come to the point where we just don't have the strength to keep on with all our projects? The petals drop one by one. A tulip is still beautiful in its own way as long as the last petal remains on the stem. It is then that the remembrance of the beautiful yellow tulip finds a place in our hearts. Life continues in its cycle of returning the strength to the bulb under the earth as it rests a while and prepares for another spring.

After 38 years of marriage, I have renewed love and fresh admiration for where we have been and how far we have come together. We stuck together because we had faith in our main goals—loving each other and wanting the best for our children. We worked through the problems we faced, and our strength deepened. It is a continuing process as we face the new generation—sharing and laughing.

We have learned to see the humor in life situations. When our family was all together at Christmas last year, we were talking over early times. Heather suddenly realized that Bob was only 22 when she was born. She said, "Do you mean that Dad was Anthony's age when I was born? The comparison is hard to make. I can't imagine Anthony as having all that responsibility and being what Dad was."

Anthony didn't think it was all that funny. Finally, we all laughed as we realized that too often we only view life from where we are today.

Later Bob spoke to Maria gruffly. She looked him in the eye and said, "Don't ever talk to me in that tone of voice again, or you won't be my friend anymore!" He was taken aback, then he looked at her and saw that she was laughing. They laughed together, but the point was well made.

We find real delight in our seven grandchildren. Watching them learn and grow is to discover life in a new and beautiful light, to see it through someone else's eyes after you thought you knew all about it. Bob bought an old Volkswagen van for driving the grandkids around the farm. They scream with delight when it's ride time. He loads them all up in the van, opens the sunroof, and away they go over the fields.

Anthony recently said to me, "You know, unless you have the smells of home, you'll never come home." He meant that there must be good memories to come back to. And all the children *have* come home! Coming home doesn't mean we all live in the same way and fit the same mold. Rather, we continue to expand and augment our spheres of interest and tolerance of individuality in others.

Our children also show an active interest in working for the company. Each one comes with unique creative talents.

There is a mellowing that has drawn us closer as a family. We are more aware of each one's strengths and weaknesses and the love we have for each other. Livingston Taylor has expressed the way we feel about each other:

> You are the way you are,
> You don't have to change.
> And if you are not perfect by tomorrow . . .
> I think I'll love you just the same.

CHAPTER 28

Treasuring Today

Every day's a "happening"
That's meant to celebrate;
Every day's a holiday,
No matter what the date!
Friendship, love, and laughter,
Dreams, and songs to sing,
These are very special gifts
That any day can bring!
So never mind the calendar,
Each morning brings your way
A world of joy to celebrate.
Celebrate today!

Connie Hiser

A dear friend called on the telephone with a huge agenda of woes. I listened. The last comment she made before the conversation ended was, "I'm so tired of this kind of life!"

I couldn't reply. I was amazed. I didn't believe she wasn't in charge of her own life.

As we celebrated another friend's birthday, I said to her, "Look at it not as being a year older, but as having another year of increased awareness and growth."

"But, Ardie, the trouble is that I don't feel that I have grown this year. I'm static." I was astonished. Why doesn't she do something about it, I thought?

Somehow that put me in mind of Farmer Alfalfa, a character in a wonderful children's story. He started out one morning all excited because time was moving fast. He chopped the wood, repaired the fence, painted the house, planted the garden, cleaned the house, took care of all the animals. He worked as if there were no tomorrow. At the end of the day he was tired but happy because all the chores were accomplished. As he sat down at his desk to finish the paperwork for the day, he discovered that he had ripped two months from the calendar that morning instead of one. The joke was on him, but he felt good just the same because he was so far ahead of the game!

How often in my life I have chuckled as I sat exhausted, calling myself "Farmer Alfalfa." It's true! There is so much to do. As I get older, it seems that I live in the fast lane—I have to if I am to accomplish all the goals on my agenda! The faucet of my heart and mind just keeps overflowing. I wouldn't have traded my life for the life of anyone I know.

I think of myself as the little pig who built his house of bricks. No matter how hard the wolf tried, he couldn't blow the house down. The little pig was secure and could not be swayed from his goals.

I am trying hard to approach life by becoming like the sun from which all experiences radiate. And the rays reflect back to make living one fantastic adventure. If one's thoughts are negative the rays don't travel far, so life is limited to only part of its potential light!

I think of how my life is every day. I see the faces of those outside my family whom I encounter every day. I appreciate sharing conversations and kind actions that give extra surprise and the nourishment to my days.

A friend at work gave David's friend Mark a book called *Celebrate the Temporary* by Clyde Reid. Mark liked it so much that he bought me a copy. It stresses the point that we are often so absorbed in the past, or in preparing for tomorrow, that we miss the wonderful joys of today.

It hit home when I went to stay at the New Farm with my six-year-old granddaughter, Maya. How long has it been since I walked barefoot in the grass or in the early morning dew, I wondered. "Maya, let's take off our shoes," I said. It felt so wonderful to feel the cool softness of the grass. Like a TV screen, my mind flicked back to memories of carefree days of growing up. Now together, Maya and I laughed, we ran, and we were quiet. We walked through the garden, smelled all the flowers, and dashed through the sprinkler for some relief from the day's heat. We stuck our feet in the stream and let the soft silt squish through our toes.

The next morning as we left—me for work and Maya for day-care—she said, "Please, Ummy, can we come back to stay tonight? I have so much more work to do."

As that day wore on, it turned hard, and I left the office for a brief visit to the mountain where David had lived. There I continued to be the inquisitive child and to experience the moment. I wondered if I could stand the shock of submerging my bare feet in the spring-fed pond in the front of the house. Screaming with delight, I felt a shock of exhilaration. It reminded me of the icy, rhododendron-encircled mountain pond of my childhood, an isolated spot we shared with the trout as we swam. I went back to the office refreshed.

Then Maya and I went back to the New Farm for our second night of Celebrating the Temporary. She pleaded to go to the farm of Ben Brubaker, our Mennonite neighbor, to see the cattle. We left the dishes in the sink and trudged over the shale-dust path that connects the two farms. We passed the spring where the Indians must have met when they inhabited this area. We passed the horses gently grazing and swishing their tails in the field, and the goats penned in by an electric fence. "Don't touch that fence!" I shouted. Of course, Maya's reply was, "Why not?"

With dusty shoes, we arrived at the barn just at feeding time. The grain was passing through a noisy funnel and coming out finely pulverized. We touched the feed to feel its softness, and then we faced the cattle. They looked at us, and as they chewed, they drooled and sometimes they seemed to be smiling. We were face to face with them, separated only by the feeding trough and the rails. We jumped over cattle dung and wet puddles, and back again, trying to find a way out of the huge barn. Every gate appeared to be locked and, in the maze, I had lost the sense of where the entrance was. Would we be locked in for a long time?

I finally found a bottom fence rail that was a bit higher than the others. "Look, Maya, maybe you can crawl under the fence." She succeeded. That left me on the other side. "Maya, do you think I can make it? Will you pull me through if I get stuck?" I pushed and shoved, and *finally* got through. Victorious, I stood up!

"Ummy, you're a mess. You're all dirty!" Would my white blouse ever be clean again?

I looked at Maya and quietly said to myself, Maya, *you're* a mess, too. Your red shirt is gray now!

We walked toward the house, and as we caught glimpses of the Brubaker grandkids, we waved. We went over to Ben, who was washing the black Mennonite buggy. "Hey, Ben, how often do you have to wash that buggy?"

"Oh, almost every day we use it," he replied.

We watched the barefooted little kids walking around—not in the grass, but in the barnyard's mud and manure. Nettie, a red-cheeked toddler of two, had just been retrieved from the animal watering trough. Her shyness was understandable when she heard us speak English, for she hears only Pennsylvania Dutch at home.

Leon, age five, stood on the buggy roof, pretending it was a surfboard. The super springs of the vehicle really made it jiggle and Leon laughed with delight. Laura, their mother, came running. "Leon, stop! That's too dangerous for you!" Ralph, the eldest, was helping with the chores in the barn.

My eyes darted back and forth between Ida and Maya. Ida is a year younger than Maya. The two girls didn't speak but viewed each other with dignity. What were their thoughts? Ida had a thick, golden braid. If Maya had a braid, Laura and I thought, it would be pencil thin. We both felt the strong braid of Ida's hair, and then the fine silk of Maya's. Laura's hair was barely visible under her Mennonite cap, but smiling and with pride she said, "You know, my hair is like Ida's. When I let it down, it touches my waist." It was my time to admire. I always wanted thick straight hair instead of being a short-haired curly top!

Reluctantly, we headed back to our place, stopping to see the nest of a robin. Maya was thrilled to see the one blue egg. The next item on the agenda was a bath that would wash away the grime, but never the memories of Celebrating the Temporary that day.

I will never forget that experience. I spend some of my happiest moments seeing life through the eyes of a child. Maya's inquisitiveness was contagious and enriching. Who says we have to live in an adult world and live life in a rut? Only *we* put limits on our experiences, forgetting that we still have most of the world to discover.

Other circles of influence have opened because of how David touched us all. His friends are very visible in my life as I continually keep close touch. It's important to me what happens in their lives.

A long time ago when my children were small, we subscribed to a magazine called *Wee Wisdom*. One wonderful story I will remember forever is about the meaning of love.

In a far away jungle in the Congo lives a tribe of Bantu natives. Their language is called Lonkundo. Many years ago, a group of kind people went to the Congo to help the Bantus to a better way of life. These people wanted to teach the Bantus to read and write. There were no books in Lonkundo, so the people had to learn the Bantus' language . . . but they could not find a Lonkundo word that meant love.

One day they heard a Bantu woman crooning to her baby. "Eoto," she murmured, holding him lovingly, "Eoto . . . I feel with you." This was it! I feel with you. What you feel, I feel too. What better word for love.

I am deeply touched by the gay people I know. In spite of a frightening future for some, they are not hysterical as one might expect of someone in jeopardy. They have a tremendous strength. They feel worth for themselves and are striving to achieve their maximum. There is a new awareness about caring for their lives in a healthful way. There is also a deepened concern for the health of others. We each reach out in love.

Our company was approached by the local AIDS service center for permission to send an informational flier to each employee. It dealt with what AIDS is, how it is transmitted, and how to protect yourself and your family. It also contained questions that most people ask about AIDS, and the answers. I gave the requested permission. The local newspaper picked up on this and called to do a story, since we were the first company in our area to provide this important information.

There were three reasons, I said, for my wanting our people to have this information: First, we care about the Rodale Press employees; second, I want our people to live; third, I believe the right information will dispel fear and prejudice. The community responded to the newspaper story in a very positive, supportive way.

I feel a stronger need to touch the lives of those who are suffering. Perhaps this has helped me to cope with the pain of losing David. We wait to send flowers until after someone leaves, but it would mean so much more for them to know while they live how much they matter in our lives.

I look into a pool of water and my reflection looks back at me. There is calmness of the water and the image of my outside self is very clear. I drop a pebble in the water and through the ripples I am able to see my inside self. Who I really am becomes very clear. As this vision of myself surfaces, I find certain statements of living that are part of myself. This is what I live by and what I see.

♥ ♥ ♥ ♥ ♥ ♥ ♥ ♥ ♥ ♥ ♥ ♥ ♥ ♥ ♥ ♥

Set goals yearly, weekly, daily. In times of strife, aim for the daily goals, but always look positively ahead.

The pioneer spirit is not dead. Breaking out of set patterns offers a tremendous satisfaction. Continually doing things the same way stifles creativity.

Adapting to life's changes and rolling with the tides makes life exciting.

As I accept myself and feel good about me, life runs more smoothly. As I learn to answer to myself, there is less need for placebos. I am responsible for my actions and blame no one.

It isn't important what others think of me. I am not in competition with anyone else. I am only competing with myself to be a better person.

Freedom to be me. I am always mindful of the freedom for growth of all people.

Never take a backseat in a discussion. Everyone has the right to question.

It is important to know when to step off life's merry-go-round to retreat to the mountain for contemplation.

When confronted with a problem, I treat it the way I treat a cold. I try to blow it out and clear my head.

When I am down, I can dance happiness into my heart.

With love, even a patch of weeds can become a beautiful garden.

Never give up.

I allow myself to feel pain as well as joy.

Be selective. Each person is capable of weighing two sides of an issue and evaluating the potential worth of an experience.

I work on myself instead of trying to teach other people lessons. Live by example.

Instant gratification must stand the test of time.

I am thankful every day for the good in life.

The sincerity that leads us to do things in life cannot be ridiculed.

It is necessary not to hurt another. Eyes must not be so intently goal-oriented that we fail to see the effects of our actions on others.

Life isn't always a bed of roses. As the road leads over the rocks and thorns, remember that there were sweet fragrances and the nourishing times, too.

Look to challenge as an expansion of life, something that goes beyond a need. It is the extra sun, the extra smile, the extra growth that puts life into the superlative.

I keep a glint in my eye as I become a child again, running through the fields breathing deeply and laughing.

I keep living on my toes. I never let myself be taken for granted.

I've thought about life as a work of art, a masterpiece, a weaving, a symphony. It can be all of these, but more than that, it is an orchestration of accomplishment. I hated playing second and third violin, and after a long time I'm finally playing first violin in my life.

Playing in the orchestra while growing up affected me tremendously. While at the time I didn't master the technique of the instrument, I did develop an ear for how that orchestra works as one and how its music can affect our lives. Listening to great music, I often catch myself playing the violin in my mind and using the correct bowing movements. I have become a master of my life's music. I can truthfully say I'm happy being Ardie.

I'm happy to be in the running stream of life. Every now and then I want to duck into an inlet of the stream for a chance to reflect in calmer water—to see if the direction is right—but still enjoying the benefits of the running stream. Perhaps this way I won't get pulled into the rapids and whisked away. A running stream takes care of its own survival—inspiring, replenishing, purifying, satisfying. Each level works in its own regenerative way, a blend and a balance. I strive for newness always, and I want to be in the "main stream" where it all happens.

When certain crystals are sprinkled on a fire in the fireplace, colors of blue, green, yellow, purple, and red leap up skyward in dancing delight. There is a message in this: We can sit back and wait for life to be kind to us . . . but each person has the power to *add* the extra magical potion to make life *more*. I know that I want that extra zest and beauty in my life and I'm ready to share it with those who will come to my banquet table.

I have polished off some of the sharp edges of my soul and put the shine back in my heart. This morning when I started to work, I was singing inside. I wound up one of the music boxes in the bedroom, and then another one. There was a tinkling of heavenly chimes all around and it was so beautiful that my heart cried out, Thanks, God!

I am lucky. There has been such tremendous change in my lifetime. Some old experiences are no longer a part of our culture. In some respects, I want to cling to the memories of them because they were so wonderful and I fear that knowledge of these experiences will be lost. They are worth sharing with future generations.

Today we have so many new things happening, so many challenges to rise above. There are new directions in thinking. They create new opportunities to reach out in humanness to care, to touch, to love. Strength to Climb Toward the Light does not come easily. It requires opening yourself up to all the tides, one wave at a time. Eventually, you get strong enough to withstand life's elements.

Is it worth the struggle? Without a doubt. We come to this life not only to be users, but mainly to make a positive difference in other people's lives, to enrich, and to grow in understanding of one another and the world.

Like the snake, we have to shed our skins periodically to discover the exhilarating freedom of growing in unbelievable ways. Instead of growing older, we can regenerate our physical, mental, and spiritual beings to stay forever healthy and young at heart.

CHAPTER 29

Lighting Up Tomorrow

As anything that cannot be touched with the hand or seen with the eye, your gift grows more powerful as you use it. At first you might use it only when you are outdoors, watching the bird with whom you fly. But later on, if you use it well, it will work with birds that you cannot see, and last of all you will find that you'll need neither ring nor bird to fly alone above the quiet of the clouds. And when that day comes to you, you must give your gift to someone who you know will use it well, and who can learn that the only things that matter are those made of truth and joy, and not of tin and glass.

Richard Bach, *There's No Such Place As Far Away*

I ask myself, What do I want to do with the rest of my life? It's OK if I don't have time to spend on my needlework, but it's not OK if I don't give more time to my grandkids. I want to spend time with them and stay young in spirit, helping with the continuity of generations by sharing my stories and experiences so that they have some sense of how previous generations orchestrated their own lives. I want to listen to them and to know what is going on in their minds. I want them to feel special when they are with me, the way I felt when I spent time with my grandmother. Even though I am at last playing first violin in my life, I feel a need to be the observer as others play their tune.

I want all my days to be worthwhile, not wasted mourning what I don't have anymore: old friendships, old ways of doing things. I want to keep reevaluating life and dreaming new dreams. I want to discover new ways to benefit others.

My life is a book, with each page showing what I have experienced and dreamed. I have gained new insight into who I am and what I still hope to accomplish. More and more I find that we don't have to master an instrument to appreciate life's symphony. We only need to know when the music should be soft and when the crescendo should rise. My music is getting stronger and wider in its scope. Like my own, each life is an unfinished symphony filled with surprises.

But I still have some deep concerns. Modern problems still touch my life and I search for solutions that will make the future better.

I worry that viewers who watch TV indiscriminately are anesthetized or hypnotized by what they see. They seem to live vicariously, instead of acting creatively on their own. Children and young adults need to be taught techniques of problem solving earlier in their lives. They should be learning to ask Why and How and What For so they can act responsibly instead of just plodding on without reevaluating their direction.

Quality of education in our schools needs to be upgraded. Though Bob attended 11 different schools in his 12 years of elementary and high school, he says his best and most interesting education was provided in a one-room country school he attended. Aside from the book learning, the learning that comes from life experiences was a major contribution there. Schools all over the country pour money into "facilities" for better education, but facilities too seldom translates into concern for the person. Among other things, schools should be teaching young people how to deal positively with anger and disappointment.

At Rodale Press, as we project space needs for the next five years, I am told that artists will be creating more and more of their work by computer, so there will be a big need for a new form of technical artist. The elevation of the technical artists may sound good, but I wonder, will artists be taught the basic rudiments? Will the art we know today fall by the wayside? Will those prized techniques be lost? Will a time come when we need the old ways and have no one who knows them? Nowadays, even music is being composed and played on a computer!

Our family has always been close and supportive of one another, but I wonder about the continuity of the family when there is no family support. Who do people turn to for the tie that binds? What about people who move and travel continually and have a hard time establishing roots?

Symptoms of a need for a deeper vision are everywhere in our society. Trouble with drugs and alcohol, suicidal adolescents, stress-related illnesses, increased psychological problems, runaways, and the homeless are all symptoms of a need for deeper vision of where the road of today's lifestyle is leading us.

I get angry when people in authority put limits on the dreams and desires of others. It makes me furious when an AIDS victim is told, "You're going to die." Where is the hope? A few of these people are surviving! Miracles happen every day.

Although they are frightened, many gay people are doing something positive to improve their life—changing diets, taking vitamins, practicing safe sex, reading books on the latest findings concerning their problem. Each day is important. They are taking responsibility for self help instead of waiting for someone else to tell them what to do.

It's easy to see that some of the best of the old values were left by the wayside when today's society emerged. This fact was brought home to me by something I discovered when I was cleaning out Mother's house. It was a little pamphlet that might have been written in the thirties, judging from its cover. The title, *Soul Film*, fascinated me and so did the contents:

> *A human being is much like a camera. Of course, a human being is more than a camera. Within every human being is a sensitive soul. From outside there comes, from birth to death, myriads of pictures. These affect the soul, make changes in it, leave impressions on it. How important it is, then, that these pictures be good, sharp and clear. An adult can choose the pictures he wants to take into his life; a little child cannot. The shutter of his soul is open to every waking moment. Pictures are going in all the time. How infinitely important that we as adults surround our children constantly with deserving pictures. When the children turn their camera toward us, let us hope that they receive pictures of persons who show trust and love, who have found peace and joy, and who show justice and mercy. . . . Soul Film! It is running through the camera of our children's lives every moment. What kinds of pictures are we helping them take?*

What we need is quality time and experiences that strengthen the inner values of our young people. Such activities take little money. In fact, most of them are free.

My goal of achieving dignity for the whole person is a goal for everyone to pursue—everyone contributing, everyone caring. We need more sensitivity and less scurrying and more ways for people to learn to help themselves. I dream of a whole community that is propelled by genuine love demonstrated through action. The *Daily Word* says it beautifully:

> *I cradle the world and all its people in my love. I see every nation as a collection of communities like my own . . . people working together for the highest good of all. I see the world as a vast community of families—mothers, fathers, and children who love each other and seek to express it. I see the world as a friendly place, in which neighbor helps neighbor in a bond of love and caring and all people are my brothers and sisters, speaking a universal language of love.*

When I was in junior high school, we had a special service at assembly period called the Order of the Light. Students who had achieved the honor roll and honorable mention entered the auditorium in a procession and gathered on the stage. As each student's name was called, the student came to the front of the darkened stage, shook hands with the principal and picked up a flashlight. The light blazed forth at the instant the torch was picked up. It was fascinating to watch one small light expand to a stage bright with light.

After the last student had picked up a light, the principal recited in a loud and clear voice: "Let your lights so shine before men that they may see your good works, and glorify your Father which is in heaven." At that moment all the students raised the torches high. This simple service inspired all of us to work hard and do our best.

A similar idea was behind the Ceremony of Light, a beloved custom at the camp I attended as a camper and later as a counselor. On the last night, each person received a candle mounted on a cross section of birch wood. After a long silent procession to the river, each camper lit the candle and made a wish. Then the candle was set afloat on the water. It was an awesome sight for us to see one candle, then two, then see them multiply to over 100 candles—representing each one of us set afloat in the stream of life and led wherever the flow would take us.

When all the lights came together in the stream they made a brighter light, enhancing the power of one another. Sometimes a candle would be pulled by an eddy out of the general flow, and I think now that sometimes we are like that lone candle. But the light of a group, or even of one, can be a beacon of inspiration for another lost in the darkness. And when you look down, your light often seems to be struggling in dark waters; but when you look up, your light appears as a bright star in a dark sky. Be it in dark waters or a dark sky, I know that my light can make a difference—and yours can, too. So it is important that we never lose sight of our dream to make this world a better place. The advice from Don Quixote in *Man of La Mancha* stands out in my mind:

> To surrender dreams—this may be madness,
> And maddest of all—
> To see life as it is and not as it should be.

From "Man of La Mancha." Reprinted with permission of Dale Wasserman.

As we strive to raise the level of consciousness for others and ourselves, we must keep climbing the mountains to get a better vision of the road beyond. Long ago, when I was in Europe, I was greatly inspired by the mountains of Switzerland, and at the end of the trip, I wrote:

> *Oh, let us always have a mountain within our soul with a peak so high that we never quite reach the top . . . for then we will always strive for greater things and will not be content with merely climbing hills.*

My faith in God as a best friend has led me through life's trials. I've become stronger and I'm still climbing—every day one step closer to the light. The light of understanding and the light of unconditional love. Today and tomorrow, as a helper of my fellow people, I feel the urgency to share the joy, the hope, and the love.

You know me now. I have invited you into my heart!